7—

BEATRICE WEBB

BEATRICE WEBB

BEATRICE WEBB

By
MARGARET COLE (Isabel Postgate)

WITH 8 ILLUSTRATIONS

LONGMANS, GREEN AND CO.
LONDON ◇ NEW YORK ◇ TORONTO

LONGMANS, GREEN AND CO. LTD.
OF PATERNOSTER ROW

43 ALBERT DRIVE, LONDON, S.W.19
NICOL ROAD, BOMBAY
17 CHITTARANJAN AVENUE, CALCUTTA
36A MOUNT ROAD, MADRAS

LONGMANS, GREEN AND CO.
55 FIFTH AVENUE, NEW YORK 3

LONGMANS, GREEN AND CO.
215 VICTORIA STREET, TORONTO 1

First published 1945
New Impression March 1946

BOOK
PRODUCTION
WAR ECONOMY
STANDARD

THIS BOOK IS PRODUCED IN
COMPLETE CONFORMITY WITH THE
AUTHORIZED ECONOMY STANDARDS

CODE NUMBER: 12520

PRINTED IN GREAT BRITAIN
BY WESTERN PRINTING SERVICES LTD., BRISTOL

PREFACE

THIS book is not a definitive Life of Beatrice Webb, nor a definitive study of the unique partnership which has had so enormous an influence upon the social and political thought and action of two generations of English life. Before either of these can be written, years will have to pass and, at the least, the remainder of Beatrice's great Diaries be made publicly available, so that she will, as she did in *My Apprenticeship*, tell her own story largely in her own words. All that the present volume claims to be is a brief account, for this generation, of the "life and times" of the greatest woman I have ever known, set down by one who had the privilege of being her friend and her fellow-worker within the Fabian Society.

It is a portrait of Beatrice, not of Sidney, and therefore deals with the great range of activities of Beatrice's husband only in so far as they were bound up with hers, or necessary in order to understand hers. It therefore, for example, passes very lightly over the story of his work for English secondary and university education and his long and effective labours in the Fabian Society and on the London County Council, which ought to be the objects of special study; it only uses them in order to build up the picture of Beatrice's own development.

In writing it I have made use, naturally, of Mrs. M. A. Hamilton's *Sidney and Beatrice Webb*, the only full-length study of the Webbs which has been written in this country, and of the articles which appeared in various periodicals immediately after Beatrice's death. I have also to thank Lord Passfield for giving me permission to quote from his own writings and their joint publications, for lending photographs, and for reading the book in MS.; Mr. Tobias Weaver for the photograph of the Webbs with Mr. Maisky, for reading chapter by chapter and making valuable suggestions in addition to being constantly available for consultation; and Miss Agnes Gibson, who worked so long for the Fabian Society, for reducing the manuscript to type. But, as everyone will realize, my main debt is to Beatrice Webb herself. Her own writing, in *My Apprenticeship* and the forthcoming volume on *Our Partnership*, combined with recollections of talk and correspondence for many years back, have provided me with sufficient

5

material to write a much longer book, had paper been available, without troubling her friends and acquaintances to dig in their recollections or their files for odd items of information to piece out a scrappy tale. It cannot have happened often that anyone who lived a life so full of impersonal labour has found the time and possessed the ability to provide in addition all the material necessary for a biographer. This book, and the Webb Memorial Trust to which reference is made on the cover, is the best tribute I can pay to her memory.

M. I. C.

Hendon
  February, 1945

CONTENTS

7

LIST OF ILLUSTRATIONS

CHAPTER I

THE BACKGROUND

BEATRICE WEBB was born on January 2nd, 1858, at Standish House, near Gloucester.

The story of Beatrice's birth and ancestry is of so much interest, both as a sample of nineteenth-century social history, and in its influence upon her own development—and therefore of the work which she did both by herself and in the Webb partnership—that even in a short biography it is worth some space. Her great-grandfather, John Potter, who died in 1802, owned a small draper's shop at Tadcaster, which he had inherited from his father, and also a small farm at Wingate Hill near by. His circumstances were thus very much those of the generation whose sons became the captains of industry in the Industrial Revolution; he was, for example, not far removed, in social and living standard, from the ironmonger and post-master of Newport who was the father of Robert Owen, and like him, sent his sons to be shop assistants. He had four sons, John, who got into debt, emigrated and died abroad, William, Thomas, and Richard, and three daughters: Richard was Beatrice Webb's grandfather.

Richard "commenced draper" in the 'nineties, not long after Robert Owen had done the same, securing posts in a variety of towns in the north and midlands. He was not so determinedly industrious an apprentice as Owen; he preferred, in his early days at any rate, to be at home and to work on the farm. "I am very fond of ploughing," he noted; "it raises such a high idea of nature";[1] and his elder brother William, who seems to have enjoyed playing mentor to his juniors, often found occasion to rebuke him for discontent, for idleness, or for having ideas and habits above his station. He was particularly incensed by young Dick's purchase of a nail-cleaner, which he declared was an instrument only suitable for a man-milliner and quite different from a toothbrush. "To keep the teeth clean is an act of decency and cannot be done without a brush, but a knife is quite sufficient

---

[1] For details of the Potter family, drawn from original letters and diaries, the reader is referred to *From Ploughshare to Parliament*, by Mrs. Georgina Meinertzhagen, an elder sister of Mrs. Webb.

for any purpose the nails may require." In spite of these faults, however, young Dick was an earnest fellow; he reflected long and frequently upon politics and public affairs, and in 1799 formed a discussion society with his shopmates in which the debates were conducted in French—and not such bad French either, if a letter of his in French which has been preserved is to be taken as a sample. He must also have progressed at his trade, for in 1802 we find him setting up a cotton warehousing business in Manchester with his brothers William and Tom. It is an ironic comment on the fate of the unco' guid that William, who had been so stern a teacher in earlier years, unfortunately took to drink and four years later was extruded by his younger brothers from the business.

Thomas and Richard, however, prospered remarkably, and before long had become leading citizens of Manchester and Lancashire in general. They were keenly interested in Reform politics;[1] Richard soon acquired the nickname of "Radical Dick," and a large room at the back of their store that of "Potter's Plotting Parlour." We find them protesting against Peterloo, helping to found the *Manchester Guardian* and subsequently the *Manchester Gazette*, both radical journals, playing a prominent role in the municipal politics of Manchester, reorganizing Manchester Grammar School, and later taking an active part in the agitation to reform the Poor Law and in the movement against the Corn Laws. Their interest in Reform, however, was reformist not revolutionary; it was the interest of the rising manufacturers whose ranks they had reached, and they were not concerned either to support adult suffrage or to enlist the help of the working classes. In 1826 Richard got together a big Reform Committee from which working-class representatives were excluded, and this first brought upon the brothers the easily earned hatred of William Cobbett—a hatred not in any way mitigated when at the first election for the Reformed Parliament Cobbett himself proposed to stand for Manchester, where the Potter influence was naturally very strong. The later volumes of Cobbett's *Register* abound in references to the "vile Tadcaster fellows," the "crew of Pipkin Palace" (Cobbett's name for Thomas's country house) and the like.

Meantime, however, the Potters were going rapidly up in the

---

[1] Their father had had his windows broken by a mob for refusing to illuminate them in celebration of a victory in the American War of Independence.

world. Both were members of the Reformed Parliament. Thomas became the first Mayor of Manchester under its new charter and acquired a knighthood; of "Radical Dick's" daughters one married Admiral Anson and another Charles Macaulay, youngest brother of the historian—their daughter Mary married Charles Booth of the great Liverpool shipping line—and his only son was educated at Clifton, where he witnessed the Bristol Reform riots, and was subsequently called to the Bar. Into Richard's family, however, a wilder strain was introduced by his marriage in 1815 to an eager dark girl named Mary Seddon. It has been suggested that Mary Seddon had gypsy, or alternatively Jewish blood in her; and though no confirmation has been established, her letters show a passionate and jealous disposition not at all suggestive of the heroines of Jane Austen. Eight years after her marriage she left her husband owing to what would to-day be described as a nervous breakdown, never returned to live with him as wife and mother, and died at a ripe old age, having at one time endeavoured to lead the Jews back to Palestine. The inheritance of this eccentric grandparent is at least visible in the later histories of some of the Potter descendants.

Richard junior, Beatrice Webb's father, was brought up in third generation style to be a gentleman of leisure. Educated at Clifton and (because he was a Unitarian) at University College, London, he was called to the Bar without intending to practise: on his father's death in 1844 he inherited a reasonable fortune and was preparing to become a country gentleman, to pursue, in the nineteenth-century manner, such intellectual studies and discussion as interested him, and probably in due course to enter politics and rise to Cabinet rank. (It is worth noticing that by middle life he was already attending Anglican services—and being asked to read the lessons!—and disapproving strongly of Disraeli's Reform Act.) Shortly after his father's death he travelled to Italy and while in Rome met and fell in love with a girl named Laurencina Heyworth, the idolized daughter of Laurence Heyworth, a Liverpool merchant who came from much the same stratum as the Potters, his forebears having been "domestic manufacturers" in Rossendale, and who also had a record in Radical politics. Laurencina Heyworth was brilliant and intelligent, a most suitable wife for an intelligent and energetic young *rentier*, and had it not been for the crash of 1847–8 they might have settled quietly down in Herefordshire, where they had bought a property.

That crash, however, removed most of Richard's inherited wealth, much of which had been invested in French *rentes*, and forced him, at the age of thirty, to go to work. It cannot be said that his fall was heavy; his father-in-law stood by him and made him a director of the Great Western Railway, while an old school-fellow, W. P. Price,[1] offered him a partnership in a timber-works at Gloucester. Before many years had passed, he had turned that partnership to great profit by persuading the British and French Governments to order vast quantities of wooden huts to shelter the soldiers in the Crimean War; and though, like any other mid-Victorian capitalist, he suffered from financial ups and downs, he was never again anything but extremely comfortably off.

The events of 1847 did, nevertheless, make this difference; they turned Richard Potter from an idle into an actively working member of the governing class. For the rest of his life, until his stroke in 1885, he was continually *busy*, directing and controlling enterprises and money transactions of all kinds, and pursuing these interests into different parts of Britain and even into the New World (for ten years he was President of the Grand Trunk Railway of Canada); his wife had to accommodate herself to this pattern of life, and his daughters were brought up in it. It was a pattern involving considerable movement, of the family from the London house taken for the Season to the Gloucestershire house at Standish, to Rusland Hall in Westmorland, to the Monmouth property called The Argoed, as well as foreign travel, business tours in which Richard Potter was accompanied by one or more of his daughters; and a corresponding movement of business and other guests in and out of the Potter home. Though events had made him a business man rather than a politician, Richard Potter was firmly settled in the ranks of the Victorian upper class, the people who, as his daughter says in her autobiography, "habi-tually *gave orders*"; and other members of that upper class, belonging to his own or to other occupations, came and went in his house and made the acquaintance of his daughters. The social range of the Potters can most easily be gauged from the marriages made by his daughters.

He had nine: Laurencina, Kate, Mary, Georgina, Blanche, Theresa, Margaret, Beatrice, and Rosalind—his only son died when a small child. All married and these were the husbands of the first seven and the youngest:

---

[1] Grandfather of Morgan Philips Price, the present M.P.

R. D. Holt, merchant of Liverpool; Leonard Courtney, who became Lord Courtney of Penwith and narrowly missed the Speakership of the House of Commons; Arthur Playne, mill-owner; Daniel Meinertzhagen, banker; William Harrison Cripps, distinguished surgeon; Alfred Cripps, barrister and subsequently Lord Parmoor; Henry Hobhouse, member of a great Liberal political family, M.P. for Somerset and Chairman of the Somerset County Council; Arthur Dyson Williams,[1] barrister. The contrast between this solid phalanx and the background of Beatrice's future husband needs no further emphasis.

Note. It would be an extremely interesting assignment for a sociologist or social historian to trace out the fortunes of the Potter blood down to the present generation, before records get lost or confused. This book, however, would not be concerned with the result, since its subject is one of the two Potter daughters who left no descendants at all.

[1] Died not long after his marriage; his widow, the youngest of the sisters, later became Mrs. George Dobbs.

CHAPTER II

CHILDHOOD AND YOUTH

1858–82

IT is a common reflection that in most large families there is one odd-man-out—one who has no particular friend among the others and is not closely knit into a family grouping. Among the Potters the odd-man-out was Beatrice. She did not, until she was nearly grown up, really make friends with Margaret, the sister next above her in age; next below her came the brother who died so young; and between her and the youngest sister, Rosalind, was a gap of seven years, which is far too much for comradeship in childhood. Her father, though exceedingly fond and proud of all his daughters, did not distinguish Beatrice, she says, with the special affection which he felt for some of her sisters; and her mother not merely disliked women, but seems to have had particularly little sympathy for her eighth daughter. She confided to her diary the statement that "Beatrice is the only one of my children who is below the general level of intelligence"—a misjudgment, as can be seen from Beatrice's own account of her early years and reflections, so startling as to suggest something almost amounting to antipathy.

Furthermore, Beatrice was a delicate child, suffering from "almost continuous illness, bouts of neuralgia, of indigestion, of inflammation of all sorts and kinds, from inflamed eyes to congested lungs," which periodically resulted in the abandonment of all formal education, confinement to bed or to the open air, or "complete change of scene," and which probably helped to produce the chronic insomnia of later years;[1] and nobody who has not experienced it can realize the extent to which ill-health in childhood can isolate its victims from the rest of their world, however kindly disposed that world may be. As a result of this, it would seem that Beatrice had next to no formal education, and in her early years was largely "brought up by servants." Her first recollection, at about four years old, is of being flung naked out

---

[1] To this insomnia, none the less, we owe the sixty years' Diary which, when published, will undoubtedly be one of the great documents of the age.

BEATRICE POTTER
as a child, aetat 5

BEATRICE POTTER
as a girl, aetat about 18

of the nursery by the nurse who was in charge of her baby brother; another, also very early, is that of sitting on the ironing board in the laundry, expounding to groups of admiring maids her intention to become a nun. Yet nobody ever suffered less harm than Beatrice from being "brought up by servants"; indeed, it may even be argued that on balance she gained. Her relations with Martha Jackson[1] ("Dada"), the children's nurse, her mother's lifelong companion and "the only saint I ever knew" was always one of deep affection and respect; it was Martha Jackson who was responsible in 1883 for her first introduction to real working-class life;[2] and it seems not unlikely that this early acquaintance with members of the lower classes as real persons helped her in later life to an ease of intercourse which is too seldom acquired by reformers who spend their energies championing "the working class", but who, owing to a more sophisticated and stereotyped upbringing, are unable to talk to an ordinary Co-operator without embarrassment. It should be emphasized, also, that there was no element of repression or resentment in Beatrice's family life—nothing for Freudians to lay hold on. She loved and admired her father intensely; she respected her mother, even if she did not much care for her, and before her death in 1882 had grown to like and understand her much better;[3] and for her sisters she had a strong family affection which lasted throughout her life. She was not in revolt, though she was often unhappy. She simply did not make friends with her family, or, apart from the maids, with anyone else except Herbert Spencer.

These circumstances, acting upon a sickly child with a strong intellect, naturally made for introspection, and the child Beatrice was certainly very introspective. In the slightly laboured opening of *My Apprenticeship* she talks at some length about "the Ego which affirms and the Ego which denies"—which, translated into simpler language, merely means that, unlike people who act upon instinct or as a result of a mental process of which they are not conscious, she had a lifelong habit of arguing with herself (mostly on paper during the night) upon the course she ought to pursue, or the opinions she ought to hold; and this tendency made its appearance very early in her life—and with a certain amount of

---

[1] Herself a distant relative.   [2] See Chapter III.

[3] Photographs show a distinct resemblance, particularly about nose and chin, between Mrs. Potter and Beatrice as a girl, though Beatrice was much the handsomer. They may have had more in common than they realized.

pomposity. Even allowing for the mid-Victorian habit of taking one's own conduct with extreme seriousness, it is difficult to believe that a girl of fourteen who could write:

"Vanity, all is vanity. I feel that I have transgressed deeply, that I have trifled with the Lord. I feel that if I continue thus I shall become a frivolous, silly, unbelieving woman, and yet every morning when I wake I have the same giddy confident feeling and every night I am miserable."[1]

was not in some danger of becoming a morbid introvert. From this fate, in her early years, she seems to have owed her deliverance mainly to Herbert Spencer.

This curious and in many ways absurd philosopher, whose theories of political society are now little more than academic dodos preserved in American university courses, first made the acquaintance of Mr. and Mrs. Potter when he was a young man of twenty-four, and was greatly attracted by both of them. With Mrs. Potter he held much intellectual discussion, sometimes continuing, according to his own account, "so long that Mr. Potter, often playing the role of listener, in despair gave it up and went to bed"; for Richard Potter he had a lifelong affection and respect, although the latter had no appreciation whatever of his philosophical theories, and summed him up as "lacking instinct, my dear, instinct. You will discover that instinct is as important as intellect." He would then add a mental note reminding himself to arrange a day's fishing with the "poor man."

Herbert Spencer was a frequent visitor to the Potter home, and was very popular with the Potter children, to whom his championship of the rights of the individual against authority caused him to appear in the guise of a natural liberator. "You can go out this morning, my dears, with Mr. Spencer," pronounced the old-fashioned governess with lips pursed up, "and mind you follow his teaching and do whatever you have a mind to"—an instruction which they occasionally obeyed to the discomfort of the philosopher.[2] But to one of the Potter girls Spencer became a real friend, a friend so trusted that he was prepared to make her his literary executor; and that friendship began while she was still a child.

---

[1] The same feeling prompted her resolution, recorded three years later, not to "come out" into Society—this determination, however, had disappeared by the following year.　　　　[2] See *My Apprenticeship*, page 26.

It would be difficult to overestimate its importance. Long before she was old enough to comprehend a line of his writings, Beatrice had found in Spencer a man who cared about her personally and was genuinely interested in what she did and felt, who was concerned about her chronic ill-health and troubled to suggest remedies, who listened to her childish discourses upon the universe and patiently criticized her "untutored scribblings about Greek and German philosophers," and who, finally, gave her every encouragement to become an intellectual worker and, as she herself says,[1] set her "the example of continuous concentrated effort in carrying out, with an heroic disregard of material prosperity and physical comfort, a task which he believed would further human progress." Undoubtedly, Spencer was the strongest intellectual influence of which Beatrice Webb was conscious in her early life; it is the greater sign of the originality and power of her own mind that her mature thinking, even before her marriage, shows so little trace of influence of the peculiar Spencerian systematization. Almost the only common factor which seems to have survived is a passion for ascertaining facts and discovering their relevance to theories of society and of human and animal behaviour. Spencer would have been horrified—as he was by her marriage—if he could have foreseen what use Beatrice was to make of this training in *The History of Trade Unionism*, to say nothing of *Soviet Communism*; nevertheless it was to him, rather than to anyone else, that she owed that delight in collecting and verifying illustrative facts to which the shelves full of the Webbs' major works bear witness.

Meantime, she was a girl, and a girl growing up in a household such as I have already described, in which visitors of eminence and importance were continually coming and going, and in which her elder sisters were "coming out," acquiring suitors, and getting married. Personal expenditure was restricted, because her mother, though not her father, had never passed out of the belief in rigid personal abstinence which characterized so many of the families who rose to affluence with the Industrial Revolution; but in matters of the mind she was not restricted at all. Her father had a great admiration for women; he genuinely believed them to be superior to men, and he encouraged his daughters to discuss and read anything they had a mind to, even advising them to buy a book in which they were interested, but which

[1] *My Apprenticeship*, page 29.

happened to be banned by the circulating libraries. "A nice-minded girl," he said, "can read anything; and the more she knows about human nature the better for her and for all the men connected with her." For this reason, her almost complete lack of formal education, save for a short period during which she was sent for reasons of health to a fashionable boarding-school, was very little handicap.[1] She learned no mathematics; but she read a great deal of stiff and serious work; she wrote, beginning in 1872, the journal which was the material of *My Apprenticeship* and must in due course become the material, not merely of any definitive life of the Webbs, but of other social studies of the period which their lives cover; and she reflected and meditated. Intellectually she was educated by herself and by Herbert Spencer; and her education was limited, therefore, by the philosopher's interests and by those which she found for herself.

It is interesting, however, to observe, in her autobiography, some faint trace of an "inferiority complex" produced by her lack of the artistic gifts which some of her sisters possessed. Therein she did herself an injustice. It is true that she could not draw and had practically no appreciation of art or of drama—her interest in Shaw's plays is the exception which proves the rule; poetry seemed to her, generally speaking, nonsense, a deliberate putting of words in the wrong order for no discoverable purpose; and it was only towards the end of her life that the B.B.C. taught her to appreciate music. But she undoubtedly had gifts as a descriptive writer which she never used to the full; the extracts from her early diaries quoted in *My Apprenticeship* fully prove it. At one time she toyed with the "vulgar wish to write a novel" and at another discussed with Auberon Herbert the joint com-position of a Utopia. It is improbable that the novel would have been very good, for her powers of imagination as regards indi-viduals were limited; and the only approach to Utopia which the Webbs ever produced—*The Constitution for a Socialist Common-wealth*—is undoubtedly the least successful of their joint products. But even the most ardent admirer of the great partnership and its literary results may spare a sigh that the monumental and inexorable style which it eventually produced crushed out Beatrice's native ability for vivid word-painting which appears, for example, in the account of the young Irishman, met on a

---

[1] Unless it might have taught her to write a tolerably readable hand, and so spared her correspondents her secretaries (and herself) some travail in later years.

climbing holiday, who was in training for the ministry, the description of social calls made on great society ladies and their conversation about the servants and the butter, or the first letters to her father from the co-operators' home at Bacup (*My Apprenticeship*, pp. 110, 121, and 155).

Intellectual pursuits apart, her education proceeded through learning to take her share in the management of a large establishment—for her mother, as she has told us, practically never spoke to any of the servants except her own maid, but exercised her authority through her daughters as deputies—and, after she had "come out" in 1876, through participation in the London Season. For in the 'seventies, for girls of Beatrice Potter's rank, the London Season and its concomitant country-house visiting, was the real equivalent of university education[1] for their brothers. Parents spent money on their daughters' balls and presentations at Court as they did on their sons' fees and allowances and for much the same reason—to train them for life in upper-class society and to equip them with the means to an adequate livelihood—in the boys' case a profession, in that of the girls a husband. Richard Potter, having no sons, spent on his daughters and reaped the success merited by a good father and wise investor; he saw eight of them safely married to the kind of husband he approved from every point of view, and his latter years were only slightly clouded by the fear that his "little Bee" would not find a good kind man of her own.

Even after fifty years, the recollection of this "university of Society" was extraordinarily vivid in Beatrice's mind. It would not be true to say she disliked it, and though small personal triumphs were not the sort of thing with which she was concerned when she wrote her autobiography, it is clear from minor indications that she was a good deal more of a social success than she allows herself to mention. She was very handsome; she talked well and intelligently—even if her intellect was alarming to some —and she could listen; since, moreover, her elder sisters all married while she was young, she was for a considerable time the only daughter, "the brilliant Beatrice Potter," and could shine unchallenged. But she early saw through the show to the purpose which lay behind it and the colossal waste, both material and

---

[1] In after years, Beatrice occasionally wondered whether she herself would have done better with a university education; but was consoled by the reflection that she might have become a Woman Don. Having regard to her character and talents, one can be very glad that the experiment was never tried.

spiritual, which it involved. "I discovered," she writes in one of the most pungent passages of her autobiography,[1] "that personal vanity was an 'occupational disease' of London Society; and that anyone who suffered as I did from constitutional excitability in this direction, the symptoms being not only painful ups and downs of inflation and depression but also little lies and careless cruelties, should avoid it as the very Devil. By the end of the season, indigestion and insomnia had undermined physical health; a distressing mental nausea, taking the form of cynicism about one's own and other people's characters, had destroyed all faith in a capacity for steady work. And when these years of irresponsible girlhood were over, and I found myself (after 1882) my father's housekeeper and hostess, I realized that the pursuit of pleasure was not only an undertaking, but also an elaborate, and to me a tiresome undertaking, entailing expensive plant, a large number of employees and innumerable decisions upon insignificant matters." The training, however, was probably worth while in more than one respect; not only did she acquire a profound distaste for spending time and money on ends not desired for their own sake but enforced by fashion or custom, but she was permanently immunized from the temptation, to which more than one eminent Labour leader has fallen victim, of being flattered and diverted by the attentions of persons in high social position.

[1] *My Apprenticeship*, page 49.

CHAPTER III

APPRENTICESHIP

1882-8

THE final paragraphs of the last chapter have taken us a little way beyond its proper scope, which was that of Beatrice's childhood and her youth as a comparatively unimportant member of a large family. With her mother's death in 1882 the picture changes; her elder sisters were already married, and she became not merely the Miss Potter in charge[1] of the household, but also her father's companion and from time to time almost his confidential secretary; he even upon occasion suggested—a proposal more revolutionary then than it would be to-day—that if she did not marry she should become his business partner. This association was of the greatest importance for the development both of Beatrice's character and of the technique which she later employed in social investigation. In the first place, it trained her in methodical organization; having once been accustomed to manage a large household without allowing it to absorb all her own time, no domestic or office ménage had henceforth any terrors for her. In the second place, she learned to treat money as a business man treats it, and not to regard it either as an unintelligible mystery, as too many women, including intelligent Socialist women, tend to do, or as a very rare commodity with which one dare take no risks—as is the almost inevitable result of having been brought up on scanty and precarious means. Much of the history of the working-class movement, whether Trade Union or Co-operative, has been adversely conditioned by the inability of the decent thrifty working man to run any risk with the hoarded pence of himself and his fellows or to spend with imagination on the chances of greater gain. Beatrice, working as the secretary and associate of a man who was concerned in many businesses and whose talents lay in speculation and planning rather than in execution, early grasped the meaning of the phrase "cut one's losses"; and the knowledge

---

[1] "In charge," as a director, not a practitioner. Beatrice had neither need nor ability to cook or mend or do household chores.

stood her in good stead in other spheres than those of finance.
She never suffered from either the timidity in action or the clinging
to institutions or projects after they have become useless or
impossible of achievement which the history of the last two
generations has, alas, shown to be such a common failure of
Social Democratic parties and governments founded on them : she
had practical as well as intellectual courage.

Thirdly, she gained a great deal of experience in personal
contact with and handling of people of many types, which when
reinforced by the East London experiences described later in this
chapter stood her in very good stead when she came to exercise
the craft of a social investigator. In the Webb partnership, she
was the interviewer, broadly speaking, and Sidney the sum-
marizer and note-taker, and she was an extremely successful
interviewer, sparing no pains to set the objects of her study at
their ease and to coax and cajole them into parting with the
information she desired to obtain. Readers who are interested
in this aspect of her work should read the illuminating essay
called "The Art of the Interviewer" in that highly personal
book, *Methods of Social Study*, which recounts, *inter alia*, how an
elementary knowledge of palmistry can upon occasion assist an
investigator. Whatever defects Beatrice showed when trying to
convert or to organize people—and she had some—when she
was merely trying to extract information from them she was
superb; and the beginnings of that ability she owed to the years
spent as her father's assistant and the head of his household.

Two main strands are visible in Beatrice's life for the next few
years; a search for a faith to live by and a search for a profession.
The first was not really satisfied until after the date at which this
chapter closes, after she had discovered, almost simultaneously,
Fabian Essays and the writer of one of them. But by the time of
her mother's death she had already practically lost her faith in
the Christian Church, and she never returned to it. In after years
she criticized the doctrines of Christianity on intellectual grounds,
and became particularly indignant over the command to "do
unto others as ye would they should do unto you," which she
said was a highly individualist precept and ran contrary to any
conception of social justice; but her original rejection of it—
which was a gradual process—was due to simple inability to
continue in acceptance either of its mythology or of its claim to
universal validity as against Buddhism or any other of the great

religions.[1] Somewhat illogically, she retained a belief in the value of individual private prayer and ascribed to its practice her ability to survive the mental and spiritual troubles of the ten years preceding her marriage.

The losing of her early faith left her, however, with the sensation of a void which she spent some years endeavouring to fill. She tried the worship of science, so strong and fervid among its votaries in the 'seventies and 'eighties, whose prophet was Spencer; she read Winwood Reade's *Martyrdom of Man*, talked with Tyndall, Huxley, and Francis Galton (for whom she had a great and admiring affection); she struggled with George Henry Lewes's *History of Philosophy*. But the Religion of Science failed to take hold; at the end of it all she confessed herself a doubting Thomas, albeit a feeble one. Later she sampled the Religion of Humanity as preached by Auguste Comte, among whose array of followers were numbered many of her acquaintances, including Frederic Harrison and his wife. The Harrisons were more than acquaintances, they were close friends for many years, and stood by her whole-heartedly at the time of her marriage when others fell away; but in spite of her affection and respect for the Harrisons and her debt to that other enthusiastic Positivist, her cousin Charles Booth, she never became a Comtist, and later summed up the Positivist philosophy as "a valiant effort to make a religion out of nothing; a pitiful attempt by poor humanity to turn its head round and worship its tail." It was not until the Fabian restatement of the philosophy of Bentham and John Stuart Mill as Socialism had fused with her own experience of working-class institutions and the realities of modern industrial society that she found any philosophic haven; and though that apparently satisfied her for a large part of her working life, those who knew her realized that in later years she found it increasingly lacking in the dynamic force of the great faiths. Her final resting-place can be clearly seen in the eleventh and twelfth chapters of *Soviet Communism*; it is one of the small ironies which are so common in history that the woman who in her early days wrote highly critical analyses of the economics of Marx[2] should have ended her days a passionate supporter of the régime inspired by his philosophy.

[1] Brian Hodgson, Gloucestershire squire, ex-Indian civil servant, and oriental scholar, played a large part in opening her eyes to the world of religious thought which lay altogether outside Christianity.
[2] See Appendix to *My Apprenticeship*.

Her choice of a career proceeded, during these years, more fruitfully, though at one point there was a real possibility that she might not have a career in the proper sense at all. In 1882 or 1883 she first met Joseph Chamberlain, then almost at the height of his success as a Radical leader, and was very strongly attracted; in fact, it is accurate to say that for some time she was in love with him. It is easy to understand the source of his attraction for her. Twenty years older than Beatrice, and coming from much the same social ancestry, he stood then in the public eye as a passionate protagonist of Radicalism, of that urge to better the condition of the people as a whole which had inspired her grandfather and great-grandfather. Furthermore, he was not merely a politician or a philosopher—a talker; he was a man of great practical ability who had already done more than many would have thought possible to bring about in his own city of Birmingham the conditions which he hoped to see extended to the whole nation; and by these efforts he had already raised himself to a position of political power in which he would be able, like Beatrice's father and his friends, to give orders and expect them to be carried out—with this difference, that the orders he would give would be aimed, not at increasing the individual wealth and personal comfort of himself or his family and friends, but deliberately at improving the standard and ordering the comfort of the whole people. The references to Chamberlain in *My Apprenticeship*, and particularly the long and vivid description[1] of a packed political demonstration in Birmingham, when "the master and the darling of his town" received a tremendous ovation, shows very clearly how exciting Beatrice found the personality and position of the man; and as he on his side was not unmoved by her personality, her looks, and her intelligence, there was a definite chance that she would become his third wife (his second had died in 1875) and his helpmate in his political career.

This did not happen. Had it happened, it could scarcely have failed to be a disaster; indeed, except for the very remote contingency that Beatrice as a stepmother might have some influence for good upon his son Neville, there seems nothing to be said in its favour. Chamberlain's Radicalism, and his enthusiasm for social reform, were at their peak in the early 'eighties; had Beatrice married him then, she would have had to watch him

[1] Page 125 et seq.

turn from a radical to an imperialist, and associate more and more closely with persons with whose views and practices she could not possibly have felt in agreement; far more important, she could not possibly have done the work which she did do. Mrs. Joseph Chamberlain, a political hostess, could have left no place for Beatrice Potter, social investigator; and Beatrice Webb, joint leader and maker of Socialist thought, could never have been born. Mrs. Joseph Chamberlain would have been comparatively useless and certainly miserable.

Even in the first glow of interest and excitement, Beatrice was not without the power of critically appraising the object of it, as the following quotations from her Diary show:

"By temperament he is an enthusiast and a despot. A deep sympathy with the misery and incompleteness of most men's lives, and an earnest desire to right this, transforms political action into a religious crusade" (the faith she had failed to find?) "but running alongside this genuine enthusiasm is a passionate desire to crush opposition to his will, a longing to feel his foot on the neck of others, as though he would persuade himself that he represents the right and his adversaries the wrong." (January, 1884.)

"In his treatment of some members of the Association (I noticed this particularly in his attitude towards Schnadhorst) he used the simple power of 'You shall, and you go to the devil if you don't.' The second power—that of attraction—is shown to a certain extent in private intercourse with his intimate friends, but chiefly in his public relationship towards his own constitutency; and it is proved by the emotional nature of their enthusiasm.. It is to this power that Chamberlain owes all the happiness of his life, and it is the reaction of the power which intensifies his sympathies and also his egotism. Whether it will develop so as to assume a form which will extend beyond the immediate influence of his personality is one of the questions which will decide his future greatness. At present he fails to express it in his written words, except in the bitterness of his hatred and contempt, which is but one side of his passion." (February, 1884.)

The emotion, however, was strong and disturbing, and her doubts of the right course of action probably great; but whatever the reasons which finally influenced either party, the Socialist and social student cannot but be profoundly grateful for the result.

This result was in part due to the fact that Beatrice in the early 'eighties was already moving on the path to her own career. The initial step was partly fortuitous and partly due to the curiosity which was so important an element in the originality of her mind. In 1882, following the example of her sister Kate (afterwards Lady Courtney), she had gone in for a little "slumming"—in her case some work for the Charity Organization Society, the body which attempted to prevent the evils attendant upon undiscriminating almsgiving by systematic investigation and separation of the deserving sheep from the undeserving goats. Voluntary social service in some form or other, ranging from active membership of the House of Lords or of a County Council to the life-work of Florence Nightingale, or "district visiting," was reckoned as a duty by a great many of the middle and upper class of Beatrice's day, and their acceptance of it played no small part in the stability of the British social system and its failure to develop a functionless parasitic class of the kind seen in France before 1789 and in Russia before 1917.[1] Beatrice herself ascribes the zeal to a "class-consciousness of sin" among property-owners, arising from the violent contrasts in standards of living between rich and poor, which produced the thunder of Carlyle and the outspoken pictures of Dickens; but it is probable that the causes lie further back. Hannah More, the Friends, and the charity school pioneers were doing "social service" long before Carlyle had uttered a syllable, and Pitt's generation was well acquainted with unpaid public work. The tradition, in the nineteenth century, was no more than carried on by the C.O.S., by Octavia Hill, and other great names.

But Beatrice Potter, though she worked for the C.O.S. intermittently for five years, felt very soon that the stratum of the indigent, the unlucky, and the shiftless, with which that body principally dealt, was only the fringe, and not a very interesting fringe of "labour." (A few years later, as a result of her work as

---

[1] Some writers, such as Professor Carr in *The Conditions of Peace*, have endeavoured to produce a contrast in this respect between the middle and the working classes and to accuse the latter of regarding the nation as an organization which provided for them such amenities as free education, but to which, in peace-time at least, they owed no service. Such criticism, assuming as it does an upper and middle-class interpretation of the term "social service," ignores all the mass of effort expended by members of the working classes in such fields as the organization of chapels, mechanics' institutes, evening classes, and the like, apart from the personal services continuously rendered by the poor to the poor without any organization at all. Even assuming its own interpretation it is nevertheless unjust, for two reasons: first, that the opportunity to undertake unpaid "social service," particularly in the day-time, is almost wholly a privilege of the well-to-do; secondly, that the encouragement offered to persons of working-class origin to serve their country—as magistrates, for example—has been, to say the least of it, very meagre indeed. "First," said the realistic Greek, "first gain an independent income, and then practise virtue."

a rent-collector, she made an interesting comparison between the "leisured class" of the poor—the careless borrowers and occasional thieves who lived by casual employment—and the leisured class of the London Society where she had been brought up.)

In her early life in her father's home she had found "labour" an abstract term, used alongside with its mate "capital," and turning up in technical journals and company reports in such revealing phrases as "water plentiful and labour docile" (from a prospectus). In her own words "right down to the time when I began to train as a social investigator, labour was an abstraction, which seemed to denote an arithmetically calculable mass of human beings, each individual a repetition of the other, very much in the same way that the capital of my father's companies consisted, I imagined, of gold sovereigns identical with all other gold sovereigns in form, weight, and colour, and also in value."[1] Her imagination getting to work, she realized that this was not a true conception, that "labour" must consist of individual persons; but she did not feel that the individual persons she met with in her social work were a true sample.

It was then that she remembered that not all the family of her grandfather Heyworth had gone up in the world; some had remained factory hands in the north and were periodically visited by Martha Jackson. The story of her decision to go and find out for herself what sort of people they were would be spoiled if it were told in any but her own words.

"Surely, Da," said I, turning my eyes for the moment from the fascinating scenes in a coal fire, "some of the Akeds must be our kin."

"Well, let's see," says our old nurse, putting her hands on her knees and meditating, "there's John Aked, he's a reedmaker, now out o' work, nephew of Mrs. Heyworth's. Then he's got two brothers, James, manager of the waterworks, and William, who is, I fancy, rather queer; I don't think he does much. Then there's Mrs. Ashworth, Miss Aked as was. I was apprenticed to her in the dressmaking line before I went to Miss Heyworth. She married James Ashworth, a rich man; she's a widow now, and what you call rather close with her money. I don't think there's any of your grandmother's relations left besides them as I have mentioned; at least I am not aware of it."

"Da," I said, as I watched a narrow bridge of black coal give

[1] *My Apprenticeship*, page 42.

way, tumble into the red hot mass below and burst into flame, "I should dearly love to go to Bacup next time you go." "Well, you know you can always go; there's no occasion to wait for that," answered the dear old woman, "but my friends up there would be astonished to see a Miss Potter coming along with me; they are not accustomed to such grand folk. I think they would be what they call 'flayed' by you." "Oh!" cried I, jumping up with the delightful consciousness of an original idea, "I wouldn't be Miss Potter, I would be Miss Jones, farmer's daughter, from near Monmouth."

So it was as Miss Jones, farmer's daughter, that Beatrice went in November, 1883, to stay in the house of John Ashworth, in a back street of Bacup in Lancashire, and there to meet, long before she had thought of writing on the Trade Union or Co-operative movements, the men and women who composed them. In this first visit (she returned to the place in 1886 and 1889 and at the close of the second visit disclosed her identity) she did not make any deep political generalizations; but she discovered the Co-operative movement and the enormous part played by it and by the dissenting chapels in the life of the Lancashire working class; and she noted that in the younger generation the strong force of religious faith was beginning to weaken and to be replaced, to some extent, by political fervour, and suggested that local government would be a field in which this fervour could be most profitably trained, as "one of the best preventives against the socialistic tendencies of the coming democracy"![1] She also found, a little to her surprise, that she was completely at home with these working men and women, that they talked to her freely and in spite of the fact of her smoking cigarettes found nothing odd about her except that she was "far more like a male than a female to talk wi'." Throughout her life, in fact, there was always a large element of what is commonly called masculinity about Beatrice's mental processes.

The first venture at Bacup led no further for the moment. Beatrice returned to social work in London. But by this time she was already disillusioned about the C.O.S., of which her autobiography contains a full and mordant criticism. By their vehement discouragement of personal charity, the medieval almsgiving which the visitor to many Eastern countries will still find in full force to-day, while at the same time they frantically

[1] *My Apprenticeship*, page 161.

opposed any organized State effort to relieve the hardships of poverty—as, for instance, by granting old-age pensions—they had, she points out, "let loose the tragic truth that, wherever society is divided into a minority of Haves and a multitude of Have-nots, charity is twice cursed, it curseth him that gives and him that takes."[1] For a time she found, or thought she had found, a more satisfying field of activity in succeeding her sister Kate as a rent-collector and manager of blocks of working-class flats. These buildings had been erected by philanthropists inspired by Octavia Hill, to provide cheap and sanitary rehousing for the poor of the dock areas whom the demolition programme of the Metropolitan Board of Works (forerunner of the L.C.C.) had removed from their appalling "homes." In association with Miss Ella Pycroft, she took over, at the beginning of 1885, the management of Katharine Buildings, near St. Katharine Dock, and continued the work, with some intervals, for nearly two years.

The experience, however, was not satisfactory. The work itself, as all rent-collectors and house property managers know, was physically extremely exhausting, and Beatrice, though her health had improved greatly since childhood, was not of the horse-like breed whom nothing can tire. The surroundings were very depressing, and the Buildings themselves even more so, partly because they were not "slum property" whose horrors everyone could deplore—and blame them upon a nameless "slum landlord" as later they blamed starvation wages upon an equally nameless "middleman sweater"—but had been deliberately planned by philanthropical human beings as places in which other human beings ought to be glad to live. Even Beatrice's aesthetic sense, which was never her strong point, was outraged by a design in which the dominant feature of the whole building was the water-closets on the landings and the easiest rendezvous for young men and women the landings by the same water-closets. "All amenity, some would say, all decency, was sacrificed to the two requirements of low rents and physically sanitary buildings." More than that, she came to feel increasingly that the whole experiment of which Katharine Buildings was a part, though it was not, like C.O.S. detective work, actively insulting to the poor, was doing nothing whatever to solve the

[1] *My Apprenticeship*, page 203. It was for this very reason that Samuel and Henrietta Barnett, two of the leading social workers of London and great personal friends of Beatrice, left the C.O.S. in 1886.

basic problem—that of their poverty; and in November, 1886, she went so far as to term it "an utter failure." Except as an enlargement of experience, therefore, the months she spent in rent-collecting must be considered a waste of time, though even here it is instructive to notice the thoroughness with which she set about her job and the instinct for organization which she brought to bear on it. An instance of the first is the brief note in her diary—following a long description of Emma Cons, Victorian philanthropist and aunt of Lilian Baylis of the Old Vic—"Desirable that I should thoroughly master details of South London Building Company management"; and in November, 1885, before she had been a year at work, she produced a proposal for the association of all the agencies which provided housing for the poor, covering about 150,000 persons, for the pooling of all the information which they could collect about the objects of their charity,[1] the publication of the results, and the provision of a central information office, which seems to have startled even the experienced Canon Barnett, who asked her to think out a detailed plan. This, however, she never did, for on the 26th of the same month her father was struck down with paralysis. For some time she was completely absorbed in attendance on him and debarred from all public activities; and when, realizing that he was likely to live for years as a helpless invalid, her married sisters decided to take turns in relieving her, it was not to rent-collecting that she returned, but to help Charles Booth in his great Inquiry into the Life and Labour of the People of London.

She had first met "Cousin Charlie," founder with his brother of the Booth Shipping Line, philanthropist, Positivist, ardent believer in science, who looked more like a priest, a university professor, or an artist, than a successful captain of industry, in the late 'seventies, when he came with his wife to stay at Standish House while recovering from a breakdown in health, and had been very much impressed by him; but the earliest mention of the great Inquiry in her autobiography is dated April, 1886. It was in the spring of the following year that, using the Friends'

---

[1] "This is the outline of what I wish to discover about the inhabitants of Katharine Buildings: number of family, dead or alive; occupation of all members; actual income from work, charity or private property; race; whether born in London; if so, belonging to London stock? If not, reason for immigration, and from what part of the country; religion. As much of previous history as obtainable." (November 8th, 1885.) Some of these questions may have been suggested by discussion with Charles Booth (see below); nevertheless, it sounds a rather formidable programme to present to the lady rent-collectors.

headquarters in Bishopsgate as her home, she began to assist Booth by making an inquiry into dock labour in Tower Hamlets.

There is no space here to describe the Booth Inquiry, which by incontrovertible and inescapable *facts* taught complacent Londoners of the comfortable classes so much about the misery and degradation which formed the ground floor and the basement of their own prosperity, and which has been the model for so many subsequent studies of similar type by Seebohm Rowntree, Lady Bell, and others; it is very fully described in *My Apprenticeship*. What is important is the influence which the methods, practical and intellectual, of Charles Booth and his able assistants, Hubert Llewellyn Smith and Ernest Aves, had on Beatrice Potter. She was instantly delighted with them, and the reasons for her delight are plain.

In the first place, Booth was one of the first nineteenth-century investigators to start without *a priori* assumptions about economic laws (which always irritated Beatrice intensely) to discover, as far as possible without bias, what were the real facts about the lives of the poor. It is said, though the authority is not very certain, that he actually began his Inquiry with a view to showing that the fierce statements of the Social Democratic Federation about the shocking condition of London were unjustified; but there is no doubt that the conclusions he reached surprised himself. Secondly, he found a way,[1] before "sampling" was invented, to combine the quantitative analysis derived from statistics obtained from the Registrar-General with qualitative description, collected by personal interview, of what life on a given wage in a particular area was like for an individual. Thirdly, by using what his apprentice calls "the method of wholesale interviewing and automatic recording" of the impressions of a very great number of helpers he managed to cancel out or to neutralize the personal predilections of any one of them. It is with obvious delight that Beatrice tells us how his inquirers, "in a wholly beneficent sense," were unable to see the wood for the trees, and that the completed results of an investigation frequently contradicted the expectations of one or other, or even of all, of the investigators. Finally, he was himself a man of great human qualities under whom it must have been a joy to work,

---

[1] To some extent, Booth here followed in the steps of Henry Mayhew, who in the 'fifties wrote anecdotic and statistical articles which were collected under the title *London Labour and the London Poor*.

who had embarked upon this giant undertaking from no selfish
motive but purely out of sympathy with human suffering, but
who at the same time was consumingly anxious that the picture
he finally presented should be true and balanced, and that the
dark patches should not be so coloured by resentment or pity as
to hide the brighter ones.[1]

In this task, Booth and his immediate assistants coped with the
statistical material. Beatrice, to whom statistics were about as
intelligible as poetry, was at first merely one of the interviewers,
though an interviewer who *enjoyed* her life and work, who was
beginning to feel her capacity and regain the faith in her own
individual capabilities which had suffered some painful weakening
—mentioned in her autobiography—during the period of her
early and abortive apprenticeship.

Pretty soon, however, her quality, demonstrated in the information which she persuaded her part in the Inquiry to yield, began
to receive more public recognition. She actually "commenced
author" in February, 1886, when the *Pall Mall Gazette* asked if
she would sign, as an article, a letter which she had sent them
on the subject of relief works for the unemployed. Admittedly,
this request came at a moment when she was spiritually at a very
low ebb; nevertheless, it is astonishing to the historian of 1945 to
find that Beatrice, at twenty-eight, could derive such comfort
from so small a crumb of recognition. In September, 1887,
however, an article of hers on "Dock Life in the East End of
London," the fruit of her Booth investigations, appeared in the
highly respectable pages of *The Nineteenth Century*; and was in due
course followed by three others, entitled "The Tailoring Trade of
East London," "Pages from a Workgirl's Diary," and "The
Lords' Committee on the Sweating System,"[2] published between
1888 and 1890. As an authority she had begun to arrive.

For Booth's use for his brilliant cousin did not end with setting
her to haunt dock gates and make acquaintance with dockers'
families, fascinating as she found it. For her next "holiday"

[1] "They refuse," he said of those who could not maintain this attitude, who pitied
the dying birds so profoundly that they forgot the living ones, "they refuse to set off
and balance the happy hours of the same class, or even of the same people, against
these miseries; much less can they consent to bring the lot of other classes into the
account, add up the opposing figures, and contentedly carry forward a credit balance.
In the arithmetic of woe they can only add or multiply; they cannot subtract or
divide"—words which many passionate propagandists might well inscribe permanently on their writing desks.

[2] The articles on the Docks and the Tailoring Trade were included in the first
volume of Booth's *Survey*, published in 1889.

(from attendance on her father) he very soon prescribed the job of investigating "sweated" labour in the East End tailoring trade, which she began in October, 1887. This gave her the only actual experience she ever had of life as an industrial worker. After her "first morning learning how to sweat" (as an investigator calling on an establishment in Oxford Street, Stepney), she got employment in several workshops as a "plain trouser hand,"[1] in the course of which she overheard the somewhat double-edged compliment: "She's no good at the sewing: if I keep her I will put her to look after the outworkers—she's got the voice and the manner to deal with that bloody lot." This investigation brought her more into the public eye, by producing a command to give evidence before the 1888 Select Committee of the House of Lords on the Sweating System; and incidentally, as a reflection upon an interview with a factory inspector who had refused information because Booth had plied him with insufficient personal compliments, gave rise to the remark, which ought to be written on the hearts of all real workers in the social services or elsewhere, "*The personal element in work is contemptible.*" To that maxim Beatrice—and Sidney also—adhered throughout their lives.

Giving evidence before the Lords' Committee was not on the whole a happy experience. Beatrice was irritated by irrelevant comments from the press on her dress and appearance, and more unpleasant comments on the facts she had to give about the social and moral conditions which were the result of starvation wages; it was her first experience of public questioning, and she seems to have been nervous and to have made blunders. But, more important than that, the conclusions which she was gradually reaching were such as to be anathema to the members of the Committee. They agreed that some wages were shockingly low —yes; and that wages which were shockingly low produced results which were very dreadful—some of which should really not have been mentioned by a nicely brought up young woman of good appearance. But, like the C.O.S. and the philanthropic flat-builders, they wanted to see the problem as a small and localized one, which could be solved by a minor piece of legislation or by strict control, and if necessary punishment, of a few

---

[1] She wrote up her experiences in the article called "Pages from a Workgirl's Diary," which had a success which rather annoyed her, as she thought it was adventitious. This article, with some others, was republished in *Problems of Modern Industry*, by S. and B. Webb (1898).

C

anti-social persons in a few selected places. Just in the same way as Hitler's dupes in pre-war Germany, though on a lesser scale and in a quieter manner, they were looking for scapegoats—primarily, then as now, Jews—on whom the evil could be fastened; and they were confronted with this Miss Potter, who, when asked "How would you define the Sweating System?" stated flatly:

"An inquiry into the Sweating System is practically an inquiry into all labour employed in manufacture which has escaped the regulation of the Factory Act and Trade Unions." (Question 3248.)

Subsequently, in her review of the Select Committee's Report, she elaborated the statement that sweating was not a special vice of middlemen or of sub-contractors, or confined to those who employed a handful of workers in backyard premises, but was equally to be found in such large-scale machine industries as textiles, engineering, or ready-made clothing—anywhere, in fact, where effective machinery had not been introduced to protect the worker from the greed of the profit-maker. She summed up the position in a phrase, *"the sweater is, in fact, the whole nation,"* which occurs in an address given to the Rochdale Co-operative Congress of 1892. But by 1892 she had discovered not merely the cause of nineteenth-century sweating but its remedy. To this aspect of her intellectual development we must now turn.

CHAPTER IV

CO-OPERATION AND SOCIALISM

THE casual observer might be rather surprised to find that a woman of Beatrice Potter's mental ability and with her immediate personal knowledge of poverty, of the results which nineteenth-century capitalism had produced on the minds and bodies of its servants, particularly on its women servants, had not become early in her career either a Socialist or a feminist. In 1884 she was still writing to a friend, in rather pompous phrasing, of her objection to "these gigantic experiments, state-education and state-intervention in other matters, which are now being inaugurated and which flavour of inadequately thought-out theories—the most dangerous of all social poisons"; even five years later she had not got beyond meditating "whether profit is not on the whole a demoralizing force"; and it was in the spring of 1889 that she was ill-considered enough to allow her name to be attached to Mrs. Humphry Ward's manifesto protesting against Votes for Women.

The latter mistake is fairly easy to understand. Beatrice never, in all her life, suffered any disadvantage from being a woman. Her father, as already related, firmly believed in the superiority of women, discussed with his daughters on equal terms, and gave them, if they wanted it, anything he would have given to his sons. Furthermore, as she very candidly acknowledges, in many ways she found being a woman a definite advantage; the public opinion of her class did not force her to train for a recognized profession, as it would have done had she been a man, but left her free to choose her own occupations; and when she took up social investigation she discovered, she says, that being a woman enabled her to get information and assistance that would have been denied to a man. (Whether a woman who did not happen to be Beatrice Potter would have met with the same experience is of course another question, and one which she does not discuss.) At any rate, she had never felt in her own person any sex disability; that there were other women not so happily situated, with whom the social worker at least ought to have sympathized, she might have discovered from her East End studies, but she does

not seem to have been looking in that direction. The demand
for women's suffrage reached her from a different source, from
ladies of the middle class who were disposed to transform a protest
against specific injustices into a generalized conviction that
women as a sex were universally superior to and oppressed by
men (which Beatrice knew to be untrue), and some of whom
further extended their cry for equal rights to a demand for the
abolition of all discriminatory legislation including the Factory
Acts—a demand which Beatrice rightly thought monstrous. In
sum, it would seem that she had come up against the sillier sort
of feminists, and that they made her impatient. All her life,
Beatrice was impatient of silliness, more especially when it was
exhibited by persons who because of their birth and education
might reasonably have been expected to know better; and one
may conjecture that it was in a fit of impatience, and without
thinking out the implications, that she signed Mrs. Humphry
Ward's letter. This conjecture is borne out by her refusal to take
up the cudgels when Millicent Garrett Fawcett wrote an indignant reply—she was not sure enough of her ground—and by her
uneasiness at finding that her Co-operative friends assumed that
she had signed the letter because she was a well-to-do woman, as
indeed was partly true. But the mistake was made, and took a
long time to repair; it was nearly twenty years before she publicly
and generously acknowledged her error.

The question of Socialism is easier. She was not a Socialist
partly because she had not yet carried her meditations upon social
evils to the only end which would satisfy her, but more because
she had not yet discovered the type of Socialist who could appeal
to her; she was like a dissatisfied believer who has yet to discover
the possibility of atheism. Such Socialism as she had come across
appeared to her to be the work of doctrinaires or of ranters, or
both. Doctrinairism—*a priorism*—she disliked and distrusted
instinctively, and by the middle 'eighties she had already become
strongly critical of its particular manifestation in classical political
economy, both because it seemed to her to ignore entirely the
human element in the production of wealth, and further because
its theorizings dealt with "only one of many social institutions
engaged in or concerned with wealth production; and it is misleading to ignore these other social institutions by which wealth
has been, and is now being produced among hundreds of millions
of people unacquainted with the 'big business' or profit-making

capitalism for which Ricardo sought to formulate the 'laws.'"[1]
She wanted any study of social questions, whether it were called
Political Economy or whatever it was called, to be based on, and
its conclusions to arise from a study of all social institutions,
including the family, Trade Unions, local governing bodies,
churches, etc., of which profit-making business would be only
one; she wanted, in fact, deductive Economics to be replaced by
inductive Sociology.

It was unfortunate, for a time, that the only part of Marx's
teaching which seems to have reached her was just the part
which she was least likely to appreciate, the labour theory of
value, of which she wrote a sharply critical essay at about the
same date. Marx's views about history and the evolution of
institutions might have found her more sympathetic had she
discovered them. It was also unfortunate that the Socialists
whom she came across were of the hot-gospeller pure-milk-of-
the-word type associated with the early days of the Social Democratic Federation and its insistence on the verbal inspiration of
Das Kapital. She does not say very much about them; but it is
clear that she considered them at least as silly as the ardent
feminists if not sillier. And though by 1888 she had just heard
of the Fabian Society, the only Fabian leader she had met was
that very un-Fabian Fabian, Annie Besant. Annie Besant was
then at her brilliant best as a public orator; but it was hardly
to be expected that the essentially rationalist Beatrice Potter,
with her continuous striving after self-control and a logical
approach to life, should be favourably impressed by the elemental
genius who began by enthusiastically marrying an unimaginative
clergyman of the Church of England, fled from him to become
with Charles Bradlaugh an apostle of Secularism, individualism,
and birth control, changed again to a strike leader and passionate
advocate of Socialism, and within less than half a dozen years
had abandoned her Socialism for an equally fervent devotion to
Theosophy. In her autobiography, Beatrice is polite to Mrs.
Besant, but her politeness barely conceals the fact that she thought
her an inspired idiot, and doubtfully inspired at that. Her near
acquaintance with the Fabian Society only began when she was
referred to another of its leaders as the kind of man who knew

---

[1] *My Apprenticeship*, Appendix: "On the Nature of Economic Science." See also
the study by G. D. H. Cole, "Beatrice Webb as an Economist," in the *Economic Journal*,
December, 1943.

everything about social subjects and had the knowledge at his fingertips.

In order to need this man's knowledge, however, she had first to enter the fields in which that knowledge would be useful; and this came about through her own explorations. After her work on sweating in the East End was done, she had to decide what she would do with her next "holiday" from her father's side. Booth made the obvious suggestion that she should follow up what she had begun by intensive study of the questions of women's labour in general, and should make herself an authority on the subject; and this suggestion was strongly backed by her friend, the economist Alfred Marshall, whom she consulted. But though she seriously considered the idea, she turned it down in favour of a more ambitious plan—to write a book on the Co-operative Movement. She wanted, in the field of social study, to work on something positive, some of the living institutions ignored by the classical economists to which she had made reference in the paper quoted above; and in the Co-operative Movement she thought she had found her subject. She knew it was a living and growing thing, for she had seen it with her own eyes; and the fact that hardly anyone she knew had ever heard of it and that Marshall discouraged her strongly, practically giving her to understand that she was a presumptuous young woman even to think of such a thing, did not deter her in the least. Early in 1889 she began work on the book which subsequently appeared as *The Co-operative Movement*, and which, despite Marshall's gloomy prophecies, was to hold the field as the only impartial study of its subject for many years to come.

It was a little book—as Sidney Webb pointed out just after it had appeared, "it ought to have taken you six weeks to write, not seven months." But it represented a great deal of labour of the characteristic Webb type as well as the mere act of putting sentences together. All during the spring and early summer of 1889, in the midst of attendance on her father,[1] Beatrice was wading through masses of reports of conferences, files of journals, balance-sheets of societies, and all the rest of it; and this she supplemented by many visits, which she recorded in her diary, to various Co-operative Societies, interviews with leading Co-opera-

---

[1] Since her mother's death and still more during her father's illness she had acquired the habit of getting up early and devoting the hours between five and eight in the morning to sustained reading.

tive personalities, with some of whom, such as Benjamin Jones, she became firm friends, and long sessions, cigarette in hand, with the Central Boards of both the Co-operative Union and the Co-operative Wholesale Society. In a criticism of dining with the latter—"A higgledy-piggledy dinner; good materials served up coarsely, and shovelled down by the partakers in a way that is not appetizing"—the reader gets an early hint of Beatrice's critical attitude towards both food and drink, which coloured a good many people's impression of the Webb partnership in its heyday. She was not an abstainer from any kind of food or drink on principle, but she did regard excess interest in, or excess time occupied in consuming food or drink as sinful waste. This was perhaps partly accounted for either by the fact that an ascetic diet best suited her own delicate constitution, or by half-conscious recollection of the enormous amount of labour which it cost to dine and wine the Society of her youth; whatever the cause, it was an ever-present factor, and at one time caused the name of the Webbs to be unfairly linked with the words "cold mutton." For though Beatrice may have held an exaggerated view of the harm done to the character by over-eating or connoisseurship in food, she could never be justly accused of starving her guests even if, in her hurry to get to more important business, she did sometimes force them to gulp down their pudding.

She began to write her book in November of 1889. By then she had already reached certain very important conclusions. The first was that "Democracies of Consumers"—by which at that time she meant distributive co-operative societies—were a very important and valuable form of organization of the economic life of society alternative to the capitalist, profit-making businesses among which she had grown up: the second, that producers' co-operation in the form of self-governing workshops such as formed the aim of many of the pioneers of Co-operation and in the mid-century of the Christian Socialists, were ineffective and undesirable, and that if the Co-operative Movement were to function in the field of production, it should be by the great distributive societies themselves taking up productive enterprise and not by independent groups of producers "commencing business" on a basis of democracy within the shop or factory.[1]

[1] Agriculture, the one great occupation within which producers' co-operation is not merely possible but an inevitable condition of democracy, does not seem to have entered her ken; it took the U.S.S.R. to convince her that under Socialist conditions producers' co-operation could be thoroughly efficient.

With these two conclusions most of her new friends of the Wholesale and the Co-operative Union were in hearty agreement; with the third they had much less sympathy.

For while she condemned the self-governing workshop as undesirable in itself and hopeless as a competitor with capitalism, and advocated a wide extension of consumers' co-operation, she also saw quite clearly that the principles of the Co-operative Movement in themselves provided no guarantee of protection for the employee, in the factory or behind the counter, who actually did the work.

"What was . . . directly relevant," she writes, "to the controversy raging in the Co-operative movement in the 'eighties was Mitchell's inability to perceive that consumers' co-operation, unless tempered by the intervention of the political State through Factory Acts, and by due participation in the management of each enterprise by powerful Trade Unions, might become an effective coadjutor of the co-existing capitalist employer in the exploitation of the worker. . . .

"For these and other reasons it became clear to me that the existence of strong Trade Unions, enforcing standard rates and the normal working day, and protecting the individual from arbitrary fines and capricious dismissal, was as essential to the economic welfare and sense of personal freedom of the workers within the consumers' Co-operative Movement as it was in profit-making industry. Thus 'government from above' had to be supplemented by 'government from below.'"[1]

The leaders of Co-operation, then as too often in the history of their movement suffering from a too profound conviction of its virtues, saw no reason for this interest in the protection of conditions for workers in their employment; but Beatrice was sufficiently convinced of the rightness of her views to make up her mind before she had even begun the writing of her book that her next study was to be Trade Unionism, and had made the acquaintance of her new subject at first hand at the Dundee Trades Union Congress of September, 1889. It was the year of the great Dock Strike, led by the Socialists Ben Tillett, Tom Mann, and John Burns, which was to have so lasting an influence in turning the Trade Unions from cautious hangers-on to the coat-tails of the Liberals into the prop of the Labour Representation Committee born eleven years later. Trade Unions and their activities were well in the public eye.

[1] *My Apprenticeship*, page 387.

Trade Unionism—a far bigger subject than Beatrice could have anticipated in 1889—was the first occupation of the great Webb partnership; but it was Co-operation that was directly responsible for the two coming together. Beatrice had been given in October a copy of the newly published *Fabian Essays*, which she read with delight, commenting in a letter to a Co-operative friend, "by far the most significant and interesting essay is the one by Sidney Webb; *he has the historic sense*."[1] When, therefore, Beatrice, finding that she needed more information about the conditions of the working class in the eighteenth century, was recommended to try Sidney Webb, who "literally pours out information," she was very willing to do so. A meeting was arranged in January, 1890, at which a list of accessible sources "was swiftly drafted, there and then, in a faultless handwriting, and handed to me." By mid-February the owner of the faultless handwriting was dining at the Devonshire House Hotel to meet the Booths, and Beatrice was confiding to her diary a first summary picture, in which his "utter disinterestedness" stands out above all.

Sidney, it would seem, fell in love, if not literally at first sight, at any rate very promptly. Beatrice must have realized that he almost certainly would; she was not a fool, and could not have been unconscious of the probable effect of her own considerable attractions when combined with their community of tastes and approach to society. In her own case, the process was much more gradual; she had been in love once, and had not long escaped from its pains; she was rapidly building up for herself an important position as a single woman; and Sidney Webb was not in appearance the type of person with whom the brilliant Beatrice Potter would be expected to fall in love. "But I like the man," she says in her first summary; and there is a good deal of significance in the little word "but." The acquaintance nevertheless progressed rapidly, with the exchange of information, of books, of ideas; by the following Whitsun they were travelling together, in company with a number of her working-men friends, to the Co-operative Congress at Glasgow. There he definitely declared himself, and among the drunken crowds of Glasgow

---

[1] By one of the charming coincidences which so seldom occur in real life, Sidney Webb, in reviewing in the previous spring the first volume of Booth's *Survey*, had remarked, "The only contributor with any literary talent is Miss Beatrice Potter."

streets on a Whit-holiday night, "two Socialists came to a working compact."[1]

"You understand," said Beatrice, "you promise me to realize that the chances are that nothing comes of it but friendship."

Much did come of it, as the world knows; but not as quickly as might have been expected or as Sidney would have chosen. It was not until the summer of the following year that they were engaged. What turned the scale, apart from Sidney's persistent patience, was, first, her appreciation of the "utter disinterestedness" which she had observed at the February dinner, and secondly her growing consciousness that she needed him, if she was to go on with the work she had marked out for herself, as much as he, quite simply, wanted her. In so many ways he was her exact complement, and supplied her deficiencies. His "faultless handwriting" could be used instead of her abominable scrawl; he could wade through an infinity of tiresome documents which made her head ache and her hand refuse to copy, summarize them and memorize all the salient points in an incredibly short space of time; he was calm and unruffleable where she was moody and impatient; he could provide the strong framework of Fabian State and municipal Socialism into which her experience of the working class and its organization could fit, and which it could fill out and enrich. Two brief quotations from letters of Sidney's may illustrate the point.

On reading Marshall's *Principles of Economics*:

"I went straight to the Club and read right through Marshall's six hundred pages—got up, staggering under it. It is a great book, nothing new—showing the way, not following it. For all that it is a great book, it will supersede Mill. But it will not make an epoch in Economics. Economics has still to be re-made. Who is to do it? Either you must help me to do it; or I must help you. . . ." (Diary, July 27th, 1890.)

And later, when she was in despair about the "ugly details and squalid misfortunes" of Trade Union branches and Trade Union secretaries:

"You are not fit to write this big book alone; you would never get through it. When I really get to work on it you will find me not only

[1] One of them a Socialist of very new vintage. The entry in the Diary which says, "At last I am a Socialist," is dated February 1st, 1890.

a help instead of a hindrance—but also *the* indispensable help which will turn a good project into a big book." (Diary, October 10th, 1891.)[1]

But let them both give their own views in their own words.

"One and one," remarked Sidney in the course of a discussion on their possible marriage, "placed in a sufficiently integrated relationship, make not two, but eleven." And Beatrice in her diary just at the time of their engagement adds: "We are both of us second-rate minds; but we are curiously combined."

Those two comments, alike in their objectivity and their modesty—for she really meant the understating adjective—go far to sum up the Webb partnership.

They became engaged in the summer of 1891; according to a member of the family, the decision was signalled by Beatrice suddenly putting an arm round Sidney during a cab-ride. The engagement could not be made public, for her father could not be told that she intended to marry a Socialist, but it became known gradually to some of their closer friends. Lord Haldane, in his autobiography, has related how he allowed himself to be used to facilitate their meetings. He would invite himself for a visit to the small country house where Richard Potter spent his last years and would ask permission to bring his friend Sidney Webb, who happened to be lecturing in the neighbourhood. In the evening, when anyone who might have acted the part of duenna had retired to bed, Haldane would say that he would not be able to sleep unless he had a turn in the fresh air, and would then go out on the common for an hour or so by himself, thus giving the lovers a chance of unhampered conversation.

They met also in less romantic and more characteristic manner. While hunting records of Trade Unionism in a mining area, for example, Beatrice hired "with our usual coolness" a private sitting-room in her own hotel, to which Sidney duly repaired, secretary-wise, every day for pleasure and duty, giving the other residents the impression that Beatrice was a nigger-driver who worked her employees unconscionably long hours—but at the same time drawing, as it were, the first sketch of the pattern for

[1] These extracts might be held to give colour to the opinion often expressed that the Webb partnership was a marriage of two machines, upon which Sidney entered in order to write a better book on Economics, and Beatrice to get an efficient assistant on Trade Unionism. This is one of the partial truths that are so misleading.

common work and living which served them for fifty years. Well before their marriage they were a team.

At length the period of waiting ended. Richard Potter died on New Year's Day, 1892. Six months later *Fabian News* of July began its "What Members are Doing" column with the laconic announcement, "Sidney Webb was married to Beatrice Potter on 23rd ult."; and the two set off together to look up Trade Union records in Dublin and Glasgow.

CHAPTER V

SIDNEY

SIDNEY JAMES WEBB, who was eighteen months younger than his wife at the date of their marriage, was in some ways a very much more finally formed person at the time. It is true that some members of Beatrice's pre-marriage entourage, including some of her brothers-in-law, would not have heard of him, which may partly account for the persistent legend that Beatrice picked him up—from the gutter, as it were—and forcibly married him, a view that we have already seen to be without foundation. But he had started life, and started definite work, much earlier; even before his marriage he had had one career and left it for another; and his views on life and politics had been much more expressly formulated.

As everyone knows, he came from a social stratum well below that of the Potters. His mother kept a retail shop for ladies in Cranbourn Street, Leicester Square, and continued to keep it after her marriage in 1854 to Sidney's father, an accountant by profession, a vestryman, a Guardian, and like his son, an inveterate unpaid worker in the public service. Here, in the heart of London, their two sons and their daughter were born; here Sidney, the middle one of the three, spent his boyhood, going to a private middle-class school and to schools in Germany and Switzerland until he was fifteen and a half, when, the time having come for him to earn his living, he got a job as a clerk in the City office of a colonial broker, being aided thereto by the knowledge of French and German which he had acquired partly by attending classes at Birkbeck College and partly by his foreign education. (That during his schooldays he won rows of prizes will come as a surprise to nobody.)

His childhood background was thus peculiarly London; as a schoolboy he walked all over the London of mingled riches and squalor nearly twenty years before Booth had begun to describe it; and he learned to know it in a way characteristically his own. For, as he has told us himself in one of his very rare incursions into autobiography, the shop-windows and their advertisements were his spelling-book, and *Kelly's Directory* his favourite reading. "In short, I grew up a patriotic Londoner, very early declaring that no place on earth (I knew nothing of any other place) would content me for habitation, other than the very middle of London that I knew."[1]

He thus had a local habitation, a place in which his roots were fixed, which was a thing which Beatrice, in common with some in her own generation and many more in ours, never knew; and it was an habitation which he grew up loving as other men love their countryside. During all his long career in public life, it is doubtful whether any work he did so deeply engaged his heart as his service on the London County Council and his efforts for the higher education of Londoners; and any attack on the working class of London moved him to a straightforward warmth of indignation stronger than he usually showed on other subjects.[2]

He had to go to work at fifteen. But he did not, therefore, abandon study. By means of evening classes—the nearest he ever got to a university education—he raised himself to the standard of sitting for the Civil Service Open Examinations in 1878, and became a Second Division Clerk in the War Office; a year later, again by examination, he reached the Office of the Surveyor of Taxes, and after another two years, passed into the First Division and selected the Colonial Office, though he had passed high enough to get into the Foreign Office had he wished. There he remained, until in the early months of 1891 (before his engagement) he decided to give up the Civil Service and live on what he had saved and what he could earn by journalism. (In 1885 he had been called to the Bar at Grays Inn.)

So rapid a rise implies an unusual power of passing examina-

---

[1] "Reminiscences" by S. and B. Webb. *St. Martin's Review*, December, 1928.

[2] In 1909, for example, after having addressed the Association of Technical Institutes on the need for the proper education of youth up to the age of twenty-one, he was asked by a questioner in the audience how, in that event, the community was to get its supply of hewers of wood and drawers of water, and flashed back the angry answer :

"I may be a dreamer of dreams, but I thought that the doctrine that education was only for a part of the nation was buried a hundred years ago; it certainly does not consort with twentieth-century ideas to imagine that there is to be a class of hewers of wood and drawers of water; no class destined to remain there, and forbidden from rising, because we do not provide for it. I cannot believe that we are only to provide the means of instruction for a certain limited number of people who we think will rise, while the rest are to toil for our convenience. For our convenience! Who is to hew? Who is to deliver our bread? *Our* convenience! *Our* comfort! Our comfort is to stand in the way of enabling these people, our fellow-citizens, to attain anything better than being mere hewers of wood and drawers of water! I must apologize for having been betrayed into a little heat, but I do object to the notion that, for our convenience, we are to keep people as hewers of wood and drawers of water."

tions, which also involves an equal power of memorizing facts, especially relevant facts; and his power of memorizing relevant facts and making rapid and effective use of them—he learned the latter skill partly by giving unpaid lectures to the Working-Men's College—was one of the most characteristic traits of Sidney, not merely in those early days, but throughout his life. Relevant facts, be it noted. Bernard Shaw, reviving in after years his first recollections of Sidney Webb at a debating society, wrote:

"He knew all about the subject of the debate; he knew more than the lecturer; knew more than anybody present; had read everything that had ever been written on the subject; and remembered all the facts that bore upon it."

There is only one thing wrong with this encomium—its fourth item. Sidney Webb would never, then or at any other date, have wasted energy reading *everything* that had ever been written on any subject; with an instinct for economy even more remarkable than his prodigious memory he would have realized which, of the infinity of books and pamphlets which had been written, were capable of affording him assistance in whatever purpose he had in mind at the moment; and his choice made, would have proceeded with incredible rapidity to dig out and transcribe from his sources exactly what he needed. This singlemindedness of application, this inability—for it really came to that—to waste time or mental or physical energy on what he did not feel to be important to his purpose (including therein the purpose of keeping reasonably well and reasonably happy) is the clue to a great deal of Sidney's life, and also accounts in part for the effectiveness both of the Fabian propaganda for which he was responsible and of the joint research work of the great partnership. As he had little use for displays of physical energy which went beyond the needs of healthy exercise, so he had no temptations to wander down bypaths of research which were irrelevant to his theme; he never ran any risk of turning into a museum-grub, the standard caricature of a professor.[1]

---

[1] His conception of useful information was, however, wider than most people's. Shaw has told a story of how, when travelling in France in his early days, he quoted to a post-office clerk the paragraph in the French postal code which made it in order for him to dispatch a large packet of official papers for a halfpenny. (See M. A. Hamilton, *Sidney and Beatrice Webb*.) After this feat, Shaw said, he could have posted the whole of his laundry home without being questioned.

He was, of course, an early member of the Fabian Society; but his intellectual life did not begin there, by any means. He is first heard of in a body calling itself the Zetetical Society, where in 1879 he met another young man who had joined it for the purpose of learning to speak in public, a struggling, lean journalist of twenty-four named Bernard Shaw. It was of this meeting that Shaw made the remark which I have quoted above, adding the very Shavian descriptive touch that Webb had "a profile that suggested . . . an improvement on Napoleon the Third." In the Zetetical Society was formed a close friendship which has lasted for more than sixty years—it was already a dozen years old at the time of his marriage—and to which were in due course added the two other members of the famous Fabian quartette, Sydney Olivier and Graham Wallas.

Neither Shaw nor Webb was a foundation member of the Fabian Society, that remarkable body which sidled into the world sixty years ago as an offshoot of Thomas Davidson's "Fellowship of the New Life"; but they both joined it during its first year, and Olivier and Wallas followed their example shortly afterwards. By 1884 Shaw, and by 1885 Webb, were members of the Society's small executive committee.

This book has no room for a history of the Fabian Society, for which there are many other sources.[1] But it is important, for the understanding of Beatrice as well as of Sidney Webb, to realize the quality of the early Fabian Society, of the work which it did and of the training which it gave. At the beginning, according to Shaw, the handful who made up the Fabian Society —only forty in 1885!—were as vaguely anarchistic and insur- rectionist in their ideas and their expression of them as any group that had existed before them. They regularly denounced capi- talists as thieves and talked about using dynamite, and they looked forward with confidence to an imminent social revolution, to take place somewhere about 1889. But the forty members, and those who joined them within the next year or two, contained a very high proportion of people who combined remarkable intellectual ability with a strong sense of practical possibilities; and they very soon, particularly after the failures of Labour agitation in the mid-'eighties, used their own critical abilities—

---

[1] Pease, *History of the Fabian Society*; Shaw, *Early History of the Fabian Society*; G. D. H. Cole, *The Fabian Society, Past and Present*; Margaret Cole, *The Fabian Society over Sixty Years*.

"the invaluable habit of freely laughing at ourselves," as Shaw calls it—to discover that neither flaming denunciation nor millennial aspirations were going to get them very far in late Victorian England. The change began with the preparation in 1886 of a series of proposals to deal with unemployment, which was "the first Tract that contained any solid information." In the manner of the early Fabian documents, it was the work not of a single hand, but of a group of five, one of whom was Sidney Webb. Even so, it was meat too weak for the revolutionary zeal of the other twoscore Fabians, who refused to let it be issued in the name of the whole Society, but published it as a report signed by the five. But in the following year came *Facts for Socialists*.

Next to *Fabian Essays, Facts for Socialists*,[1] of which the fifteenth edition was issued in 1944, is the most characteristic of Fabian publications; it is also deeply characteristic of the Webb partnership and of Sidney's contribution thereto. The title itself is revealing, for equal emphasis should be laid on both nouns. The pamphlet consists of *facts*, i.e. true statements drawn from authoritative sources, which are meant to stand up to all criticisms; but it does not consist of facts selected at random. The facts are *for Socialists*; that is to say, they are facts about subjects in which Socialists, *qua* Socialists, will be interested, and they are facts for Socialists to use in converting the country to their views. Led by Shaw and Webb, the Fabian Society had come to believe that out of the mouths of the other side, out of their own papers, their own records and their own statistics, Socialists could convict capitalism of inefficiency as well as immorality and leave it, in the minds of those who could read and listen, without a leg to stand on. *Facts for Socialists* was the first fruit of this belief, which the Webbs in the 'twenties coined into a phrase, "Measurement and Publicity"; and if the meaning of the words is generously interpreted, it may fairly be said that the immense mass of the published work of the Webbs is in fact a vast expansion of *Facts for Socialists*.

But the Fabians were well aware that it was not enough to collect facts; they must also bring the facts to the notice of those who might be influenced by them, and they must make clear, at some point, the philosophy which lay behind the collection of

[1] *Facts for Londoners*, a tract for which Webb was responsible and which must have been a subject very near his heart, followed in 1888, and paid an immediate dividend in the results of the election to the new London County Council.

D

facts. The agitation came first. In the late 'eighties, this handful of Fabians worked at their job of propaganda and of learning how to conduct propaganda, as few groups, at any rate of the middle classes, have worked before or since. Let Shaw speak for himself.[1]

"My own experience may be taken as typical. For some years I attended the Hampstead Historic Club (a study circle formed to read Marx and Proudhon) once a fortnight, and spent a night in the alternate weeks at a private circle of economists which has since blossomed into the British Economic Association. . . . I made all my acquaintances think me madder than usual by the pertinacity with which I attended debating societies and haunted all sorts of hole-and-corner debates and public meetings and made speeches at them. I was President of the Local Government Board at an amateur Parliament where a Fabian ministry had to put its proposals into black and white in the shape of Parliamentary Bills. Every Sunday I lectured on some subject which I wanted to teach to myself; and it was not until I had come to the point of being able to deliver separate lectures, without notes, on Rent, Interests, Profits, Wages, Toryism, Liberalism, Socialism, Communism, Anarchism, Trade Unionism, Co-operation, Democracy, the Division of Society into Classes, and the Suitability of Human Nature to Systems of Just Distribution, that I was able to handle Social Democracy as it must be handled before it can be preached in such a way as to present it to every sort of man from his own particular point of view."

The list is a grand one; and if the nineteen-forties demand from the embryo Fabian lecturer a rather different selection of subjects the principle is nevertheless the same.

"I do not hesitate," he continues, "to say that all our best lecturers have two or three old lectures at the back of every single point in their best new speeches; and this means that they have spent a certain number of years plodding away at footling little meetings and dull discussions, doggedly placing these before all private engagements, however tempting. A man's Socialistic acquisitiveness must be keen enough to make him actually prefer spending two or three nights a week in speaking and debating, or in picking up social information even in the most dingy and scrappy way, to going to the theatre, or dancing or drinking, or even sweethearting, if he is to become a really competent propagandist—unless, of course, his daily life is of such a

[1] *Early History of the Fabian Society*, Fabian Tract 41, 1892.

nature as to be in itself a training for political life; and that, we know is the case with very few of us indeed."

It was in work of this kind that all the Fabians, not merely the half-dozen leaders, learned their jobs; it took them, incidentally, into local government circles and made them see the big possibilities of municipal enterprise—"gas-and-water Socialism"—which had been neglected since Joseph Chamberlain moved into wider and more dubious spheres than municipal Radicalism. It is a curious chance that it was not Beatrice, his former admirer, but Sidney, who brought into the partnership the idea of the State and the Town Council as associations of consumers for the common good, born to function alongside the Co-operative Movement which she had been the first to discover.

The Fabians were extremely busy, both at learning and at teaching. Being very well equipped, they were also most effective, and being effective they were able to produce an impression of being far more numerous than they were. Like a stage army, their individual persons and voices kept appearing and reappearing in one place after another, and almost succeeded in persuading people that they were the active and coming wing of the Liberal Party—there was of course no Labour Party at that date. One of their successes was in getting hold of the *Star*, whose assistant editor was the brilliant journalist Henry Massingham, and filling it with Socialist propaganda.[1] Another, more solid and more lasting, was the securing of a Progressive majority in 1889 on the newly established London County Council—a majority which endured until 1907. This was peculiarly the work of Sidney Webb, who was not himself a candidate and was in fact travelling in the United States when the election came on. But by his expert and long-standing knowledge of London, expressed both in *Facts for Londoners* and in a remarkable questionnaire which he prepared for presentation to all candidates for the Council, he did in effect equip the Progressives with a Fabian municipal policy which they had not known they possessed, and by his "bewildering conjuring tricks with the Liberal thimbles and the Fabian peas" (Shaw) made the Fabians the leaders of London government. By 1892, when the second election was held, he had left the Colonial Office, believing that on what he had saved and what he

---

[1] When the proprietors of the *Star* put a stop to this, Massingham continued his efforts on a morning paper, the *Chronicle*.

could earn by journalism he would be able to keep himself and play a part in voluntary public service. He stood for Deptford —not then a "safe" Labour seat—and got in by a handsome majority. But before then *Fabian Essays* had appeared.

It is perhaps characteristic of the Fabians that they worked for five years as propagandists before they felt the need to make a public definition of the philosophy for which they stood. As soon as they did so, however, it was plain that they were expressing the views, not only of themselves but of thousands of others who had outgrown the arid, individualist, secularist Radicalism of Bradlaugh and G. W. Foote, but had no sympathy with the nearly as arid dogmatic Marxism of H. M. Hyndman and his Social Democratic Federation. *Fabian Essays in Socialism*, delivered first as an unadvertised series of lectures in London,[1] edited by Bernard Shaw, and published by the little Society at its own expense, was an instant success, and has gone on selling in successive reprints right down to our own day. It had not, of course, the mass appeal of emotional propaganda; it did not secure a circulation like that of Henry George's *Progress and Poverty*, which denounced the landowner as having stolen the land from the people, or Robert Blatchford's *Merrie England*, which in hundreds of thousands of copies priced at a penny told the ordinary working man what might be made of his own country. Neither Shaw nor Webb had any gift, or much use for emotional appeals, and Olivier's chapter on the morals of Socialism is easily the dullest of the essays. But it appealed strongly and immediately to anyone of Radical leanings who was in need of a philosophy; and when the Independent Labour Party was born four years later it took its philosophy, as well as many of the facts it used in propaganda, direct from Fabian sources.

Sidney Webb's contribution to the collection is entitled *Historic*; its first sub-title is "The Development of the Democratic Ideal," and its purpose is to show that the democratic ideal cannot be fulfilled by mere extensions of political democracy, but that

[1] The seven essayists were Bernard Shaw, Sidney Webb, William Clarke, who died in 1901, Sydney Olivier of the Colonial Office, who became Governor of Jamaica and was made a peer by the first Labour Government, Graham Wallas, author of *Human Nature in Politics*, and long a pillar of the London School of Economics, Annie Besant, who has been mentioned in an earlier chapter, and Hubert Bland, treasurer of the Fabian Society for thirty years. It is worth noting that they were all thirty or over; it was not a group of bright young men looking round for something to do who went through the stiff course of learning and teaching which the Fabian way of life prescribed, but people with their careers chosen and their livings to earn, who thought the drudgery and the effort of thought worth while.

economic democracy, brought about through the socialization of private property, must be added. As this lesson, notwithstanding the achievements of the U.S.S.R., is still largely unlearned in the Britain of 1945, Webb's fifty-five year old essay retains a freshness of application which some of the others have lost.

It is interesting, also, in other ways. It shows quite clearly the pedigree of Fabian thought, and its direct derivation from the Utilitarians in politics—as Shaw's contribution shows its derivation from Ricardo in economics. Webb's masters are Bentham and John Stuart Mill, and though he criticizes Bentham, he is not criticizing Bentham's ideals, but the inadequacy, in modern industrial society, of the suggestions he makes for realizing them. "The greatest happiness of the greatest number" is a good enough slogan for Sidney Webb; he merely points out that the greatest happiness of the greatest number can only be achieved through Socialism. And, like the great Utilitarians, he believes that the best institutions can only be made to work for human good if the best people will come out from their studies and work them; he does not think that County Councils—created in 1888 and then hailed as rather larger instalments of democracy than they have since turned out to be—will prove of much use unless there are public-spirited County Councillors to sit upon them. Furthermore, the essay is firmly and explicitly gradualist and anti-catastrophic. Having observed the course of history for some generations, Webb states flatly that "no philosopher now looks for anything but the gradual evolution of the old order from the new, without breach of continuity or abrupt change of the entire social tissue at any point during the process. The new becomes itself old, often before it is consciously recognized as new; and history shows us no example of the sudden substitution of Utopias and revolutionary romance." "The inevitability of gradualness" was thus a part of Webb's philosophy thirty years before he used the phrase in a presidential address to the Labour Party Conference; and this partly accounts for the Webbs' hostile attitude to the Russian Revolution in its early days. They believed the hard-headed Bolsheviks to be guilty of giving the lie to the orderly development of history and of attempting a revolutionary romance.

It is remarkable, however, that Webb's conception of economic democracy envisages only collective ownership—state and municipal enterprise—and entirely ignores the functional side, the part that could be played by associations of producers, whether Trade Unions or professional organizations. In fact, the complete over-looking of Trade Unionism by the Essayists (an omission which they afterwards handsomely acknowledged) is one of the sur-prising features of the book, when one considers the date at which it was written. Even Annie Besant, fresh from organizing the Bryant and May match-girls' strike, makes only a passing refer-ence to "Trade Union minimum rates"; and of the three other references to Trade Unionism one (by Graham Wallas) is dis-tinctly hostile. References to Co-operation are rather more intelligent; but they too fail to show a tithe of the understanding of Beatrice Potter's diaries.

As a literary product, Webb's essay is rather more vivid and concise than some of the later writings of the partnership. Webb never scintillated like Shaw, but such phrases as "the evangeliza-tion of the earth by the sale of grey shirtings," as a description of the benefits of the industrial revolution, stand out sharply memor-able. The tendency, however, to catalogue, as fully but less rhythmically than Walt Whitman, which was always one of the defects of the Webbs' writing, makes its first appearance here. Two pages of a not very long essay are practically taken up with catalogue, ending with the magnificent paragraph:

"Nor is the registration a mere form. Most of the foregoing [a huge catalogue] are also inspected and criticized, as are all railways, tram-ways, ships, mines, factories, canal-boats, public conveyances, fisheries, slaughter-houses, dairies, milkshops, bakeries, baby-farms, gasometers, schools of anatomy, vivisection laboratories, explosive works, Scotch herrings, and common lodging-houses."

Students of style may be interested to compare this Fabian essay with the quotations from Beatrice's diary in *My Apprenticeship*, and with one or other of the joint works produced by the partner-ship. Beatrice's own style is not impeccable; but it does not suggest that her favourite reading was the Classified Index of the London Telephone Directory.

One other point should be noticed before we leave *Fabian Essays* and the early Fabian Society. The *Essays*, even though they were signed with the names of their individual authors, were a collaboration; each separate contribution was criticized by the other contributors and by the editor before it was admitted in final form. And this "collaborativism" went much further in many of the other early publications of the Society, which were circulated in proof to all members for comment and criticism before being published. This practice made for a remarkable lack of egotism among the members, which is particularly noticeable in the case of Sidney Webb. He was a very efficient and rapid drafter of resolutions, manifestoes, statements, reports, pamphlets, or what not. "In the absence of any evidence to the contrary," writes Pease, "it is to be assumed of any report that Webb drafted it." But he was entirely devoid of any desire to claim credit for his own work; if the pamphlet or whatever it was would be more effective if it appeared anonymously, let it appear anonymously—or under the name of anyone, carrying more weight or appearing more impartial, who would be prepared to sign it. This disinterestedness, this utter lack of personal vanity of any kind, has been, for all his life, one of the most marked characteristics of Sidney Webb. He has never minded at all, provided that the work was done, who got the credit for it; and though this trait has occasionally caused him to underestimate, and to be impatient with, the results of personal vanity in persons other than himself, it is certain that it acted as a perfect antidote to any personal vanity in Beatrice which survived her own ruthless analysis of it. On this, as on many other points, they were complementary.

CHAPTER VI

THE PARTNERSHIP BEGINS

FABIAN ESSAYS put the Fabian Society on the map of people's political consciousness, and in the ensuing two or three years it enrolled members at a speed which astonished itself—though the bulk of those living in the provinces drifted away to the I.L.P. after the foundation of the latter body. During the late 'eighties and early 'nineties it was, by all the evidence, a full and satisfying life to be a member of the Fabian Society: one enjoyed the conviction of being right, the conscious-ness of success, and the pleasure of close collaboration and keen discussion with sharp-witted and like-thinking fellow-workers. When Beatrice Potter married Sidney Webb, she did not merely marry a man, she married into a group of which she was not herself a member. Though she had, of course, met Sidney's close friends, and had attended at least one Fabian conference, she did not join the Society until the middle of 1893.

This point needs emphasizing. When Beatrice married, it was she who resigned her career—if only for a time—and not Sidney. Her income enabled him to abandon his intention of living by journalism, set him free, in effect, from the necessity of earning; but he still had the Fabian Society, with its executive committee meeting twice a week and the demands which it made on him for lectures, pamphlets, the answering of inquiries and the running of campaigns, and in his afternoons he was engaged with the London County Council, and particularly with its Technical Education Committee, of which he became the first chairman. In none of this work had Beatrice any part; and she had stepped out of her own native circle in order to join him. It would not be true to say that she had given up the opportunity of a brilliant marriage, for that, if it had ever tempted her, had long ceased to do so. But she had moved right out of the *milieu* in which brilliant marriages were made, in which she could shine and be complimented on her looks and her wits; and that sacrifice, however consciously and however wisely it was made, was nevertheless a real one. Several of her former acquaintances thought she must have gone mad, to marry beneath her, to marry a Socialist, and a Socialist, moreover, who was barely presentable, who was ugly, not with a craggy ugliness like Lincoln's, which one might perversely admire, but with a small and insignificant ugliness that associated itself with shiny suits and pince-nez with a broken cord. Her brothers-in-law, for the most part, disapproved; such old and tried collaborators as Charles Booth and his wife severed connections; and though some friends like the Frederic Harrisons stood by her, they were, for the moment, in the minority. Exit, definitely, "the brilliant Beatrice Potter"; it is symptomatic that she made no attempt to retain her maiden name, and was inclined in after years to be slightly contemptuous of public women who retained theirs, declaring that it was confusing and inconvenient. From henceforth she was Mrs. Sidney Webb, the wife and collaborator of a public man.

She accepted the position; she gave up those of her former friends who could not swallow her marriage, and took on Sidney's name and Sidney's friends as part of her future life, and she did it very well. It is matter for some credit that the introduction of her powerful personality did not interfere in the slightest degree with Sidney's own friendships, particularly that with Shaw, whom at first she found very perplexing. He was like nothing she had ever seen before; she grasped some of his jokes with difficulty; she was doubtful whether he was serious at heart, and she could make nothing of his ways with women. After some meditation, however, she decided that Shaw was a "Sprite"—a sort of Undine with only a slender connection with the world of mortals, of Trade Union inquiries and the really serious business of life; and on that understanding built up a relationship of critical goodwill to which Shaw has time and again paid tribute in his own writings, while making clear his conviction that she would at any time have sacrificed him to save Sidney's little finger.[1]

Shaw being by far the most original and difficult to assimilate of Sidney's friends, the other Fabians were plain sailing; but she was not, and could not be indifferent to the falling-away of some of those whom she had thought her own. The defection of Charles Booth, her cousin and her first instructor in the craft of social

---

[1] E.g., when she emphatically refused to let Sidney mount a bicycle from which she had gleefully watched Shaw having a series of tumbles. (M. A. Hamilton, *Sidney and Beatrice Webb*.)

investigation, cut deep;[1] and though she was able to see the comic side of it, the horrified reaction of Herbert Spencer, her oldest friend, took her rather in the wind.

In 1887, Spencer, after a good deal of preliminary fuss, had asked Beatrice Potter to be his literary executor. "I was taken aback," Beatrice wrote in her Diary "but it was evident that he had set his heart on it and hoped, poor old man, that someone who cared for him should write his life." So she agreed, and he declared in a letter that "I can say with literal truth that with no choice could I have been more content." But five years later he learned that his executor-designate was about to marry a Socialist, of all horrors, and a Socialist, moreover, who had made slighting remarks about Herbert Spencer in *Fabian Essays*. His consternation—expressed in the Albemarle Club—was extreme.

"It would not do for my reputation," he twittered, "that I should be openly connected with an avowed and prominent Socialist—that is impossible. Inferences would be drawn however much I protested that the relationship was purely personal with you."

"I quite agree with you, Mr. Spencer," Beatrice answered sympathetically. "I fully realized that I should have to give up the literary executorship."

"But what can *I* do?" he wailed. "Grant Allen, whom I once thought of, has become a Fabian! There is no one who possesses at once the literary gift, the personal intimacy with my past life and the right opinions, to undertake the task."

"What about Howard Collins? He is sound; would he not do?"

"He would be the proper person—but then he has no gift like you have of making his subject interesting."

"But I should be delighted to help him in any way you like to propose, either acknowledged or not."

The Philosopher (says Beatrice) lay back in his chair with a sigh

---

[1] Booth was certainly no Socialist, or friend to calculated planning against poverty. As late as 1903 he wrote of cyclical unemployment:

"Looked at from afar, these cycles of depression have a distinctly harmful and even a cruel aspect; but from a more distant point of view, 'afar from the sphere of our sorrow' they seem less malignant. . . . There are some victims, but those who are able and willing to provide in times of prosperity for the lean years which seem inevitably to follow, do not suffer at all; and, if the alternation of good and bad times be not too sudden or too great, the community gains not only by the strengthening of character under stress, but also by a direct effect on enterprise. As to character, the effect, especially on wage-earners, is *very similar to that exercised on a population by the recurrence of winter as compared to the enervation of continued summer*." (Italics mine.)

Holding such views, Booth would naturally find the Fabian Society anathema; but Beatrice felt that he and his wife need not have dropped her so abruptly, like a hot coal.

of relief. "That arrangement would be admirable—that is exactly what I should desire—the Life would appear under his name and you would add reminiscences and arrange the material. That would quite satisfy me."[1]

And, notwithstanding the shock of her marriage and her deplorable views, the friendship between them survived. She visited him often, and eleven years later, when he lay on his death-bed at Brighton, went down week after week to sit by his side. This attention paid to the gnarled, disappointed, and morose old man that Spencer had become should be remembered by those who do not sufficiently appreciate Beatrice's capacity for ordinary human friendship.

The Webbs' plan for their joint life after their marriage was formulated very quickly and remained singularly unchanged for fifty years. As far as work itself was concerned, the collaboration had effectively begun some months before the wedding. They had already engaged a secretary, F. W. Galton;[2] they had toiled together over Trade Union documents and Trade Union secretaries, and had even begun to develop their devastating technique of joint interview,[3] in which they battered from either side the object of their attentions—sometimes a political opponent, sometimes an official who had not devoted much thought to the underlying implications of his official actions—with a steady left-right of question, argument, assertion, and contradiction, and left him converted, bewildered, or indignant, as the case might be. The work which they did on Trade Unionism in Dublin and Glasgow differed very little from that which they had done earlier in the Durham coalfield, except that they stayed in the same and not in separate hotels.

But for joint living a new plan was needed. They had between them an unearned income, mainly Beatrice's, of roughly a thousand a year, with income tax at sixpence in the pound. On that they decided they could live comfortably and without ostentation, but with sufficient margin to keep a secretary and a domestic staff and to provide for fairly frequent holidays away from home. They did not intend to have children. Sidney, it was settled, was to give up the thought of journalism as a profession

---

[1] *My Apprenticeship*, page 34.
[2] General Secretary of the Fabian Society from 1919 to 1939.
[3] Not mentioned in Beatrice's essay on "The Art of the Interviewer," but well known to all who came in contact with the Webbs in their heyday.

and to devote the time not taken up in public service to the work
of joint research. The resulting books would, they hoped, pay for
themselves in the long run; but meantime they would take the
risk and be their own publishers, paying an established firm a
commission to act as their agents. Messrs. Longmans, Green & Co.,
the publishers of this memoir, in fact saw by far the greater part
of the Webb output into the world. They would live simply,
but not on the margin of subsistence; they—or rather Beatrice,
who took the initiative in matters aesthetic—were prepared to
spend a reasonable amount on making their dwelling-place
pleasant in their own eyes. Originally it was their intention to
live very regular lives and to go to bed early, to spend little or no
time in entertaining or in being entertained. As the "permeation" and political activity described in subsequent chapters
increased, this intention was modified in some degree. They
asked people to dinner, and dined out themselves; but "evening
amusement" of the play or concert type tempted them very little.
One of the best and most characteristic Webb stories, for which
I am indebted to Alderman Emil Davies, tells of their going to a
performance of *Parsifal* for which they had been given free
tickets. Meeting Sidney on the following day, Mr. Davies asked
how they had enjoyed it, and was somewhat surprised to receive
the answer "Very much indeed."

"Our seats," Sidney added, "were just behind Herbert
Samuel's, and during the interval we had a very interesting
discussion on the incidence of sickness during pregnancy"! (It
was at the time when the National Health Insurance Act was
passing through Parliament.)

Immediately after their marriage they lived in a flat in Hampstead; but they were already making inquiries after a permanent
home, and very soon fixed upon the famous Number 41 Grosvenor
Road, which was to house them until they retired to the Hampshire countryside in their old age. They acquired a long lease
at an all-in rent of £110 per annum, which was little more than
the ten per cent of total income which in the latter days of
Victoria the middle class agreed was the right proportion to be
devoted to houseroom.

Forty-one Grosvenor Road—subsequently rechristened forty-
one Millbank and rendered uninhabitable in the blitz of 1940–1
—was never a beautiful house. It was a bad specimen of a bad
period, too narrow and too high, wasteful of space inside, and

externally cumbered with meaningless decoration which a dull creeper strove unsuccessfully to conceal. Nor were its surroundings—except for the river, admittedly a large exception—particularly attractive in 1893. The visitor coming from the House of Lords and the garden by its side soon found himself in what was almost a slum—dirty houses of varying sizes, some half-tumbling down, occupying the sites where the vast modern buildings of the I.C.I., etc. now stand, and facing the old Lambeth Bridge, a footway on wooden piles. Such was the beginning of old Grosvenor Road: then came a terrace of ugly but respectable houses which included number forty-one, and beyond them, where the Tate Gallery now stands, the old Millbank Penitentiary. Across the river the inhabitants of this terrace had an unimpeded view of the pretentiously hideous tower of Doulton's Pottery works. There was, however, plenty of light and air in Grosvenor Road; and it was for this, for its cheapness, for its comparative quiet before the days of motor-cars—the trams were well away on the other side of the river—and for its accessibility that Beatrice chose it. It was within easy walking distance for Sidney of the offices of the L.C.C., then in Spring Gardens by Cockspur Street; it was not impossibly far from the meeting-place of the Fabian Executive; and a number of friends, such as Mrs. J. R. Green (one of Beatrice's old acquaintances who had stood by her), Logan Pearsall Smith and his sister, and H. W. Massingham were near neighbours.

Their technique of joint working was quickly established. They breakfasted early—Beatrice, it will be remembered, was a bad sleeper—and their secretary was frequently bidden to breakfast to receive his instructions for the day. Breakfast being cleared, they "commenced operations" on the dining-room table, the secretary having been sent off, either to collect information or to sort, file, and extract from documents in a little upstairs room, which served them as a cross between a small library and a large filing cabinet. They then started upon their own work, which in the earliest days was the history of Trade Unionism, going through the mass of notes which they had accumulated, and hammering out, not always without sharp disagreement, the conclusions which they thought should be drawn and the terms in which they should be expressed.

In one of the most personal of their joint works, *Methods of Social Study* (1932), Beatrice gives an elaborate description of their methods in a chapter entitled "The Art of Note-taking," in which she advises all students of the social sciences to follow their own example in such detail as writing down each separate fact acquired on a separate sheet of paper of uniform size, with the source clearly stated in one corner and the date in another, and then shuffling and reshuffling these sheets, like packs of cards, until they yielded a conclusion satisfying to both partners—a conclusion which sometimes, she adds with an evident recollection of her earlier work with Booth, was not what either would have expected. The interest of this chapter of the book lies rather in the picture which it gives of highly individual researchers at work (as it were a glimpse into a painter's studio) than as a model; for other labourers in the field will undoubtedly choose their own methods. One certain result, however, is that any conclusions they reached were always thoroughly well documented; and that if they were challenged on any point they knew exactly where to look for their reply. How far they were "impartial" is a question which different critics will answer according to their own views and personalities. Absolute impartiality is a quality they would never have claimed, for they did not believe it could exist; and the views which they gradually came to hold must undoubtedly have influenced them to some extent in their selection, in the decision to give prominence to one fact rather than another.[1] But every historian must select, to some extent; the question is how far the facts are checked and how far the readers are given the opportunity of re-checking them from the original sources. Herein the Webbs reach a very high standard; their big books are fully documented in footnotes and bibliography.

This work of discussion and composition, generally speaking, occupied the morning until lunch-time; after lunch, on five days of the week, Sidney went off to the London County Council, and Beatrice occupied herself in various ways. It must be remembered that, for most of her life, she was not a strong woman; in addition to her insomnia, she suffered periodically from digestive trouble, and was more than once seriously ill. This meant that she had not the physical capacity to do a regular full day's work, day in and day out, as Sidney had, though in fact she got through

---

[1] For example, in the *History of Trade Unionism* they regarded the Junta, the group of leading Trade Unionists who formed the London Trades Council in the 'sixties, as of much more historically formative importance than its rival and enemy George Potter, editor of the *Beehive*. Hence, it has been suggested, they devoted an altogether unfairly small space to Potter in the *History*.

BEATRICE & SIDNEY WEBB
in the dining room at 41 Grosvenor Road

BEATRICE & SIDNEY WEBB
After the first World War

much more—even when she was not sitting on a Royal Commission or doing some particular intensive job—than is achieved by most ordinary full-time workers: it also meant that, being free from any routine other than that imposed by their own plan of living, she was the more able to keep her mind fresh and open to ideas and projects which might be used or carried out then or at a later time. It is important, for a comprehension of the Webbs' lives, to appreciate that they did not believe in the merits of overwork. They often tired themselves, no doubt, in interviewing and in searching through documents which were old, dirty, or dreary—or all three at once. But they never tried to go all out for any length of time; the student of their lives receives no such impression of frenzied scrambling, of burning the candle at both ends, as, to take two well-known examples, was the case with both Scott and Dickens. Nor, on the other hand, is there any trace of their having to flog themselves unwillingly into creative composition, as Arnold Bennett always complained of having to do; if they followed any other author's example, it was Anthony Trollope's. They enjoyed their work, it is probable, more than any two people ever did. But they enjoyed it in moderation, and arranged to plan.

They followed their plan not merely at home, but on holiday, so far as circumstances permitted. They took holidays frequently, sometimes going to The Argoed, one of the homes of Beatrice's childhood, sometimes taking a house in the country, which they often shared, particularly in the early days, with Shaw and other Fabian friends.[1] But on any holiday of more than a short duration they took with them their current work and their plan of living. Shaw's *Letters to Ellen Terry* give the clearest short pictures of the typical ménage.

"The Fabian old gang," he writes in 1896, ". . . can only afford a country house for our holiday because one of us has a wife with a thousand a year. This time we have been joined by an Irish million-airess[2] who has had cleverness and character enough to decline her station in life—'a great catch for somebody'—to which it pleased God to call her, and whom we have incorporated into our Fabian family with great success. I am going to refresh my heart by falling in love with her. I love falling in love—but mind, only with her, not with

---

[1] Sometimes they went abroad for holidays; but their investigating tours, of which the last and greatest was to the U.S.S.R., are referred to in later chapters.
[2] Miss Charlotte Payne-Townshend, afterwards Mrs. Bernard Shaw.

the million; so someone else must marry her if she can stand him after me. . . ."

"Four hours writing in the morning; four hours bicycling in the afternoon every day. . . .

"I have to spend a lot of time mending punctures in female bicycle tyres."

And in 1897:

"I wonder what you would think of our life—our eternal political shop; our mornings of dogged writing, all in our separate rooms; our ravenous plain meals; our bicycling; the Webbs' incorrigible spooning over their industrial and political science. . . .

"Miss Payne-Townshend, Irish, shrewd and green-eyed, finding everything 'very interesting,' myself always tired and careworn and always supposed to be 'writing to Ellen.'"

The bicycles had been bought in 1895. They were a marvellous new toy—see H. G. Wells's early novel, *The Wheels of Chance*, for the romance of early bicycling days—and in September of that year Beatrice and Sidney rode triumphantly a distance of forty miles to attend the Trades Union Congress at Cardiff.

The "spooning over their industrial and political science" was a fact, testified to by Beatrice herself. The reasoned calculation of happiness on which she had married developed very quickly into a deep and abiding love which expressed itself in demonstrative affection as readily as that of any pair of youngsters in their first flight. But the rather comic verb used by Shaw (though less comic in 1897 than it would be to-day) is not without point. The Webb partnership, throughout its long and excellent life, always had something slightly funny about it, which is partly, but only partly accounted for by their resolute disregard of fashion and public taste when they did not agree with it. "Unconventional," in the common sense of the word, they never were; people would have found them less amusing if they had been. They did not go in for eccentricities of dress or food; and Beatrice, though she thoroughly appreciated a good gossip—particularly after her retirement to Passfield Corner—disapproved of sexual irregularities nearly as strongly as she did of over-indulgence in food and drink, mainly, one feels, because they were a nuisance, because they interfered with planned, sensible living, the work of the world, and the road to Socialism. When in 1932 she went to the Soviet Union, she observed with obvious approval that "there is no 'spooning' in the Parks of Culture and Rest." Whether the observation was strictly accurate or not is irrelevant; the point is that she felt (and the Russian Communist Party largely agreed with her) that with a new world in the building there was so much excitement and interest in work that time and energy spent in personal emotion was time and energy wasted. This view was reinforced, no doubt, by her own natural puritanism; it is impossible to imagine Beatrice Webb finding any pleasure whatever in getting drunk or in telling a dirty story. But it had a rational basis.

Up to a point, therefore, the Webbs were highly conventional —conservative, even, in not challenging the accepted habits built up in English society over a long period. Beatrice, though she became a lifelong friend of Shaw's and learned to appreciate his jokes and prods at English conventions, thought and said on more than one occasion that Socialists ought to be respectable, that those who were preaching a fundamental change in the economic and political structure of society ought not to discomfort their audience (and possibly defeat their own ends) by indulging in irrelevant personal whims.[1] But they saw absolutely no reason why they should "follow the crowd" in matters of fashion and passing taste, why they should chase pleasures which they did not find pleasurable, go to the theatre if they did not like plays or sitting up late, travel to see monuments of art or past culture if they preferred to see the American House of Representatives in session. A good few of their contemporaries and of the generation which followed them found the Webbs' choice of pleasures peculiar and rather funny, and the impression was enhanced rather than diminished by their complete and avowed satisfaction with each other and with their way of life. There was a basic innocence about their happiness which in a world of strife and discontent was in itself a trifle humorous.

One other characteristic may properly be discussed at this point. Beatrice, in conversation in her middle and later years, was fond of describing herself and her husband as belonging to "the B's of the world," who, she explained were "bourgeois,

---

[1] In the same spirit the early Fabian Society proclaimed its policy to an international Conference of Socialists in proudly restrictive phrases:

"The Fabian Society endeavours to pursue its Socialist and Democratic objects with complete singleness of aim. For example:

"It has no distinctive opinions on the Marriage Question, Religion, Art, Abstract Economics, Historic Evolution, Currency, or any other subject than its own special business of practical Democracy and Socialism." (Tract 70.)

E

bureaucratic, and benevolent," in contrast to the "A's"—as for example Bertrand Russell, G. D. H. Cole, and a good many others, who were "aristocratic, anarchist, and artistic." This description shows to what an extent she had become "Mrs. Sidney Webb" and subordinated, in so far as she was able, her own personality to his. For the three B qualities are far more characteristic of Sidney than of Beatrice. If she was bourgeois, it was in the sense of the *haute*, not the ordinary bourgeoisie; her manners and her habit of thought had in fact much more suggestion of the aristocracy. And whatever she was, she was not a bureaucrat. She was not an anarchist, certainly; and she disliked inefficiency and sloppiness either in thought or action. Much of her strong prejudice against the I.L.P. arose from the fact that she thought Keir Hardie and his friends were incurably woolly-minded and would not trouble to learn their own business. But to call her a bureaucrat, *in sensu obsceno*, is ridiculous; on the Poor Law Commission, to say nothing of many other occasions, she was the terror of the bureaucrat proper, the type of official who busily endeavours to find official excuses for doing nothing, and seeks to use a public inquiry as a smoke screen.[1] As to "benevolence," Beatrice was benevolent in the sense that she worked increasingly for the good of humanity, and also in the sense of having strong attachments and being extremely kind and helpful to other and younger workers in her own field—even to those who attacked her violently. But she had definite views, and she expressed them definitely; and some of those who came into collision with her in her heyday would not have felt that the unqualified word benevolent, with its suggestion of imperturbability, was a completely adequate description.

Finally, though she disclaimed "artistry," there was in fact a good deal of the artist in her methods of social study as well as in the native ability to write which is shown in *My Apprenticeship*, in the flashes in which she would sometimes see a solution to her problems,[2] and in the intuitive way in which she would sum up people and movements—not always correctly or finally. The Webb partnership was not interested in art in the ordinary sense: a very friendly critic once observed that if they had written a study of Elizabethan England they would have lumped together

[1] See below, Chapter IX.
[2] Such as when, while listening to a lecture by H. G. Wells, the institutional basis of the *Constitution for a Socialist Commonwealth* suddenly sprang to her mind. See p. 146.

Shakespeare and the poets, the madrigalists, and the building regulations for London into a single chapter and called it "Amenities of the Elizabethan Age." But that they possessed the creative qualities of the artist no one who has read *Methods of Social Study*, with its vivid account of the joys of the investigator's life, can possibly doubt.

"Here," she writes on page 126, "we must end this dry dissertation on the right use of historical sources, conscious that we have failed to express the joy of life to be found in these diggings into documents and soundings and nettings of contemporaneous literature. . . . It may be doubted whether there is any sport, any game, so alluring and so continuously absorbing as the hazards of sociological research. . . . To spend hour after hour in the chancel of an old parish church, in the veiled light of an ancient muniment, in the hard little office of a solicitor, in the ugly and bare anteroom of the council chamber of a local authority, or even in a dungeon without ventilation or daylight (which was once our lot), with a stack of manuscripts, or a pile of printed volumes, to get through in a given time, induces an indescribably stimulated state of mind. The illusion arises that one has not one brain but several, each enjoying a life of its own. There is, first, the curiously concentrated satisfaction of the rapid rush through manuscript and printed pages, brain and hand combining to detect and to record, from among the 'common form' with which the records are filled, new features in the constitutions or activities of the organization, or unexpected reactions between it and its environment. This interest in social structure is enlivened by an exciting chase after the human factor; the discovery of the leader or leaders; the play of the hand of this man or that; the emergence in the dry annals of pecuniary self-interest, personal ambition or personal vanity; as well as of some continuously expressed policy or ideal. Meanwhile another active part of the brain is alert for indications of additional sources of information. Is there a collection of pamphlets? Is there a local newssheet of old date, and where are the files to be found? What are the relevant biographies, autobiographies, travels, diaries, legal text-books, or other technical treatises? . . . Meanwhile, between all this intense but largely automatic activity of the intellectual craftsman, there runs the more tranquil and deeper current of philosophic brooding: the underlying but continuously running controversy between the ego that affirms and the ego that denies. Apart from the satisfaction of scientific curiosity, has the product social value? Will the discovery of the past help the conduct of the present? Assuming that we have discovered and identified the poison secreted by the decaying vocational organizations of the eighteenth century, will this knowledge enable the modern man to find the antidote for similar poisons at work to-day in the life of a Trade Union or a professional association? . . . And underlying all these detailed questions there is the fundamental issue: can these secular movements of successive social expediencies be translated into ever rising ethical values? Is morality, as it has been suggested, actually part of the nature of things?"

Beatrice Webb was not a mystic; but in the foregoing passage there is something, both in the physical setting and in the moral passion, which suggests to some extent a lay version of mysticism: at all events there is nothing of the bureaucrat in it.

CHAPTER VII

TRADE UNIONISM

THE Webbs lived at Grosvenor Road continuously from 1893 to 1923, when they acquired their country cottage at Passfield Corner in Hampshire, to which, after having used it increasingly, for week-ends, for holidays, and as a home for Beatrice during a good deal of Sidney's political life, they finally retired after the crash of the second Labour Government. During the thirty years, however, several different periods of activity may be discerned; these are described in more detail in this and the following chapters.

During the first, which was really a continuance of their pre-marriage partnership, they were working on Trade Unionism and its implications. Their tour to Canada and the United States, undertaken in 1898, divided this period from the second one, during which they were beginning the great series of local government studies which ended with the publication of the last volumes on the Poor Law, while at the same time they were taking a great practical interest in educational reform, and were working with and endeavouring to influence, important members of the Liberal Party and even some of the Tories. Fabian tactics in general have been described as "permeation"; and until their retirement from English politics, most of the Webbs' political work might fairly have been described as permeation of one sort or another. But the period around the turn of the century was really, as far as they were concerned, the time of "permeation" in the stricter sense—the time when they had hopes of so working upon the capitalist parties from within as to make them Socialists unawares.

This period began to come to an end with the appointment, in 1905, of Beatrice to the famous Royal Commission on the Poor Laws, which led to the great battles, first on the Commission itself, and then, after the Majority and Minority Reports had been issued, to convince the country. In the organization then set up to secure the adoption of the Minority Report, the National Committee for the Prevention of Destitution, the Webbs for the first time turned propagandist on a large scale—and found out what they were up against. The failure of the great campaign dealt the death-blow to the prospects of "permeation"; it led the Webbs to turn to Labour, to whose possibilities they had not, since the 'nineties, paid much attention. After a second world tour, undertaken in 1911–12, they began an attempt to build a collectivist political movement which failed in the wild cross-winds of opinion which were blowing just before the war. When war came, they, particularly Sidney, turned their attention to advising the Labour movement and helping to plan policy and action during the war and after—they liked to think of themselves as "clerks," in the medieval sense, to the movement, though they combined with their Labour "clerking" service on many Government inquiries and committees. When, after the war, Labour emerged as a national party and His Majesty's Opposition, its new programme was drafted by Sidney; and the post-war years were years of Labour politics, which included such high-lights as the Sankey Coal Commission, the Seaham election, and Sidney's service in the two Labour Governments. This last period came abruptly to an end in the middle of 1931; but the Webbs had little time to mourn MacDonald's betrayal—though time enough to write a slashing criticism of it—for by that time their minds, and soon after their bodies, were set eastwards, towards the Union of Socialist Soviet Republics. In this and the remaining chapters of this book we shall be traversing the story of Beatrice Webb stage by stage through all these periods.

· · · · · · ·

The first of the great works was to write the history and the philosophy of Trade Unionism. The collection of material had been begun by Beatrice before her engagement; thereafter it continued rapidly, and the first book, *The History of Trade Unionism*, was begun on Christmas Eve, 1892, and published on May Day, 1894. The companion volume, *Industrial Democracy*, which contained the description of the philosophy and practice of Trade Unionism, as observed in its workings, appeared in 1897.

It is interesting to observe how the collaboration of the Fabian group which I have mentioned earlier was manifest in these two books. Other members of the Society played a considerable part in their writing. As Beatrice herself has told us, Graham Wallas rewrote the first chapter of the *History*, and Bernard Shaw the second and third; and Shaw in a letter to Ellen Terry later speaks of "the Webbs' new treatise on Democracy which I have to help in revising." It may be that the comparatively smooth flow of the narrative in the *History* owes something to the help of these distinguished collaborators, which inevitably was not maintained, to anything like the same extent, in later publications, although the Webbs made a practice of submitting drafts of their books to those who might be interested or critical, and took very careful note of any suggestions, even the most hostile or the most rudely expressed; at all events, the *History*, apart from its originality and its authoritativeness, is one of the easiest to read of all their great books.

Its originality needs some stressing. This generation, which has seen Trade Unions become a recognized and important part of society, and Trade Union leaders knighted and consulted beforehand over Government proposals for legislation or regulation, can with difficulty realize the extent to which Trade Unionism, at the time when the Webbs began to study it, was a country unknown to ordinary people, studied only by those who had been members of it, such as George Howell, and a few interested outsiders. To the old tradition of Liberal individualism as represented, for example, by John Bright, Trade Unions were an outrage on the face of nature, and ought not really to exist at all, though as unfortunately they did exist, and continued to exist, it fell to the Government to take steps to regulate them, to restrain the more unpleasant specimens and to give mild encouragement to the nicer ones. Others, less reflective, regarded them simply as nuisances, which led the working people to have ideas above their station, which in the past, in the days of Robert Owen, had been a danger to society, and, like an endemic disease, every now and again gave trouble, in times of "labour unrest" or "bad trade"; but the great majority of thinking people literally did not think about them at all. As we have seen, the writers of *Fabian Essays* passed them by; and it is worth recalling, as a sample of a common attitude, that when *Industrial Democracy* appeared, some critics "ridiculed the idea of attaching even so much importance to the workmen's organizations as to write a book about them."

Time has passed; no one would nowadays echo the words of those critics. Many a book has been written about "the workmen's organizations," and much has been found out that the Webbs, in their first patient researches into the old records of Trade Unions and the old memories of Trade Unionists, did not discover; but nothing that has appeared since has rivalled in scope, precision of design, and sheer interest combined the 1894 edition of the *History of Trade Unionism*.[1] In it they pointed out not without some cunning, considering the audience of traditionally minded Britons for whom they were writing, that Trade Unions were not a new-fangled invention of the devil and the late nineteenth century, but an institution already comparatively venerable.

"A Trade Union, as we understand the term, is a continuous association of wage-earners for the purpose of maintaining or improving the conditions of their employment.[2] This form of association has, as we shall see, existed in England for over two centuries, and cannot be supposed to have sprung at once fully developed into existence."

They went on to say that, though they had been "unable to discover the existence within the British Isles of anything falling within our definition" before the late seventeenth century, the spirit, if not the form, of Trade Unionism went back to the associations of journeymen in the Middle Ages and possibly even beyond. Finally, and more important, they showed to those students of politics who were continually complaining that the scanty number and brief history of modern republican states gave them too little scope for observing democratic government in working, that under their noses existed thousands of small democratic, and self-governing institutions at which they had never looked. Of this world they gave a picture, vivid to-day as it was then, of what it meant to be a member of a "trade society," of how such Societies chose their officials and what the officials were like, of how the Societies worked and what had been their fortunes over a couple of hundred years.

The picture which they drew was, of course, their own interpretation, and apart from new facts which have come to light since 1894 it would not now be universally accepted *in toto*. The present writer, for example, is of the opinion that their dislike of anarchistic behaviour and their preference for self-controlled efficiency over dynamic untidiness of thought and organization

---

[1] It was revised and re-issued, with several additional chapters, in 1920. But in the meantime the authors had lost the close and intimate contact with their subject which they had had in the 'nineties, and the 1920 edition, though still invaluable to the student, has not the full vigour and finality of the earlier one.

[2] *History of Trade Unionism*, page 1. In the 1920 edition, as a result of criticism, the phrase "working lives" was substituted for the word "employment."

caused them to pass a judgment on Robert Owen that was definitely unfair, that the unpracticality of Owen as an organizer obscured for them the enormously powerful influence of Owen's ideas, which continue to have explosive force down to the present day, when the Webbs' heroes of the London Trade Union Junta such as Robert Applegarth have long ceased to be anything but names in a specialized historical course; and there are other instances in which their views may be questioned. But nobody expects the discoverer of a new continent to get all its features correct in the first description; and if the Webbs had never done anything else, they would go down to history as having discovered and mapped out, in these two books, a whole new continent of democracy.

They were able to show what Trade Union officials were like —and to give vigorous pen-pictures of some of them—because they themselves were at the time of their writing in the closest association with most of the leading Trade Unionists. Beatrice, before her engagement, had made the first contacts; but Sidney eagerly took them up, and very shortly after their marriage we find him in the very characteristic role of acting as "scribe" for one of them—Tom Mann.

In 1892 the Government of Lord Rosebery, perplexed and bothered by the appearance of the "New Unionism," the great force of hitherto unorganized labour which had jumped so spectacularly into the news in the great Dock Strike of 1889, and feeling vaguely that something ought to be done about it, appointed under the chairmanship of the Duke of Devonshire, K.G., a vast Royal Commission on Labour, consisting of a great many persons of all sorts and opinions, which dithered along, taking evidence from persons of all sorts and opinions (including Sidney Webb) for some three years, at the end of which it produced a mountainous *Report* running to seventeen volumes and containing practically no conclusions which were of any value to anyone. One of its members, however, was the fiery young Trade Union leader, Tom Mann, who had played a prominent part in the 1889 strikes. Mann was naturally in strong disagreement with most of the Royal Commission; and the first practical job which Sidney Webb found for himself in the Trade Union world was to write a Minority Report for Tom Mann, and subsequently—a very Webb-like achievement—to get this Minority Report accepted and supported by James Mawdsley, the leader of the Lancashire cotton-spinners, also a member of the Commission and also a Trade Unionist—but a Trade Unionist of very different and much more conservative views than Mann's. In the last quarter of the last century the leaders of the cotton unions were as far to the right of the movement as they are to-day, but they stood at the head of a much more relatively numerous and economically powerful section. They and the miners held out staunchly against the innovators and Socialists of the New Unionism. "Coal and Cotton," said Beatrice of the 1895 Trade Union Congress, when the representatives of the local Trades Councils (who were suspected of generally radical leanings) were finally extruded from Congress, "Coal and Cotton silently voted them down."

The possibility of establishing, under firm intellectual guidance, a working arrangement between the left and right wings of the Trade Union movement, was one which appealed strongly to Beatrice in the 'nineties, and might have seemed to have a chance of success. The Webbs, particularly Beatrice, knew and understood the organizational side of Trade Unionism as none of their contemporary intellectuals, and few of those who have followed them, have ever known it; they had eaten and drunk and talked with General Secretaries, branch secretaries, and members of lodges and executive committees. They knew what it was like to be an official of a Trade Union, what sort of work and problems it involved, and they were very unlikely to sponsor or to support wild-cat suggestions which postulated as a preliminary that Trade Unionists and Trade Union Committees should turn into something quite different from what they were; they could be trusted, up to a point, by the honest and disinterested, if not very intelligent official who had been chosen for his post primarily in order that he might serve his own members. At the same time, they were definitely and uncompromisingly Socialist, and the left-winger might feel confidence that any influence they had on such men as Mawdsley and Henry Broadhurst[1] would be exercised in the direction of making them more Socialist. With social reform in the air and in part on the way, with the effects of Forster's Education Act just beginning to be felt, with a system of local government by vote instead of by privilege finally established and the parliamentary franchise recently extended to

---

[1] Of the Stonemasons' Society. General Secretary for fourteen years of the Trades Union Congress, and one of the initiators of the largely unsuccessful movement to persuade the Liberal Party to adopt working men as Parliamentary candidates.

miners and agricultural workers, with Sir William Harcourt saying "we are all Socialists now"—above all, with the respectable classes still staggering under the combined impact of Booth's revelations of poverty and the startling explosion of the 1889 strikes—it might well have seemed that the time was ripe for the new democracy which the Webbs had discovered and charted to be wisely shaped into a great new political force.

This did not happen: though the Webbs gained the confidence of the Union leaders, wrote reports and drafted resolutions for them, and had plenty of private and interesting discussions, they did not make them into a political party. Looking back, the chronicler finds several explanations for this result. In the first place, the material was inadequate—and the Webbs really knew it. Beatrice, at any rate, was never sentimental about Trade Unionism and Trade Unionists after the manner of some cataclysmic social revolutionaries. She realized that the average Union official was more interested in employment, in creating a labour scarcity in his own particular trade,[1] in serving, in fact, a vested interest in employment, than in anything else; that honesty in handling the funds was practically the only quality continuously demanded of him, and embezzlement the only crime serious enough to warrant dismissal;[2] and that members of the Trades Union Congress, or of any other representative gathering, were liable to be stupid and obstinate and to clog their minds with beer and whisky. They were scarcely, she felt, the stuff of which, even under Fabian guidance, a new world could be fashioned; and even if she did not express her opinions directly, her personality was not so opaque as she sometimes seems to have imagined.

Secondly, the left wing—the Socialists—were much more emotional and much more in a hurry than the Webbs were prepared to be. The heroes of 1889 soon slipped away from them. Tom Mann, though he maintained an interest in London municipal politics, gradually returned to the Social Democratic Federation, the Marxist body which was undoubtedly his spiritual home; and the rank-and-file of the Socialist-minded Trade

---

[1] Even if his restrictive policies tended to create, as Engels pointed out, a pool of potential blacklegs outside the pale of his own organization.

[2] The unwillingness of men who have known the bitterness of unemployment and who cannot afford to pay pensions to throw their servants on the streets for any other reason is of course human and intelligible. But it does not make for efficiency, or for giving youth a chance.

Unionists followed, not the Fabians, but Keir Hardie's Independent Labour Party, founded in 1893. The Fabian Society itself sent delegates, with Shaw as spokesman, to the conference at Bradford which founded the I.L.P., and pronounced an attitude of benevolent interest while refusing to merge its own separate identity or to abandon its policy of permeation by encouraging Fabian membership of Tory and Liberal organizations—an attitude which very nearly resulted in the expulsion of the Fabian delegates from the conference. Beatrice, however, was herself considerably less sympathetic. She did not like either of the gods of the I.L.P., Keir Hardie or his successor Ramsay MacDonald; and it would seem that she made little or no attempt, as she did later in the case of the Guild Socialists to get on terms with them.[1] She thought them geese, and potentially dangerous geese; and it is true that during the early years of its existence the I.L.P. made little political headway save in municipal elections, though it must be remembered that it was founded at an unfortunate moment, when the upward movement of trade had stopped and the impetus of 1889 was nearly exhausted. Advanced political parties are apt to look weak and ineffective in political doldrums.

As important a factor as any, however, and important not merely for the 'nineties, but for its after-influence on the work of the Webbs, was their complete failure, in the end, to get on terms with the biggest bulking figure in the Labour movement of the day—John Burns. Long before his death in 1942, John Burns had been completely forgotten by all save a few friends and a few connoisseurs of Labour history; but in the 'eighties and 'nineties the egotistical, flamboyant, and forceful personality of "the Man with the Red Flag,"[2] which burst upon the general public in the unemployed demonstrations of the mid-'eighties and the 1889 strikes, seemed to mark him out as the future leader of Labour. It certainly seemed so to Burns himself; even in 1918 he still dreamed of heading a new Labour Party, and in the 'nineties he was already suspicious of anyone near his throne. He had broken away from his earliest comrades, the Social Democratic Federation, with a great deal of sound and abuse, and he would have nothing to do with Keir Hardie or the I.L.P. As far as can be made out, what Burns then looked for was a

---

[1] See Chapter XI.
[2] The best short account of Burns's life is in G. D. H. Cole's Fabian pamphlet, *John Burns*.

political organization based entirely upon the Trade Unions, with a Socialist or semi-Socialist programme of sorts—and with himself as sole leader. To a certain extent, the Fabians might have been inclined to agree with him; at the end of 1893, in a mood of sudden impatience with the old political parties, they had issued a manifesto drafted by Webb and Shaw and entitled *To Your Tents, O Israel!* in which they told the working classes (thereby infuriating their Liberal friends) that neither Tories nor Liberals would be any further use to them, and that they must organize politically for themselves. But Burns would have had no use for a party controlled or guided by Fabians; and his own idea was not, either in 1893 or at any subsequent date, a practical possibility. A party confined to Trade Unions and Trade Unionists and excluding from membership or influence all political Radicals who are ineligible for admission to a Trade Union, however attractive it may sometimes seem to Trade Union leaders suffering from middle-class criticism, is bound to be still-born. All Burns achieved in the end was gradually and vociferously to separate himself from his own class until he became an officer of the established system; and though when Campbell-Bannerman invited him to become President of the Local Government Board, he exclaimed with characteristic lack of modesty, "Bravo! Sir Henry. This is the most popular thing you have done!" he turned out to be mistaken. But in 1894, though his feet were already set on the road to this end, he was still a big figure; and his vain horror of being managed or "got at" in any way, and his jealous fear of any rival, was an important factor in the failure of the Webbs to bring off their original idea, and to become at that date "the clerks to the Labour movement."

There was no abrupt severance; they quarrelled with nobody. But after the publication of *Industrial Democracy* they turned their eyes elsewhere; and the formation in 1900 of the federation of Socialist Societies and Trade Unions, backed by the Trades Union Congress, which called itself the Labour Representation Committee, though the Fabian Society sent Edward Pease to assist in its birth and to be a member of its executive committee, seems to have engaged little of the Webbs' attention.

CHAPTER VIII

EDUCATION, POLITICS, LOCAL GOVERNMENT

IN 1898, having finished *Industrial Democracy*, the Webbs departed on a six months' tour of Canada and the United States, in order to take a look at modern democracies in working. They enjoyed themselves very much, interviewing politicians, attending meetings of Congress and of State legislatures, etc., and collected a good deal of information, useful to themselves, about the working of political machinery in the New World; but it cannot be said that their travels were of much importance to the outside world, and the same criticism applies to the tour of Japan, China, and India which they undertook thirteen years later. They were too British to assimilate easily non-British habits of thought, and at the same time they were too intent upon their own particular job to take in, or to evaluate, anything in other countries or other civilizations which did not seem to have direct bearing upon the working-out of Socialist democracy for Great Britain; with the result that their judgments upon other countries have a certain superficiality, a failure to appreciate what they understood so well in their own, the historical roots of political and social institutions. Only in the case of the U.S.S.R., where they had already an eager appreciation and desire to understand, did they bring back anything that was of great value to the British to learn—and in justice it must be said that they did not pretend that they had in other instances; they published no hasty impressions of the U.S.A. or of Japan.

When they returned, their main immediate concern was with public education. This concern was no new thing. As chairman of the Technical Education Committee of the L.C.C., Sidney was in point of fact largely responsible for whatever there was in the way of education for London children who had passed their twelfth birthday; and though less directly responsible, he was no less concerned both with university education and with the raising of the elementary school standard above the inconceivably mean and parsimonious level of the nineteenth century.

The detail of these activities belongs to Sidney's life rather than to Beatrice's, since from the nature of the case she was an adjutant rather than a prime mover. But the work done or initiated is of such importance, including as it does the largest physical monument to the Webbs' labours—the London School of Economics—that space must be found for a brief survey.

. The London School was actually in existence, albeit in a humble way, before they left England. Its whole history is a remarkable example of two things: the impression of trustworthiness produced—and rightly produced—by the early Fabians, and the genius which the Webbs had for building four-square, when they understood the materials at their disposal, erections which would stand the test of time.[1] After being in existence ten years, the Fabian Society had established itself as a body which could be trusted to do more with half a crown than any other of its kind; and in 1894 it suddenly found itself possessed, by the will of a cantankerous old member who was known to its executive committee mainly for the frequency and violence of his grumbles, of a sum of about £10,000 to be expended over ten years. Such a windfall as this, the executive committee decided, must not be thrown into the general pool of the Society's funds; the Hutchinson Trust, as it was called, was devoted partly to financing provincial lectures on Socialism (the lecturers included Lord Snell and Ramsay MacDonald) and partly to founding an institution for the study of political economy in London.

"It is to-day amazing," wrote Sidney[2] in 1928, "to think how minute was the provision for economic teaching, and how lacking that for economic research, in the London of the last decade of the century. King's College had a nominal professorship which was suspended. Professor Foxwell held a chair at University College, but had only a score of students, reported to be 'one-half coloured.' A rather elementary course of lectures (which I had attended in my youth) was annually repeated at the Birkbeck College. That was all that existed in the capital of the British Empire for a population comparable to that of the whole of Scotland (or Belgium or Holland) each of them having several universities. Nor was there any dissatisfaction. The pundits solemnly declared that the existing provision met the entire demand; and, as they also suggested, amply supplied the whole need."

[1] Besides the Fabian Society and the L.S.E., the historian must take notice of the *New Statesman* and the Labour Research Department—both mentioned on later pages —as institutions which have long outlived their founders' participation.
[2] "Reminiscences" by S. and B. Webb, *St. Martin's Review*, December, 1928.

It is amazing. But it is no less amazing to set out to cure the economic ignorance of London with a fund consisting of some portion of ten thousand pounds; and that is what the Webbs did. From a modest beginning in two rooms in the Adelphi they set a college of economics and political science on the road to becoming the vast building with thousands of students and many professors,[1] of which Sidney once observed, apropos of its rapid growth, "it is said that on the buildings of the School of Economics the concrete never sets." With the aid of Haldane, they succeeded in getting the new college recognized as a constituent part of the new University of London, and in getting the subject of Economics recognized as a science for the purpose of obtaining a degree. The tens of thousands of ex-university students who now write the letters B.Sc.Econ. (London) after their names owe it to the Webbs.

Beatrice from the outset played a considerable part in the school. It was her first experience of trying to raise money on a large scale for purposes she had at heart. She began with Shaw's "Irish millionairess," Miss Payne-Townshend, from whom she got a thousand pounds, and proceeded to endeavour to "milk" other persons of means, sometimes successfully, sometimes not. Beatrice's technique of begging was her own and bordered sometimes upon the minatory. The present writer had for long in her possession a slip of paper once attached to a cheque signed Bernard Shaw, which bore the inscription "Extracted by Beatrice Webb"; and undoubtedly men of great possessions were sometimes put off by her assumption—however true it might be—that she knew how they ought to use their money better than they did themselves. Nevertheless, she did raise a good deal for the School; and furthermore took a great and continuous interest in its progress. Regularly she entertained its teachers to dinner, and had At Homes for its students, even when these had reached the total of several hundreds; and for some time the School was popularly known as "the Webberies." But it would be quite incorrect to conclude from this that either Beatrice or Sidney used, or intended to use, the School as a means of covert Socialist propaganda. Its first director, W. A. S. Hewins, was so far from being an orthodox Socialist that he severed connections in order to devote himself to Chamberlain's campaign for Tariff

---

[1] Sidney himself was for many years Professor of Public Administration (unpaid) in the School.

Reform; and although it is probably true that the School, in the course of its short life, has included more Socialists on its staff than say, Trinity College, Cambridge, this merely reflects the fact that Socialists have been more interested in economic subjects than persons of other political persuasions, and is in no way due to discrimination on the part either of the Webbs or of those who followed them.

At the same time, Sidney, in co-operation with Haldane, was working and "rushing about all over London," in order to secure the passage of the 1898 University of London Act, which put a real teaching university in place of the mere external-examining and degree-conferring body which had previously borne that name,[1] and was taking a prominent part in the discussions and agitations which resulted in the Balfour Education Act of 1902 and its successor, the 1903 Education Act for London. Therein he scored perhaps the largest success ever achieved by the representative of a propagandist body with less than a thousand members. In 1901 there appeared a Fabian Tract—anonymous, but written by Sidney Webb—entitled *The Education Muddle and the Way Out*. At this time, preparation for a new Education Bill were well under way, and Sir John Gorst, who was then Vice-President of the Board of Education, having read the advance proofs of the Tract, took the unprecedented—and as far as I know, unsequelled—step of ordering fifty copies of the galleys to be pondered over by his permanent officials. The suggestions made by the Fabian Society thus received full consideration in the drafting of the two Acts.

It is not necessary to go into detail about the 1902 reforms in education, whose three principal effects were first, to initiate a system of State secondary schools, secondly, to remove the control of public elementary education from the old School Boards and to put it under the local authorities; and thirdly, to fasten the "dual system" firmly on elementary education by re-enacting the grant of public money to schools run by religious denominations—the largest of these being naturally the Church of England. As chairman of the Technical Education Committee (whose functions came to an end with the passing of the Balfour Acts) Sidney's main concern was with secondary education, and he worked tremendously hard to secure for London an adequate

---

[1] He became a member of the Senate of the new body, of which Lord Rosebery was Chancellor.

F

secondary system. Typical of his efforts was the proposal which
he brought before the Council, in his very early days in its service,
for a scheme of free scholarships to enable intelligent children
from the Board Schools to continue their education. This proposal, put forward with all the battery of facts of which he was a
master, proving how badly the greatest and richest capital city
in the world lagged behind other centres of considerably less
wealth and importance in the education of its children, captured
the imagination of his fellow councillors, who enthusiastically
voted for scholarships on a surprisingly generous scale. It was
only after the vote had been taken that the chairman of the
Technical Education Committee, drawing his facts from a survey
prepared for him by a brilliant young Civil Servant, Hubert
Llewellyn Smith, pointed out to the enthusiastic councillors that
there was only one fly in their ointment—there were practically
no secondary schools for the scholarship children to go to. This
state of things was largely remedied in subsequent years, and the
high standard of London's secondary education owes a very
great deal to Sidney Webb's preparatory work, before the Balfour
Act was thought of, and to his insistence that when it was passed
it should be used to the full.

His experience in relation to the other parts of the Acts was
less fortunate and led to estrangement, both from old friends like
Graham Wallas, who was an eager and enthusiastic member of
the old London School Board and passionately resented its
abolition, contending that the handing over of education to a
generally-elected authority, even though provision was made for
the co-option of specialists to the Education Committee, would
inevitably result in the domination of education by extraneous
and irrelevant interests; and from the Nonconformist wing of the
Liberals, who would have nothing to do with State aid to religious
institutions.

At this time, the attitude of the Webbs to religion might
reasonably be described as "non-militant atheism"; they themselves had no belief in any revealed religion, but they neither
hoped nor desired to convert the country to their opinions. This
being so, their attitude to the quarrels of Church and Chapel
was rather "a plague on both your houses," or to put it more
positively, a desire for toleration even if toleration implied the
exacting from Nonconformists of a financial contribution to
Anglican and Catholic schools.

"I thought," Sidney wrote in later years, "the imposition of 'undenominational Christianity' as unfair to the Jews, Unitarians, and Secularists, as the imposition of the Anglican Church Catechism on Roman Catholics and Nonconformists, or of the Roman Catholic formularies on Protestants. Moreover, I knew that the result would be not the closing of the Roman Catholic schools, but (as in the United States) their continuance at private cost at a still lower level of efficiency, which would be calamitous for the very large and perhaps growing number of children who would resort to them. Above all, I wanted to preserve variety in education, rather than an officially prescribed uniformity—variety in methods of teaching, variety in the subjects taught, and variety in 'atmosphere.' I wanted to leave the door open to new and unthought-of experiments in the schools."

For this reason he supported the "dual system" as laid down in the Balfour Acts, with all its implications; and his desire to preserve "variety and experiment" in the elementary schools has certainly been fulfilled, in comparison with the strict prescription of curricula, etc. which has obtained in many Continental countries with more "advanced" systems. But the attitude of the Webbs, rational as it might seem, failed to take account of the deep emotional hostility among the Nonconformist part of the community to anything which savoured of concessions to Rome. Sidney's support of the dual system in the Balfour Acts aroused bitter opposition among the Progressives on the L.C.C.; and though it did not prevent them offering him the chairmanship of the new Education Committee—after he had been returned unopposed for Deptford in the 1904 elections—it resulted in his being turned off the inner committee of the Party, and contributed to the gradual alienation of the Webbs from the official Liberals, which was completed in the first decade of the new century.

For the time, however, these activities brought the Webbs, on their return from their New World tour, into much closer social and organizational contact with a group of leading Liberal politicians, as well as with some Tories. The main link was their old friend Haldane, the same as had acted as chaperon to them in the days of their engagement, and whose deep interest in higher education—on which the rank and file of his own party were lukewarm, at the best—led him to ally himself on the one side with Balfour and Gorst and on the other with Sidney Webb and his friends. Haldane and Beatrice did not always see eye to eye, by any means. She thought that he was woolly-minded and that he ate and drank a great deal too much, and he did not regard the Webbs as immune from criticism, though, as he wrote in his *Autobiography*, "Whatever their failings socially, they are splendid workers, and I should be proud to have given up so much." Their main link was their common enthusiasm for higher education, and a common interest in seeing the work of administration efficiently done.[1]

Haldane was associated, in his own Party, with a group of men who wanted the Liberals to develop a strong forward policy both at home and abroad. Towards the close of the century, the great party of Gladstone was in a bad way; the Liberal Unionists had been lost to it through the dispute over Irish Home Rule, the leader's mantle had fallen, not without considerable bickering, upon the undecided shoulders of Lord Rosebery, and within the Party quarrels about education, about liquor licensing, about colonial policy, and about personal prestige, seemed endemic. From 1895 to 1905—an enormous stretch of time in those days—the Tories were uninterruptedly in power; and round about the time of the Boer War many knowledgeable persons, whose vision of the future was not equal to their knowledge of the present confidently predicted that the Liberal Party would very shortly fall to pieces. In this period the Webbs made friends with a small group of Liberal Imperialists (called familiarly "Limps"), whose leading figures were Haldane himself, Asquith, Asquith's brother-in-law Tennant, and Edward Grey, later Lord Grey of Fallodon. The name Liberal Imperialists derives from the attitude of this group to the Boer War, when they refused to join in the anti-war "pro-Boer" agitation of other Liberals such as Lloyd George and Massingham. On this point the Webbs definitely agreed with them; their own view, which was adopted, after a sharp clash of opinion, by the majority of the Fabian Society,[2] was that there was little to choose between the two sides in the fray, that neither gold-digging companies on the Rand nor patriarchal Dutch farmers cared two hoots either for the values of human freedom

---

[1] This interest was partly, though not entirely, responsible for Haldane's unlucky remark that Germany was his "spiritual home," which caused him to be hounded from office during the first world war; it is paralleled by the Webbs' uncritical admiration, over a period of many years, for the Japanese.

[2] Some twoscore members, including Ramsay MacDonald, resigned over this issue. See Bernard Shaw, *Fabianism and the Empire*.

A similar dispute developed over the fiscal question, on which the Fabians refused to be lined up behind the doctrinaire Free Traders.

or, more specifically, for the minds and bodies of the Kaffir population; and on the narrow issue they were unquestionably correct, though they underestimated, or failed to observe, the emotional indignation of Englishmen who did not like the appearance of their country in the guise of a large gangster bullying a small and poor people at the behest of a gang of shady financiers.[1] It seemed to them, for a time, as though the "Limps" might provide the means of permeation for which the Fabians were looking, upon a political level more lofty than that of local government, even of the London County Council, and that it might be possible to combine them with an admixture of the more progressive Tories and the more intelligent Trade Unionists into a force capable of forming a Government acceptable to Fabians in the sense of tending towards Socialist practices: accordingly, their quiet and regular life in Grosvenor Road became diversified with quasi-political social events, with lunches, dinners, and discussions, until the unexpectedly overwhelming Liberal victory of 1906 put an end to Haldane's manœuvres.[2]

Neither education, nor the County Council, nor political permeation, however, exhausts the tale of the Webbs' activity during those years. In the spring of 1899 they began their studies in English Local Government.

By that date the local government of England and Wales had emerged, but only just fully emerged, from the jungle of ancient, overlapping, illogical, and unintelligible jurisdictions of pre-Reform times, when manors, leet courts, hundreds, parishes, vestries, and dozens of other institutions drove not merely the observer or the student of politics but even the specialist lawyer nearly out of his mind with their complications. The sweeping series of reforms which began with the Municipal Corporations Act of 1835 and which substituted for the former tangle an intelligible if not a wholly satisfactory system was only completed with the setting up of the County Councils in 1888, the Parish Councils in 1894, and the Metropolitan Borough Councils in 1899; and the last-named had not reached statutory existence by the time the Webbs began their study.

The Fabian Society—the "gas-and-water Socialists"—had

---

[1] For the point of view of the non-imperialist type of Liberal see Hilaire Belloc, *Verses to a Lord who, in the House of Lords said that those who Opposed the South African Adventure Confused Soldiers with Money Grubbers*, republished in Belloc's *Verses*.

[2] He had intended, *inter alia*, that Campbell-Bannerman should go to the Lords and Asquith be leader of the Commons. See Haldane, *Autobiography*.

seized on the possibilities of the new local authorities, and not merely of the London County Council. In leaflets and tracts dealing with borough councils, urban and rural councils, and parish councils, they explained to their members and to all others who were interested the powers and possibilities of these Demo-cracies of Consumers, as Webb called them, and what use Socialists and Radicals might make of them. But these Fabian efforts were, quite rightly, related to the present and the future; what the Webbs proceeded to do was to go back into the past, to plunge again into the uncharted pre-Reform jungle, and from the specimens they found therein to construct as it were an historical biology of English local political institutions in the same way as they had already constructed an historical biology of the associations of producers.

It was a task of the same type, pursued by the same methods, by searching through documents, by interviewing officials and "informed persons," by attending meetings, and by writing down and sorting and re-sorting innumerable sheets of notes. But it was a very much bigger task. The field was as unexplored, save for specialist studies, as had been the field of Trade Unionism, but it covered a very much wider area, embraced a great many more organizations of widely differing types, and also stretched much further back in time. As the Webbs themselves said, in one of the later books in which they published the results of their research,[1] "When we turned to the subject of Local Government, nearly a quarter of a century ago, our object was to describe the organiza-tion and working of the existing local governing authorities, with a view to ascertaining how they could be improved. We realized from the outset that a merely statistical investigation of what was going on around us would reveal little or nothing of the lasting conditions of disease or health in the social organizations that we were considering. We knew that, in order to find the causes of their imperfections and the directions in which they could be improved, we had to study, not only their present but also their past; not merely what they were doing but also how they came to be doing it. Somewhat naïvely, we accepted as our starting-point the beginning of the nineteenth century. But after *a year's work* [italics mine] on the records, it became apparent to us that the local institutions of the first quarter of that century were either in the last stages of decay or in the earliest years of infancy.

[1] *Statutory Authorities for Special Purposes* (1922), chapter v.

We saw that it was impossible to appreciate the drastic innovations of 1834–6, and their subsequent developments, without going much further back. After some reconnoitring of the seventeenth century, we decided that the Revolution of 1689 ranked, in the evolution of English Local Government, as the beginning of a distinct era which continued until the Reform Bill of 1832. . . .

"In the next chapter we shall set forth the gradual evolution of a new set of principles arising out of the circumstances and thought of the new age: principles destined to become dominant in the Local Government of the nineteenth century."

The work began in the spring of 1899; a year later, as the above extract indicates, its scope was widened in the light of the information so far gathered. Two years after its inception the Webbs began to write the first of their books on Local Government, *The Parish and the County*; it is a measure of the amount of labour involved that the book was not ready for press until the autumn of 1905. It was published in the following year; *The Manor and the Borough* followed two years later; but the research and the writing-up of the results of the research continued steadily, alongside all their subsequent political and social activities, right up to 1929, in which year the second part of *English Poor Law History* was issued. Perhaps the easiest way to indicate the magnitude of the task which the Webbs projected and performed is simply to give the list of the published volumes.

The main bulk is contained in ten major books, grouped under two headings, Structure and Functions. Under the first we find (1) *The Parish and the County* (1906. 1 volume. 664 pages); (2) and (3) *The Manor and the Borough* (1908. 2 volumes, 858 pages); (4) *Statutory Authorities for Special Purposes* (1922. 1 volume, 486 pages).

Under this last peculiarly uneuphonious title, which suggests a police-court test for suspected drunks rather than a book which anyone could conceivably want to read, the Webbs concealed some of their most fascinating accounts and most profound study of the organic development of English local institutions from the medieval to the nineteenth century. Few, indeed, of the leading political economists would have thought to look for the sources of the great local government services of to-day in the early history of such bodies as Commissioners of Sewers, Turnpike Trusts, Lighting and Paving Commissioners, and others created for the abatement of nuisance to the citizens at large; the Webbs did, and triumphantly traced the pedigree.

The second heading contains the following: (5) *The Story of the King's Highway* (1913. 1 volume, 279 pages); (6) *English Prisons under Local Government* (1922. 1 volume, 261 pages, with Preface by Bernard Shaw); (7) *The History of Liquor Licensing in England* (1903. 1 volume, 162 pages); (8) *English Poor Law History: The Old Poor Law* (1927. 1 volume, 447 pages); (9) and (10) *English Poor Law History: The Last Hundred Years* (1929. 2 volumes, 1,055 pages).

A total of 4,212 pages in all, containing in addition to the text, footnotes and bibliographical references of more than usual fullness. When one adds to this total the two books which contain the Minority Report of the Poor Law Commission (for which see the next chapter) and five other by-products, *London Education* (1904), *The State and the Doctor* (1910), *English Poor Law Policy* (1910), *The Prevention of Destitution* (1911), and *Grants in Aid* (1911) —apart from the Fabian Tracts on local government written by Sidney—one may be pardoned for thinking that the contribution to knowledge made by the Webbs on the single subject of local government would be a full life's work for most people. It is not without significance that whereas the trail they blazed for Trade Unionism has been followed by many others who have written longer or shorter histories of the working class, no one, so far as I am aware, has yet ventured to write a definitive history of English local government.

CHAPTER IX

POOR LAW I: THE ROYAL COMMISSION

IN the Webb activities described in the last chapter Sidney, generally speaking, took the lead; at all events, it was Sidney who appeared most in the public eye—Sidney who was on the L.C.C. and responsible, not merely for its education policy but in large measure for its Standing Orders, and the methods it adopted for conducting its business, Sidney who was Professor at the School of Economics, Sidney who sat on the Fabian Executive, Sidney who was responsible for the Education Bill and University agitations. Beatrice, during those years, was playing the part of helpmeet, though an unusually effective and independent helpmeet. What she did "on her own" was of much less importance. In 1895 she published a long article on *State Regulation of Women's Labour*, in which she again attacked the demand of the extreme feminists that no industrial protective legislation (such as restriction of hours or night work) should be laid down for women unless it applied also to men, and for a year or two she was on the executive committee of a mixed body called the National Union of Women Workers, which was not a Trade Union, as its name would seem to imply, but a collection of women of all sorts who were interested in women's work. She resigned from the executive, and a year later from the Union itself, after she had unsuccessfully tried to induce them to abandon their practice of opening their meetings with prayer—not because she was an atheist, but, characteristically, on the ground that it was an insult to their Jewish and Mohammedan members. It does not appear, however, that she felt happy or at home with purely feminine organizations, either then or at any other time. But in December, 1905, the Balfour Government, almost with its dying breath, appointed a Royal Commission on the Poor Law, and named as one of its members Mrs. Sidney Webb. From that date her public personality began, and with the ending of the Commission's labours and the publication of the Minority Report for which she was almost entirely responsible—though the actual drafting was done by Sidney—she came full into the limelight.

No general inquiry into the working of the Poor Law had been made for seventy years, since the great reforming Commission forced upon the country the rigours of the "New Poor Law" of 1834. The Commissioners of that date, the Whigs, the philosophical and business Radicals who had come to power as a result of the Reform Act, knew exactly what they wanted. They wanted to end the practice now known as the Speenhamland system, under which the Poor Law was in effect used to provide subsidies for low wages, and, more important, they wanted to force men under the threat of heavy penalties to work in the hungry factories of the north. As justification for their course of action they had three main beliefs, all of which commanded considerable assent among the "advanced thinkers" of the time. The first, deriving from Puritan and manufacturing sources, was that, save for exceptional acts of God, a man's poverty and destitution were his own fault. Riches, as Nassau Senior and his like taught, were the reward of hard work and abstinence; conversely, poverty must be the result of idleness and indulgence. Anyone, therefore, who attempted to mitigate poverty by any other means than by driving the poor to hard work and abstinence was doing them a great moral disservice as well as undermining the foundations of the community.

Secondly, they believed in the "iron law of wages" and in the existence of a fixed Wages Fund of limited amount, which belief involved that any money paid out in poor relief in the rural areas came inevitably out of the pockets of those in work—the more money doled out to paupers, the lower the wages would be for the decent respectable labourer. And thirdly, taught by the Reverend Malthus, they believed in the bogy of population continually tending to outrun the means of subsistence, and that any relief given to destitute persons, by encouraging them to breed, would produce more and more hungry mouths to eat into the livelihood of their sober and industrious neighbours.

The logical conclusion of the Commissioners' beliefs, of course, would have been a policy of simple starvation, of letting those persons who could not or would not find work die out, along with their wives and families. But people are not, in general, quite so cruel as their logical beliefs, and even in 1834 it was too much for public opinion—as well as being contrary to the laws of England —simply to starve the workless. The most that could be done, therefore, was to grant relief, but on such conditions that the hardest and worst-paid job would be a comparatively pleasurable alternative—this was the famous "principle of less eligibility." This conclusion the Commissioners, aided by a furious propaganda whose efficiency the Webbs might well have envied and a series of hastily compiled and tendentious regional investigations, forced rapidly upon a not unwilling Parliament, and summarized them in the prohibition of "all relief whatever to able-bodied persons or their families other than in well-conducted workhouses,"[1] in which old married couples were separated and children torn from their parents. This was the system against which William Cobbett fought to his last hours, which was responsible for the furious Chartist riots of the 'forties, and which was held up to execration in the works of many writers—above all by Dickens in *Oliver Twist*. Of all the social institutions devised by the century of triumphant industrialism, none was so bitterly hated by its victims as the Poor Law. As the Majority of the 1905 Commission—those who were in disagreement with Beatrice—somewhat sadly remarked, "It has been impressed upon us in the course of our inquiry that the name 'Poor Law' has gathered about it associations of harshness and still more of hopelessness, which we fear might seriously obstruct the reforms which we desire to see initiated"; and though before the coming of the violent trade depressions of the present century, the number of those destitute and seeking relief at any one moment was a comparatively tiny proportion of the population, nevertheless Charles Booth's Inquiry showed that no less than thirty per cent of the people of London came under the Poor Law at some time during the course of their lives—which obviously meant that many more lived in the fear of it. It is only within very recent years that the shadow of "the House" has been lifted from the lives of the working classes.

This is no place to recount the history of the Poor Law between 1834 and 1905, which has been the subject of many books.[2] Suffice it to say that, without any serious changes in the law, the stark cruelty of the "principles of 1834" had been modified in many respects by administrative action, sometimes by the central officials of the Local Government Board, which had charge of the Poor Law, sometimes by the elected Guardians of the Poor

[1] For the meaning, in practice, of the word "well-conducted" the reader is referred to many examples studied in the second part of the Webbs' *English Poor Law History*. Bastilles was the name the poor gave to the workhouses.

[2] The Webbs' own *English Poor Law Policy* (1910) gives an effective summary in less detail than the three major volumes. Many biographies of Labour leaders, such as the *Life of Will Crooks*, show what the policy involved on the human side.

who until 1929 carried the responsibility in the different localities. This came about partly through the growth of humane sentiment and the relaxation of the fierce competition which marked the first half of the nineteenth century, partly because economic beliefs gradually changed. Belief in the iron law of wages, for example, faded out as the general level of wages rose steadily without any group of workers being penalized for increases won by their fellows; and Malthus's population law had proved definitely false, as improving conditions and a growing knowledge of birth control showed beyond doubt that it was not among the better-off workers, but among the destitute, the ignorant, and the hopeless that the flood of human births which his disciples feared so much was to be found, that, in fact, the best way to prevent the poor from breeding indiscriminately was not to refuse them any help but purposively to raise their standards. (It should not be assumed, however, that holders of these beliefs had ceased to exist; then as now there were political dinosaurs who could do no more than reiterate, in a mutter or a scream, what they had learned from others fifty years back.)

The belief that destitution was a man's own fault and should be treated as a crime save in exceptional cases died much harder. It gained a certain reinforcement from the misapplication of Darwin's biological theories by men like Sir Henry Maine, who took the phrase "survival of the fittest" to imply that it was dysgenic and inimical to the welfare of the State to give any help out of public funds to its weaker members, overlooking, or deliberately ignoring, the fact that the weaker members were not a separate species and did not, if unhelped, die out like good Darwinian reptiles, but continued to breed and to remain in existence as a focal centre of dirt and disease for their superior neighbours. It was assisted also by the efforts of the Charity Organization Society, with their attempts to prevent the "undeserving poor" from receiving any alms from private charity, to rewrite *Oliver Twist* with a more efficient Bumble and no Mr. Brownlow. But though these two influences did something to check the change of opinion and to offer comfort and justification to those who wished to keep the poor in poverty but to hide them somewhere where they could not be seen or smelt, they could not really stem the tide, partly because private charity was so manifestly unequal to helping more than a fraction of even the "deserving" poor, and by the late 'nineties Boards of

Guardians all over the country—and not by any means only Boards which contained working-class members or working-class sympathizers—were softening, in one way or another, the rigours of the "principles of 1834," were granting a shilling or two a week to old persons without forcing them to enter "the House," were giving out-relief to those who had fallen upon sudden disaster without insisting that they should first pawn or sell every stick of their possessions above the minimum, and were even conniving at failures to disfranchise poor people who had fallen ill and had been sent to a Poor Law Infirmary.[1]

These modifications, however, had been made almost at haphazard and according to no recognizable principle; further, they were made to a much greater degree in some Unions[2] than in others, with the result that the out-of-works, the tramps, and the sick, often received quite different treatment for no reason except that they applied for relief in one place rather than another. It was high time, said the senior administrators of the Poor Law, that something should be done to rationalize procedure and to bring the variationalists into line.

There was another reason also for "doing something about the Poor Law." By 1905, the terrible shadow of mass-unemployment, which became a reality after the first world war, had begun to fall upon society. "Cyclical unemployment" had appeared as a recognized phenomenon in the depression of 1879 and again in 1886–7; and "cyclical unemployment" meant that thousands of able-bodied and willing workers, whose temporary destitution, whatever the C.O.S. might say, was quite evidently no fault of their own, were going to come to the Boards of Guardians asking for relief. Moreover, the persons over whom this fate hung were voters; they were the people who at the end of 1905 wiped the floor with the Conservatives, and returned a huge Liberal majority and thirty Labour M.P.s. They could not be ignored; already Boards of Guardians such as Poplar (under the leadership of Will Crooks and George Lansbury) had defiantly announced that they considered their duty as Guardians was to

[1] Until 1918, the receipt of *any* benefit from the Poor Law services could be held to disqualify the recipient from voting in a national or municipal election. A perfectly solvent individual who met with a street accident, and was conveyed to a Poor Law hospital because that happened to be the nearest might find himself disqualified as a "pauper."

[2] The "Union" (of parishes) was the unit of election for Boards of Guardians. It might coincide with the area of a Borough Council, or it might not. The West Derby Union included the whole of Liverpool.

relieve destitution and not to enter upon inquisitorial inquiries
as to how that destitution had come about; furthermore, Radical
politicians had started asking pertinent questions about the
responsibility of the Government for its citizens in time of trade
depression, and had actually forced through Parliament a small
measure, the Unemployed Workmen Act of 1905, which, tiny
though it was, established the principle that the Government
could not wash its hands entirely of the causes of destitution;
there was a vague fear abroad that if something were not done
about the Poor Law the unemployed riots of 1886 might be
repeated on a much more dangerous scale. These fears were
mild in comparison with the reality to come, as those who
remember the storming of the Employment Exchanges in 1921,
the battle over "Poplarism," and the unemployed marches of
1931-2 will know; but to some observers the faint writing on the
wall was plain enough to be read.

Under these circumstances, as a result of a vague feeling of
disquietude and a general sense of muddle rather than in response
to any large-scale agitation, the Royal Commission of 1905 was
set up. It consisted of twenty members, under the chairmanship
of Lord George Hamilton, a Conservative ex-Cabinet Minister.
Nine of the members were officials responsible in one way or
another for Poor Law administration; half a dozen or so were
prominent members or supporters of the C.O.S; two were political economists; one was Charles Booth—who retired owing to
ill-health before the deliberations of the committee were finished;
four, including some of those already mentioned, represented the
Churches. To express the point of view of the working classes
there were George Lansbury and Francis Chandler, the secretary
of the Carpenters' Union; there was also Mrs. Sidney Webb.
It might well seem that the Balfour Government had succeeded
in getting together a body whose report would, in all essentials,
stand faithfully by the "principles of 1834" and those hard-
worked and often misunderstood officials who were trying consistently to carry them out, while making due provision for any
minor modifications which the experience and changing conditions of seventy years had shown to be really necessary.

This, at any rate, seems to have been the opinion of Mr. (later
Sir James) Davy, the head of the Poor Law Division of the Local
Government Board. Unwisely, however, and not realizing the
quality and temper of the mind with which he was in contact,

he gave away his intentions in a preliminary talk with one of the members of the Commission.

"I had extracted from Davy," Beatrice Webb wrote in her Diary,[1] "in a little interview I had with him, the intention of the Local Government Board officials as to the purpose and procedure they intended to be followed by the Commission. They were going to use us to get certain radical reforms of structure: the Boards of Guardians were to be swept away, judicial officers appointed, and possibly the institutions transferred to the county authorities—with all of which I am inclined to agree. But we were also to recommend reversion to the 'Principles of 1834' as regards policy, to stem the tide of philanthropic influence that was sweeping away the old embankment of deterrent tests to the recipient of relief. . . . Having settled the conclusions to which we are to be led, the L.G.B. officials (on and off the Commission) have pre-determined the procedure. We were to be 'spoon-fed' by evidence carefully selected and prepared; they were to draft the circular to the Board of Guardians; they were to select the Inspectors who were to give evidence; they were virtually to select the Guardians who were to be called in support of this evidence. Assistant Commissioners were to be appointed, who were to give evidence illustrative of these theories. And, above all, we were to be given *opinions* and not facts. . . . To-day at lunch I put Mr. Lansbury on his guard against this policy."

She had been warned; and she made ample use of the warning.

This appointment to the Royal Commission came at exactly the right moment in Beatrice's career. Sidney's interest in the Poor Law went back for many years; as long ago as 1894 he had written Henry Broadhurst's Minority Report for the Royal Commission on the Aged Poor, of which Charles Booth and the Prince of Wales were both members, and during their six and a half years' research work on local government Beatrice had come into contact at first-hand with many of the problems of the Poor Law and with the more fundamental problems of destitution and unemployment out of which they arose. Moreover, she was at that time, in her mid-forties, just rising to the height of her powers —although from time to time, influenced either by Victorian ideas of the span of active life for women, which seem to have confined it to what the Census calls "the child-bearing period," or by fluctuations in her own health, she felt that she might be "growing old"; and having for over thirteen years played second

[1] Quoted in *English Poor Law History*, Part II, page 472.

fiddle, albeit a loud and imposing second fiddle, she was more than ready to make an advance in her own proper person.

Almost at the start, Beatrice seems to have made up her mind that as far as she was able to influence the Commission, it should follow the precedent of 1834, that is to say, it should present a carefully thought-out report on the causes of destitution and the remedies for them, based upon and buttressed by special inquiries made by or on behalf of members of the Commission itself. In the first purpose she failed, and before the end of the first year of the Commission's life she was beginning to realize that she would fail. The personnel of the Commission was far too heterogeneous to come to any agreement either on principles or on remedies, and Beatrice's final Minority Report was only signed by herself, Chandler, and Lansbury, and one convert from the Church representatives, the Rev. Russell Wakefield. On the question of special reports, however, she was much more successful; she literally bullied the Commissioners into promoting or permitting an enormous series of particular investigations, many of which were printed as Appendices to the final report. These investigations had three important effects; they forced even the most *entêtés* Commissioners to take account of the facts about the Poor Law as well as the opinions of Davy and his staff, they provided inexhaustible stores of factual ammunition for those who conducted the fight against the Poor Law both at the time of publication of the Report and for a generation afterwards, and they were a first training-ground for many, such as Mr. Thomas Jones, now secretary of the Pilgrim Trust and for long secretary to the War Cabinet, who subsequently spent long lives in political and social work.

The job of appointing these investigators began during the first five months of the Commission, when Davy, supported by his assistants, was giving his own forthright and unmistakable views of what ought to happen. He told the Commission that the condition of the pauper should be, or any rate should appear to be, inferior to that of the poorest independent labourer. If the pauper, that is to say, for whom food, shelter, and clothing of a sort had by law to be provided, should imagine himself to be in any way better off than "the poorest independent labourer," who was not entitled to receive any of these things without paying for them, further steps must be taken in order to disabuse him of that idea. He should suffer "first, the loss of personal reputation (what is understood by the stigma of pauperism)"—which did result in many poor people starving themselves to death rather than have recourse to the Poor Law; "secondly, the loss of personal freedom which is secured by detention in a workhouse; and thirdly, the loss of political freedom by suffering disfranchisement." Nor was Davy contented that the workhouse should be a prison; he wanted it also to be a penal prison. "The work (in the workhouse) should be both monotonous and unskilled. . . . You have got to find work which anybody can do, and which nearly everybody dislikes doing. . . . You have got to give him something like corn-grinding or flint-crushing, cross-cut sawing, or some work of that sort, which is laborious and which is wholly unskilled"—one feels that, if the treadmill had not by then been abolished for criminals, it would have been Mr. Davy's ideal occupation for paupers. As to disfranchisement, he wished to see it applied strictly, in both parliamentary and municipal elections, to anyone who had had any public assistance of any kind, including anyone who worked for wages in any of the schemes set up under the new Unemployed Workmen Act. When George Lansbury suggested that this would be rather hard on men thrown out of work in a trade depression through no fault of their own, Davy replied bluntly, "The unemployed man must stand by his accidents; he must suffer for the general good of the body politic." So uncompromising an attitude, which the Local Government Board's own Medical Inspector for the Provinces, Dr. Fuller, found himself unable to accept, at least as regards the sick,[1] was rather too much for even the Majority of the Commission to swallow, and resulted in the conclusion of all parties that the name, at least, of the Poor Law ought to go.

While Davy and his subordinates were being examined and cross-examined, the special investigations were getting under way, and the Commission, largely prodded by Beatrice, was making the arrangements for conducting its own business. Extensive inquiries into such various subjects as the effect of out-relief on rates of wages, the conditions of the children of families on relief, the treatment of sick paupers, and the chief causes of destitution were set on foot; and the Commission appointed three committees, a Statistical Committee, an Evidence Committee, and a

---

[1] "It is not possible," he said, "to make the condition of the sick pauper less eligible than that of the independent wage-earner; the patient must be treated with a view to cure, and that means, in practice, extra comforts, good nursing and skilled medical and surgical treatment."

G

Documents Committee, the last of which is on record as having "asked for an analysis of all the Parliamentary Reports and Papers since 1834 dealing with the Poor Law, and instructed Mrs. Sidney Webb to carry out an analysis of all the Poor Law Statutes, General and Special Orders, and other instructions issued by the Poor Law Commissioners, the Poor Law Board and the Local Government Board from 1834 to 1906"—in itself no paltry assignment.

What all this meant in practice can best be seen from Beatrice's own diary, as quoted in Part II of *English Poor Law History*, which also incidentally provides excellent glimpses into the methods of "permeation" as employed by her. On March 11th, 1906, she writes (italics mine):

"The three Committees that I pressed for on the Procedure Committee have been appointed and have set to work. . . . I am trying to guide the Committee on Documents into making an analysis of all the documents of the Central Authority, statutes, Orders, reports, with a view of writing a memorandum on the attitude of the State towards each class of pauper. Lord George gives me unhesitating support; my difficulty is with Sir Samuel Provis. But I had the most friendly chat with him this afternoon, *and he comes to dine to meet a carefully selected party on Wednesday.*"

And again on July 17th:

"A new hare that I have recently started. In listening to the evidence brought by the C.O.S. members in favour of restricting medical relief to the technically destitute, it suddenly flashed across my mind[1] that what we had to do was to adopt the exactly contrary attitude, and make medical inspection and medical treatment compulsory on all sick persons—to treat illness, in fact, as a Public Nuisance to be suppressed in the interests of the community. At once I began to cross-examine on this assumption, bringing out the existing conflict between the Poor Law and Public Health authorities and making the unfortunate Poor Law witnesses say that they were in favour of the Public Health attitude! *Of course Sidney supplied me with some instances,* and I hurried off to consult M.O.H.s—Dr. X. . . . Dr. Y. As luck would have it, Dr. Z. had to give evidence, and was puzzled to know what to talk about. *He dined here, and I brought forward all my instances of conflict.* . . . With S.'s help I drew up a memorandum emphasizing all my points. . . . I am elaborating an inquiry of my own, with funds supplied by Charlotte Shaw [Mrs. Bernard Shaw]; so I merely said

[1] A very good example of the intuitive working of Beatrice's intellect.

that I should, in the course of the next six months, present the Commission with a further memorandum. 'You might elaborate with a few more details the one you have already presented,' said Lord George in a frightened way. And so it was left. . . . Meantime, despairing of any action on the part of the Commission, *I have undertaken, unknown to them, an investigation into the administration of the Boards of Guardians*. I shall put Mrs. Spencer to analyse the documents that are pouring in to me by every post; and Miss Bulkeley shall go through minutes."

There is no doubt at all, in my mind, that Beatrice bullied and harried her fellow Commissioners—and with intention. Indeed, she admits as much in her diary, and confesses to having lost her temper with them upon occasion, adding the rather comic aspiration, "Dignified silence I will set before me, *except when the public good requires me to come forward*" (italics mine). She was endeavouring by every means to force or cajole the Commissioners to agree with her own conclusions, to produce a Report which should be as forthright, original, and authoritative for the conditions of 1906 as the earlier Report was for the conditions of 1834; and though, as we have seen, she failed, she failed magnificently. The Minority Report, which she sponsored and Sidney wrote in the country house of Sir Julius Wernher, although it had only four signatures, takes rank as one of the great State Papers of the century, and was fittingly rewarded by the honorary doctorate given to Beatrice in 1909 by the University of Manchester. The Majority Report of the sixteen others, whose main recommendation was that the destitute should be relieved by voluntary charity organized and systematized, to be supplemented by State relief only when charity had manifestly proved unequal to the situation, was so inadequate to twentieth-century problems as to be to all intents and purposes still-born, and it need detain us no further. No one of any importance ever proposed to implement it. It can seldom have happened that the Majority Report of a major Royal Commission has been so completely eclipsed by the work of a dissentient handful.

CHAPTER X

POOR LAW II: THE CAMPAIGN

THE two Reports were completed and issued in 1909. Of the Minority Report the outstanding feature was that it struck straight to the heart of the problem by asserting the need for prevention rather than cure, for finding out why people became destitute, and attacking the causes of their destitution at the roots, rather than attempting to relieve—or not to relieve—their destitution once it had become a fact. As, when giving evidence before the Commission on Sweating, Beatrice had reached the conclusion that "the whole nation is the sweater," so now she maintained that the whole nation was responsible for poverty and that it was the business of the whole nation to set it right.

During the thirty-five years which have passed since the Minority Report was issued, a host of social workers such as Mr. Seebohm Rowntree and Sir William Beveridge, to take only two examples, have explored the causes of poverty, with the result that much of what was new in the Report has now become a commonplace of discussion and need not be recapitulated here. Briefly, the Report stated that people became destitute from a variety of causes, from old age, from ill-health or accident, from mental disease, from the loss of the breadwinner, from wages that were too low to support the family, or from inability to find work. All these causes, it said, should be tackled at source, by responsible people with expert knowledge, and the various forms of prevention and relief co-ordinated into a nation-wide plan. E.g., old age should be provided for by a State pension system.[1] The local authorities, through their medical and educational services, should arrange for the help needed by children, by sick and crippled people, or by lunatics; the problem of those whose wages were too low should be tackled by national fixing of minimum rates of pay;[2] and that of the unemployed by a policy of public works administered nationally and locally. The Poor Law as such, should disappear altogether, and the local authorities should appoint Registrars of Public Assistance whose function

[1] This was actually done, though on a very meagre scale, by the Old Age Pensions Act, while the Commission was still in session.

[2] The Trade Boards Act of 1909 made a very small beginning in this direction.

would be, in the first place, to keep a register of all who were receiving public funds from any source whatsoever, and secondly, to assist with relief grants persons who had fallen into destitution and were not adequately catered for through any of the sources mentioned above. The Report assumed that this last class would not be very numerous; in 1909 the idea of a million or more unemployed even at peaks of national prosperity would have seemed a fantastic nightmare. But it is interesting to observe how much of the assumptions of the Beveridge Report—the need for full employment, for example, for State medical services, and for a national minimum wage—was set out by Beatrice Webb thirty-five years ago.

Apart from its specific proposals, the two most fundamental ideas of the Report were that prevention is both better and cheaper than cure, and that the proper sphere for voluntary social activity is in co-operation with a public system and public officials. As regards the first, it pointed out that the existing Poor Law could only tackle such social evils as disease and drunkenness at the point at which they had already done, if not their worst, something nearly approaching to it. They could not prevent a man taking to drink; they could only get at him when his drinking had already reduced his wife and children to misery and starvation. They could not prevent disease or promote health; they could only relieve, in an inadequate and expensive manner, the poverty produced by disease. To take the responsibility, as far as possible, away from *relieving* bodies and Relieving Officers, and to put it squarely on the shoulders of authorities responsible for public health, etc., would, the Report maintained, be in the long run a strictly economic policy and, as well as saving human material, would actually save public money then being wastefully expended in patching and repairing damage. As to voluntary effort, the Report entirely agreed with the C.O.S. that the indiscriminate and uncoordinated charity of persons anxious to buy themselves a comfortable conscience at a low fee was harmful and demoralizing; but it pointed out that a great extension of social services would provide an immense opportunity for people to use their charitable instincts, not in money payments but in personal service, on Children's Care Committees and the like, for public ends. Beatrice stressed, and rightly stressed, the sound old doctrine of Works as a means to Grace, rather than the purchase of indulgences, though it may be argued that she did not quite sufficiently understand or emphasize the need for skill and training for any form of social work, and thereby tended to lower its standards and to make it necessary for a later generation to fight the battle of the trained social worker against the well-meaning amateur.

Here, then, was the Minority Report; and long before it appeared, it was certain that it would be a minority report. The first round had been lost; and the Webbs, therefore, decided in effect to appeal to the country, to set on foot an agitation, backed by members of all parties and all classes, which would force the Government to enact legislation on the lines of the Minority Report. The historical precedent which they had for such an agitation was probably the highly successful Anti-Corn Law League of Bright and Cobden.

Beatrice was new to large-scale public agitation; but with Sidney at her side she took to it like a duck to water. The first thing was to make sure that the Minority Report was available to the public to read in a handy form, not pushed to the back of an expensive and unappetizing Blue Book. The Webbs therefore prepared their own annotated edition of the Report for publication, and lent the plates to the Fabian Society in order that it might print off its own special edition costing only two or three shillings. This startled the Treasury, whose solicitor threatened the Fabian Society with an injunction for infringement of Crown copyright; but was defeated through Sidney's caution and his uncanny gift for remembering useful facts. He drew the attention of the solicitor to a minute of My Lords of the Treasury, dated 1887 and never rescinded, in which My Lords had disclaimed any privilege of copyright monopoly over Blue Books, holding that the reprinting of them would be to the public advantage: he also pointed out gently that the manuscript of the Report was in his handwriting, and that the copyright belonged to him. Beaten thus, the Treasury reduced the price of its own Blue Book—though not to the Fabian level—and for two years various editions of the Minority Report were merrily circulating at all sorts of different prices. The total sales were estimated to reach between twenty-five and thirty thousand copies—an astonishing figure, in those days, for a Government Report which is certainly not easy reading.

The Report had an excellent Press reception, though Beatrice was much disappointed to find that some of the commentators did not observe the profound difference between it and the proposals of the Majority. To those who had not closely studied the subject, the fact that both Reports proposed to make an end of the Poor Law was the thing that mattered, whatever they proposed to put in its place; and if Beatrice had realized the significance of that first unthinking reaction, she might have been less disappointed in the event.

The Report having been made available, the next item on the programme was to make its proposals widely known throughout the country and to get the expected support made vocal. This necessitated an organization, and in April, 1909, two months after the publication of the Report, there was formed the National Committee for the Break-up of the Poor Law, which later became the National Committee for the Prevention of Destitution. By the summer this organization was well under way; by the autumn it was housed in an office of considerable size in Norfolk Street, Strand—"just in between the Fabian Society and the London School of Economics," as Beatrice said chuckling; by December it had over 16,000 members.

The N.C.P.D. was a remarkable body. Its 16,000 membership, though enrolled with extraordinary speed, was the least remarkable thing about it. It made a speciality of collecting the distinguished, the influential, and the hard-working. Trade Unions and other bodies which could give guidance to their members were among its subscribers; practically all the Labour M.P.s were members, as well as Liberals like Sir Alfred Mond and John (now Lord) Simon, and Conservatives like J. W. Hills and Gilbert Parker. The list of "distinguished patrons" was long enough to permit of their being grouped under their several professions, as representatives of Literature, Drama, Economics, Religion, etc.; and the distinguished representatives were really distinguished, not "stuffing," and were expected both to work and to speak for the Committee, or to preside over meetings. But behind them were the thousands of enthusiastic rank-and-filers, who were the most remarkable part of the organization, the volunteers who poured into Norfolk Street to address envelopes, fold circulars and what not, who acted as stewards at meetings, who raced about collecting subscriptions, delivering pamphlets and the organization's monthly paper, *The Crusade*,[1] who organ-

---

[1] "The difference between the trade terms and sale prices is quite sufficient or rather more than sufficient to cover the personal expenses incidental to such work," said the paper—a very characteristic sample of Webb economy.

ized study groups and small meetings and spoke at them, who
helped to answer the innumerable questions on the Minority
Report which came into the office, and collected facts about the
Poor Law and about destitution. Its organizers, C. M. Lloyd,
later head of the Social Science Department of the London
School of Economics, and Clifford Sharp, editor of *The Crusade*,
and subsequently the first editor of the *New Statesman*, together
with the Webbs, directed all this activity, which a year after the
Committee had been founded required a central staff of eleven
paid members as well as the hosts of volunteers. "You look as
if you were running a general election," remarked a member of
the Majority who visited the offices in the summer of 1910—and
went away to form a rival organization to promote the proposals
of his own side, which, however, came to little. It was in the
course of this agitation that Beatrice came first into effective
contact with a social group which, owing largely to her own and
Sidney's upbringing, she had hitherto missed, the Socialist and
progressive young men (and young women) at universities.
Rupert Brooke acting as postman of N.C.P.D. leaflets on a bicycle
over the countryside has, for obvious reasons, received most
attention, but Rupert Brooke was only one of many. When the
quarrel within the Fabian Society, described in the next chapter,
came to a head, many of the protagonists were those who had
been trained in the N.C.P.D.

The secret of the rapid growth of the N.C.P.D. movement,
apart from the passionate conviction and single-minded purpose
of its founders, was the extraordinary capacity they showed
collectively for planning and attention to detail of all kinds.
They worked out their campaign almost as though it had been
a military operation, and applied their intelligence service beforehand. They took pains to find out who were the key people and
how they ought best to be approached—whether Beatrice should
put on her best clothes and invite them to lunch, whether Sidney
should arrange to be asked to deliver a private talk to a few
bankers or industrialists, or whether Professor Gilbert Murray or
Sir Oliver Lodge or Canon Scott Holland, or any other of their
distinguished supporters, should be turned on. Sidney and his
fellow Fabians knew how to draft leaflets and articles, simple and
compound, and how to teach others to do it; Beatrice knew how
to approach Trade Unions and Co-operative Societies and the
type of resolution which they could most easily be induced to

pass. Both of them knew or rapidly discovered how to set willing workers to work at the jobs most suited to their capacities; and both of them had the supreme gift of quick decision, which in running a campaign is invaluable. They never havered.

In so far as efficient planning and eager and enthusiastic service can make a campaign a success, the campaign of the N.C.P.D. was a huge success; within the first six months of its existence, for example, it had got printed a Bill, drafted by a young Socialist barrister, Henry Slesser, for putting the Minority Report into effect, and had secured a Second Reading for it. But even before the campaign had reached its peak the purpose of the organization had begun to undergo changes, exemplified by its change of name, which indicated part of the reason for its ultimate failure. It had started, like the Anti-Corn Law League, with a definite and avowed single purpose, to abolish the Poor Law and the Boards of Guardians; but by the beginning of 1910, as the Webbs wrote later in *English Poor Law History*, it was becoming quite clear that the Asquith Government had no intention of abolishing the Boards of Guardians, whose defenders included not merely the C.O.S. champions and the officials of the Poor Law—who nevertheless under the shock of the Minority Report made great efforts to put their own houses more in order—but also other groups which disliked the idea of tampering with long-established institutions, including important sections of the local authorities who were invited to take over the burden of the Poor Law. Though on the London County Council, even with a Moderate majority, the Webb influence was strong enough to secure the passage of a favourable resolution, the decision, in mid-1910, of the powerful County Councils' Association to oppose the programme of the Report was a bitter blow, not the less bitter because the decision was influenced by Beatrice's own brother-in-law, Henry Hobhouse.

Accordingly, the National Committee began to shift the emphasis of its propaganda from abolishing the Poor Law to the Prevention of Destitution by attacking poverty at its source—a very much larger task and one which, as subsequent history has shown beyond a doubt, could not be achieved without making enormous changes in the organization and assumptions of society. "Prevention of Destitution," in effect, implied at the least a considerable dose of Socialism; and while that fact added inspiration and enthusiasm to many of the younger recruits to the campaign, it could not be expected to do the same for its Liberal and Tory backers, and though the meetings continued to be packed with ardent supporters, it gradually became increasingly clear that the speakers were preaching to the already converted, and that the converted were on the Left.

In fact, "permeation" of the capitalist system from outside, by means of a large supposedly non-party public agitation, proved ultimately as unsuccessful as permeation from within, through small groups of influential persons. Nor do I believe that any other result was possible, even had not public attention been distracted, first by Lloyd George's 1909 Budget and the quarrel with the House of Lords, and secondly by the Insurance Act. Edwardian England was not prepared even for instalments of social revolution; but it is no discredit to the Webbs that they did not realize this, or see how much of social revolution was implied in their proposals. For hardly anyone else among their supporters realized it either.

The Insurance Act was the means by which John Burns, as he gleefully proclaimed, "dished the Webbs"; and the man who brought it into being was Lloyd George, the Chancellor of the Exchequer.

Lloyd George had never subscribed to the Minority Report—though Winston Churchill took some part in the campaign in its early days—and John Burns, since 1906 the President of the Local Government Board, was unequivocally hostile both to it and to its authors—and very much, though he did not know it, in the hands of his own able officials with their rooted hatred of either relief or prevention provided out of public funds. Nevertheless, something had to be done; the public feeling aroused by the Report and the campaign was too strong to be ignored or met with a re-enactment of "the principles of 1834," and the proposals of the Majority were hopeless. Accordingly, an idea was borrowed from Bismarck's social legislation in Germany; one of the main causes of destitution, old age, having been dealt with by the Pensions Act, the second great cause, ill-health, was to be tackled by a system of contributory insurance, to which the workers, the employers, and the State would all subscribe. (And in the same measure a small experiment was to be made, for a few trades, with insurance against the third cause, unemployment.) The provision, by this means, of a few shillings a week to help to save the sick poor from the workhouse would, it was calculated, get rid of the great mass of cases which had shocked the well-meaning philanthropic, without entering upon any dangerous social experiment and without upsetting too seriously either the C.O.S. or the officials of the Local Government Board. And it would be, in the immediate run, much cheaper. "Ninepence for four-pence," and a heated discussion on whether society ladies ought to be demeaned by having to lick stamps for servant-girls, replaced the slogans of the Committee in the public mind.

There is no need to describe the passage of the 1911 Insurance Act, or the fierce and successful actions fought against parts of it by the insurance companies and the British Medical Association (neither of which groupings seem to have forgotten their cunning during thirty years). The Bill became law, and Burns was right; it did dish the Webbs. A good deal of primary poverty was of course relieved; but it was relieved by a method which they thought fundamentally wrong, which put plasters on the wounds but made no attempt to prevent either ill-health or unemployment; and the Boards of Guardians and the "stigma of the Poor Law" remained, not to be swept away until the economic storms of the inter-war years and the unflinching resistance of such people as Lansbury and his Poplar Guardians had made their retention impossible. Worse, a good many of their previous supporters could not grasp the difference of principle, and could not understand what *The Crusade* was making such a fuss about, why it could not gracefully accept the concessions offered. As the Webbs themselves said, "All the steam went out of the movement"; by 1912 the staff of the committee was heavily cut and appeals for new subscriptions were discontinued. *The Crusade* ceased publication in 1913. The great campaign, as a campaign, had failed.

It had failed; but so sound was the thinking on which it was based that the years which followed forced Conservative Governments gradually to the abolition of the Poor Law. A brief post-script here may be of service to readers. The Insurance Act, applying insurance against sickness to all employed persons and insurance against unemployment to a few experimental industries, became law in 1911; in 1916 an amending Act brought the bulk of the munitions trades under the unemployment provisions. In 1917 the Maclean Committee on the reform of local government (of which Beatrice was a member) again pressed for the abolition of the Poor Law and the Boards of Guardians; but in the flush of full war-time employment no one was interested in the Poor Law, and the Maclean Report was one of the many documents which were forgotten as soon as the war was over. All that was done by way of reform was that in 1920 insurance against unemployment was extended to cover practically the whole of the wage-earners (and salary-earners below a certain low level) with the exception of domestic servants, agricultural workers, civil servants, and railwaymen.

When the Act of 1920 was passed the post-war boom was still in being. But by the end of the year it broke, and within a short space of time the first great depression had blown the actuarial basis of unemployment benefit to smithereens and had swept away finally the "principles of 1834." Hundreds of thousands of men who were out of work and had exhausted their right to benefit under the new Act stormed the Employment Exchanges and the Guardians' offices, demanding work or out-relief at a rate on which they and their families could live. In the "depressed areas" all question of individual discrimination or imposition of punitive conditions of relief became out of the question; the Boards of Guardians had to pour out thousands of pounds weekly on scales very roughly fixed. Some became completely bankrupt; in all cases rates went soaring up; in London the Poplar Board of Guardians, led by George Lansbury and Charles Key, went on a strike which sent them to jail but eventually forced an adjustment of rating burdens which made the richer parts of London enlarge their contribution to the burdens of the poor ones.

After a time the economic storm subsided a little, and by means of Government subsidies to the Insurance Fund, enabling those whose claims to benefit had been exhausted to receive "uncovenanted benefit"[1]—in effect, out-relief under another name and outwith the Poor Law—the immediate danger was surmounted. But the crisis of 1921–2 had clearly demonstrated the economic and social obsolescence of the Boards of Guardians; and when at length the Government of Stanley Baldwin worked out its reform of local government, the Act of 1929 removed them from the political map. The relief of destitution, as the Minority Report had proposed twenty years before, became part of the ordinary duties of county and county borough councils; and though the family Means Test and other devices were used to try

[1] This was one of the main achievements of the short-lived Labour Government of 1924.

and save the principle of "less eligibility," to keep down the relief given to a man who had "run out of benefit" to a level below what he could have earned in employment and to make his earning sons and daughters support him, when the great depression began in 1931 a combination of the public conscience[1] with the furious and forceful protests of unemployed marchers and the National Unemployed Workers' Committee Movement, rapidly forced a modification. Furthermore, by setting up, in 1934, what is now the Assistance Board, the National Government in effect accepted the contention that the maintenance of unemployed workers was in the last resort the responsibility of the State—an admission which must have made Sir James Davy turn in his grave—and in the years which followed more and more persons were in practice brought under the care of the Board and its officers. As the Beveridge Report showed, there were many anomalies left; many thousands of persons went through life without any security whatever, and those who obtained help obtained it in a widely differing degree, without any logical reason, but merely because their destitution had arisen from one cause rather than another; moreover, the State had still not accepted any real responsibility for the *prevention* of destitution. The *White Paper* of 1944, with all its defects, carried the Government policy some distance beyond that of ten years back. Had they continued their story of *English Poor Law History* for another decade, the Webbs would have been able to chronicle a good deal of progress towards the policy they had outlined in 1909.

But in 1911 all this was far in the future, and what was immediately apparent was that the campaign of the National Committee was going to end in failure. In the summer of that year the Webbs set off for their second world tour. Beatrice, on the eve of her departure, considered the lessons she had learned from her strenuous and exciting life over the past six years, and drew the entirely correct conclusion that what was needed now was to form a strong and independent Socialist political party.

---

[1] See, for example, the reception given to Walter Greenwood's *Love on the Dole*.

CHAPTER XI

FABIANISM AND CONFLICT

FROM June, 1911, to April, 1912, the Webbs for the second time travelled the world. They went *via* Canada to Japan, about whose people they were as enthusiastic as they had been at the time of the Russo-Japanese War; they found them intelligent, efficient, polite, and clean. Beatrice noticed particularly that Japanese slums did not smell. From there they went to China, which they thoroughly disliked, and on to India, about which their feelings were mixed. On one occasion in a Native State Sidney, all unwitting, set off on an expedition to view the sculptures in a particularly venerable temple, all of which turned out to be meticulous representations of various forms of unnatural vice! Their chief solid gain, however, which they brought home from their tour was the large sum of money from the Bombay steel firm of Ratan Tata which laid the foundations of the Social Science Department of the London School of Economics. By the autumn, Beatrice was ready for a new experiment in political organization, to abandon, finally, the older parties and the policy of permeation, to wind up the N.C.P.D., and to create an independent Socialist Party—the nucleus for which might seem to be the Fabian Society.

In order to understand why this was not so simple or so easy as it appeared we must retrace our steps for a short while, chronicle what had been happening in politics while Beatrice was engaged with the Poor Law, and also try to re-create the atmosphere of the decade which preceded the first world war. Those who have grown up in the shadow of two wars within a generation and of the period of frustration and tragedy which separated them often tend to look back to the reign of Edward VII as a golden age in which everyone was prosperous, unrestrained, and happy. But many of those who lived through it did not see it at all in that light. They saw the great masses of poverty which in spite of nineteenth-century improvements still underlay and supported the prosperous class, the sweated trades among which Mary Macarthur toiled and organized, where wages were so low that a Trade Board minimum of $2\frac{1}{2}d$. *an hour* for women was a real

advance, and whole industries, such as the railways, in which,
during the early years of the century, hardly anyone was able
to earn a decent living; and they observed, rather less clearly but
with growing perplexity, that since the Boer War the decline in
prices, food prices particularly, had ceased. The cost of living
was slowly but steadily rising. The worker was faced not only
with continued fluctuations in trade, but with a mysterious and
inexplicable power which made the actual money in his pocket
worth less and less, and though the rise in the cost of living was
of course minute in comparison with what happened later, it
must be remembered that wages in general were lower and masses
were living at a standard at which a rise of a halfpenny in the
price of bread was something very serious indeed.

More bewildering, they saw British parliamentary politics, the
march of progress, and the processes of democracy show signs of
failing to work. They saw women asking for the franchise, getting
Bills in its favour voted by Parliament and the Bills strangled
deliberately by Ministers of the Crown. They saw the women,
cheated by the formulae of democracy, turning to force where
reason had failed, breaking windows, setting fire to post-offices
and throwing chairs and insults at Cabinet Ministers. They saw
the country asking for the end of the Poor Law, and being given
instead an Insurance Act for which nobody had asked. They saw
Army officers refusing to obey orders and put down gun-running
in Ulster, and members of Parliament declaring that the officers
were doing no more than their duty and saying that if Home
Rule were passed by Parliament, "Ulster Will Fight, and Ulster
Will be Right." They saw, at Liverpool in 1911, and still more
spectacularly at Dublin in 1913, strikes of a kind which really
could be held to be "a danger to the community"—such as had
not been the case since the Chartist strikes of the 'forties—and
they saw these strikes officered and supported by men who
declared that strike upon strike, leading up to one final burst of
revolutionary violence, was the only proper goal. They smelt,
through the very mild "revelations" of the Marconi scandal and
the growlings of Chesterton and Belloc, that there was a money-
power which was playing a much greater part than people knew
in affairs of State; and though very few of them had any inkling
of the disaster brewing on the continent of Europe, they were
vaguely worried by things they observed abroad, the anti-
semitism which even in 1908 caused Dreyfus to be shot at in a

French street, the militarism and navalism of Germany—and the
war scares which it produced—and the alliance of their own
country with the blood-stained autocracy of the Tsar. Later
historians can trace in that period the seeds of much that was to
grow to gigantic heights in later years;[1] although they were not
apparent then, the Edwardian age was one of much confusion
and discontent—well expressed in H. G. Wells's earlier novels
and well described in George Dangerfield's *Strange Death of
Liberal England*—even if it got no further than wondering why a
strong Liberal Government, elected as the result of a great popular
landslide, could not make a better job of it.

The Liberal majority of 1906 was to Beatrice unexpected and
not particularly interesting. All their lives the Webbs were
insufficiently aware of the deeper currents of irrational popular
opinion—they were equally surprised by the violence of the 1931
reaction—and she seems to have done little more than observe
the existence of the Liberal Government during the first vigorous
reforming years, before Lloyd George tripped up over the stubborn
feet of landowners. But it was a real popular storm which struck
down the Tories, which brought that sturdy old radical Campbell-
Bannerman to the Premiership, and carried into Parliament a
tail of thirty avowed Labour members (soon to be joined by
thirteen miners elected on a Liberal-Labour ticket), which for the
first year or two energetically and effectively wagged the large
Liberal dog; and while its impetus lasted and the fear inspired
by its enormous vote kept the possessing classes in awe it achieved
a good deal of reform, the Trade Disputes Act, the Old Age
Pensions Act, the Trade Boards Act, the Children's Act, medical
inspection in schools, the Education (Provision of Meals) Act,[2]
etc., and appointed civil servants of the bolder type to see that

---

[1] It was in 1912 that Hilaire Belloc wrote: "That arrangement of Society in which
so considerable a number of the families and individuals are constrained by positive
law to labour for the advantage of other families and individuals as to stamp the
whole community with the mark of such labour we call *The Servile State*"—which is
a good enough description of the social ideal of Fascism. As, however, the principal
danger-sign which Belloc quoted was the passing of the Insurance Act, most people
thought he was making a perverse and unnecessary fuss.

[2] Of the operation of the last-named, a leading member of the C.O.S. wrote in
1911: "London, *with its ill-considered and wholesale feeding of school children*, set the
country a bad example, and has made the work, the 'care' of school children, much
harder than it might have been; for in this neighbourhood I have, as it were, *been
on guard night and day with a pistol in one hand and a bayonet in the other*, to prevent the
starting of feeding out of the rates; and, in addition, have been hampered in finding
the requisite help for legitimate case-work. . . . *Now comes the further danger of rate-
paid and State-subsidized medical treatment*." Italics mine; the C.O.S. attitude dies hard.

its work was done. All this was not, of course, the doing of the Labour handful; but it was largely due to their presence in the House and to the consciousness of many Liberals that they had gained their seats by working-class votes which might be withdrawn from them as they had been withdrawn from Gladstone in 1874.

The group which in 1906 changed its name from Labour Representation Committee to Labour Party was, however, very different from the Labour Party of 1939 or even of 1918. It had no clear policy and no individual membership. When, in 1900, Keir Hardie persuaded the Trades Union Congress and some of the leading Trade Unions to enter into a federation for the purpose of returning Labour members to Parliament, the most definite statement to which he could induce them to agree was the following:

"That this Conference is in favour of establishing a distinct Labour group in Parliament who shall have their own whips and agree upon their policy, which must embrace a readiness to co-operate with any party which, for the time being, may be engaged in promoting legislation in the direct interest of Labour, and be equally ready to associate themselves with any party in opposing measures having an opposite tendency"

which is not exactly a clarion call to action, and certainly did not commit the constituent bodies to Socialism, or indeed to anything else. Furthermore, this modest little creature was a federation of various bodies, including Trade Unions, which paid a general subscription on behalf of their members until the Osborne Judgment of 1909 and the subsequent legislation enforced a more stringent procedure, and Socialist societies such as the Fabian Society and the I.L.P. (The representation of these bodies, with their handful of members, on the Executive Committee of the federation suggests that it was a little more Socialist in practice than would be gathered from the resolution quoted above.) An individual, therefore, who wanted to join the Labour Party and to play a part in its counsels, had, if he was not a Trade Unionist —and in many cases if he was—to join one of the Socialist societies.

As a result of the election, and somewhat to Beatrice's surprise, the membership of the Fabian Society, which had been stagnating and tending to decline since the Boer War, took a sudden

H

upward turn. From 730 in 1903-4, it rose to over 2,000 in 1907-8, and to something under 4,000 (including about a quarter who were enrolled in local groups only) by the outbreak of the war. And this membership, small though it may appear in sum, was a passionately keen and excited membership; in one year 78 per cent of the total roll voted in the elections for the Executive Committee. Anyone with experience of the working of voluntary societies will realize that this is an astonishing proportion.

But, though it was growing and enthusiastic, the Fabian Society of Edwardian days was not the straightforward, single-minded group of collaborators which Sidney had helped to build and to which Beatrice had first been introduced. From the earliest days of the revival, the Fabian Society was blown about by the winds of social uneasiness to which I have previously referred, and was torn, from time to time, by fierce disputes which only just failed of destroying the Society altogether. The Fabian Basis, which in the 'nineties had been a calm statement of the basic minima on which all Fabians, to whatsoever party they belonged, were in agreement, had become ten years later a confession of faith which was disputed as bitterly as any other creed.

H. G. Wells was the first of the stormy petrels. After a period spent in sampling various brands of Socialist propaganda, in William Morris's house at Hammersmith and elsewhere,[1] Wells joined the Fabian Society, and in 1903 made his debut with a paper bearing the remarkably forbidding (almost Webbian!) title of *The Question of Scientific Areas in Relation to Municipal Undertakings*.[2] In his *Autobiography*, Wells says that the Fabians paid no attention to his efforts. As far as one Fabian at least was concerned, he is wrong; Beatrice, whose attention had been already attracted by his brilliant essay, *Anticipations*, listened to his paper with great interest, and "in a flash" envisaged an arrangement of local government areas, largely derived from that paper, which she was later to elaborate in *A Constitution for the Socialist Commonwealth of Great Britain*. It is possible that she did not tell him so at the time; it is even likely, seeing that on his own confession, he was then attacking the Webbs' local government research as futile grubbings in the institutions of the horse-and-buggy age.

But Wells, having entered the Fabian Society, was not going to

---

[1] See Wells, *Experiment in Autobiography*.
[2] Reprinted as an appendix to *Mankind in the Making*.

stop at remarks about local government—from which, incidentally, derived the Society's "New Heptarchy" series of pamphlets which are still worth studying by regionalists and other local government reformers. Very soon—in 1906, to be exact—he burst into the limelight with a paper entitled "The Faults of the Fabian," and with an equally brilliant, but less controversial contribution called "This Misery of Boots," which still had a sale in the Fabian Bookshop in 1944.

The paper on "The Faults of the Fabian" was read to a meeting ("confined strictly to members of the Society") on February 9th, 1906. It was a cheerfully abusive effort, indicting the Fabian Society for being small and scrubby in its appearance and in its ideas; it suggested that the Society ought to behave in a vast and impressive way befitting a body which was really setting out to reform the universe, that it ought to have vast and impressive offices, hold its head high, and spread its propaganda wide. *A Modern Utopia*, published in 1905, expresses fairly well the view which Wells had of what a proper Fabian Society should be aiming at. He succeeded as far as getting appointed a special committee, whose membership was mainly nominated by himself, to discuss his proposals for reform—its Report was subsequently rejected—and in adding to the Fabian Basis a phrase affirming the equal citizenship of men and women;[1] in 1907 and 1908 he was elected by large votes to the Executive Committee.

But the Fabian Society, under the leadership of Shaw and Webb, was no place for Wells. His brilliantly critical, anarchic mind, which has always managed to combine a continuous demand for a Plan and an orderly development of society with an instant and instinctive opposition to any plan and to any order which human beings have ever made for themselves, was fundamentally alien to the quiet controlled development envisaged by the Fabian leaders; and though a persuasive writer, he was an ineffective speaker and debater and made no headway against Shaw's trained virtuosity and Sidney's cruel command of facts— "myself," as he says, being nothing if not candid,[2] "speaking haltingly on the verge of the inaudible, addressing my tie through

---

[1] Beatrice supported this change, and took the opportunity to retract publicly her earlier attitude with regard to women's suffrage. Unkind commentators said that the threat of the women members of the Fabian Society to support Wells in a body if the amendment was rejected had something to do with this; but there is no doubt that she had genuinely changed her mind.

[2] Wells, *Experiment in Autobiography*, page 661.

a cascade of moustache that was no sort of help at all, correcting myself as though I were a manuscript under treatment, making ill-judged departures into parenthesis." After various ineffectual attempts to shake the domination of Webb and Shaw and their friends over the Society he resigned in the autumn of 1908, after a rather obscure dispute concerning the upbringing of children. He had decided that the Fabian Society was not a body which would produce the Samurai of whom he had dreamed in *A Modern Utopia*.

He had gone; but he left a scar. Beatrice was angry at what she felt to be an ill-judged, anarchistic, and impertinent attempt to swing the Fabian Society over to his own loosely defined purposes, to destroy the work of twenty years and to discredit its authors. She also disliked instinctively his views upon marriage and the relations of the sexes, as exemplified both in his own personal life and in novels like *Ann Veronica*. He, for his part, was bitterly resentful at having been steam-rollered, and took his revenge in *The New Machiavelli* (1911), an untidy, rather long-winded novel whose most readable section to-day is the unfriendly satire upon the Webbs and their Grosvenor Road ménage under the names of Oscar and Altiora Bailey. (It should be recorded that, though the satire was sharp and must have hurt, neither of the Webbs ever exhibited any public resentment; both continued to follow their critic's work with interest, and in later years their friendship with Wells was renewed and restored.)

Wells had been defeated, partly because he was unable to formulate his genuine but wide and vague dislike of what *Punch* subsequently called "Sidneywebbicalism" in terms sufficiently precise to be put to a vote at a meeting. But the subsequent history of the Society shows a greater sympathy with Wells's uneasiness than would appear on the surface. There were constant debates on its principles and practice, on whether it should tie itself closely to the Labour Party and turn out all its Liberal and Tory members, whether it should itself run a large number of Fabian candidates for Parliament, or should abjure political affiliations altogether—and the like.

In the autumn of the year in which Beatrice and Sidney sailed for their Eastern tour, a group of younger members calling themselves the Fabian Reform Committee, whose leading lights included the present Lord Slesser and the late Dr. Marion Phillips, long the Chief Woman Officer of the Labour Party, put forward a series of propositions designed *inter alia* to tie the Society closer to the Labour Party, and thus to commit it implicitly to the opinion that the Labour Party could be made into a Socialist Party. The proposals caused a considerable to-do in the ranks, and were finally rejected—as Pease, the historian of the Fabian Society, put it, "the Old Gang triumphed"—and the committee disbanded itself late in 1912; but the unrest did not cease to exist.

Up to that time, Beatrice herself had played little direct part in the Fabian Society. She had lectured for it, and written a tract; and she had been to the Fabian Summer School[1] in 1908 and 1909 and in 1910 had acted as its director. She had also thrown out, at a meeting of the grouping of younger Fabians which called itself the Fabian Nursery, the suggestion—one cannot be sure how seriously it was meant—that she was not to be reckoned as a member of the "Old Gang," i.e. Sidney, Shaw, Pease, Olivier, etc., but would henceforward lead the Nursery, though she was fifty-one at the time. In 1912, however, she stood for the first time for election to the Executive Committee, and came out second, just below her husband. She was prepared to take the Fabian Society seriously.

It was not, however, a very auspicious moment. As I have already said, unrest and discontent were abroad; the 1911 strikes of rail and transport workers, which frightened members of the middle classes out of their wits and produced in Liverpool a miniature and short-lived civil war, were only just over, and during the spring of 1912 the first national strike in the coalfields made itself felt in many other industries. "Labour unrest" was rapidly coming to a peak; and had the war not intervened we might well have seen a series of industrial battles comparable in scale to the General Strike of 1926. At the same time, the Parliamentary Labour Party, which between 1906 and 1909 had been able to wag the dog, had since the indecisive elections of

---

[1] Some student of social history ought some time to write a monograph on the Fabian Summer School, which was started as a private venture in 1907, taken over by the Society in 1911, and has been held uninterruptedly, wars or no wars, until the present time. Stories of its laxity of conduct—and alternatively, of the stern discipline imposed by Miss Mary Hankinson, who for many years managed it and captained its cricket team—still survive in the memories of many Fabians. The report on its first session, printed in *Fabian News* of November, 1907, comments rather sadly on the "rather unduly grey-headed" membership of the School, which was only tempered by "eight or ten delightful young members," who apparently received free board in return for doing the housework. Beatrice herself was anxious to lower the age-level and to remit unnecessary restrictions, though as will be seen she was not particularly well pleased with the attendance of youth when she achieved it.

1910 become the indispensable prop of a Government anxious to
pass a Home Rule Bill for Ireland, and was therefore bound to
the general support of politicians like Asquith and Grey who were
no more Socialists than they were Flat-Earthers. One of the
young Fabian rebels of 1912–15 has described how, on a visit to
Parliament designed to convince him of the sterling worth and
independent spirit of the Parliamentary Labour Party, his
mentor's discourse was interrupted by the sound of a division-bell
and an urgent cry from one of his colleagues—"Barnes! Barnes!
Come and save the Government!"

The discontent was not without its theorists and canalizers.
From France had come the half-mystical Syndicalism of Georges
Sorel, which may be roughly summed up as an adjuration to the
workers to "Strike, strike, and go on striking—until the last final
strike will put the power of the State into your hands." It was
reinforced by propaganda from the United States, formulated
by Daniel De Leon and Eugene Debs, which demanded that the
hordes of workers of every nationality who were oppressed by the
huge combinations of capital in steel-plants, textile mills, and
stockyards should leave Theodore Roosevelt's "trust-busting"
campaign to perish of its own futility and should unite themselves
into One Big Union to fight the bosses. Tom Mann, strike leader
of 1889, came back from Australia and South Africa to lead
bigger and better strikes in Great Britain; a pamphlet literature
of syndicalism, industrial unionism, and Marxism sprang up and
circulated, and Dennis Hird led a breakaway from Ruskin
College (founded in 1900) to form the Central Labour College,[1]
which offered to the working class a Marxist education without
taint of assistance from the capitalist State or middle-class universities. Among members and likely adherents of the Fabian
Society, the new ideas eventually took shape, under the influence
of Arthur Penty, S. G. Hobson, A. R. Orage (editor of the
New Age weekly), and G. D. H. Cole, as the doctrine of Guild
Socialism, which sought to combine ownership of industry, etc.
by public bodies with its administration by self-governing bodies
of workers founded on the Trade Unions.[2]

The Webbs, at that time, were wholly unsympathetic to any
suggestions for control of industry by producers, from whatever

[1] Forerunner of the National Council of Labour Colleges.
[2] See *National Guilds*, by S. G. Hobson; *Self-Government in Industry* and *Guild Socialism
Restated*, by G. D. H. Cole, as well as much other literature.

source they came. At that stage of their development, Sidney's
mind, with its strong bias towards pure collectivism, towards an
economy based on "consumer-democracy" of State and local
governing bodies, with a niche for co-operative societies, was in
the ascendant. Beatrice had forgotten much of her early Trade
Union studies and remembered only that "producers' co-operation" in Great Britain had turned out almost uniformly unsuccessful. Further, they disliked very strongly the tang of unreason, of
violence, mysticism, and disorderliness, which flavoured all these
movements; it seemed to them dangerous and rather disgusting,
and they condemned it without really understanding its sources.
(They had, it must be remembered, been out of England for the
greater part of a most important year.) Finally, when the new
theories turned up within the Fabian Society itself—and just at
the moment when Beatrice had decided to devote serious attention
to it!—they were not unnaturally astonished and disconcerted.
Previous oppositions within the Society had been either concerned
with definite but minor points, or so chaotic that they defeated
their own ends; the opposition which began in 1912 and fought
until in 1915 its chief leader flung out of the Society in a rage,
carrying with him much of its effective fighting vigour, was able,
coherent, and armed with a clear rival policy—the first the Webbs
had encountered on their own ground. As G. D. H. Cole wrote,
in the opening chapter of his first book, *The World of Labour*
(1913):

"It is the most striking contrast between the British and the Continental Labour movements that here the intellectuals seem to have so
little influence as to be almost negligible. Socialist theory, so fruitful
of quarrels abroad, has been in England, at least till quite lately,
unimportant. . . . But in reality we have been saved from important
divergences within the Labour movement not because our intellectuals
have had no influence, but because a single and very practically
minded body of them long ago carried the day. The first leaders of
the Fabian Society, and in particular Mr. and Mrs. Sidney Webb, were
able so completely, through the Independent Labour Party, to impose
their conception of society on the Labour movement that it seemed
unnecessary for anyone to do any further thinking."

This conception was now to be violently and rudely challenged.
On her return to England, Beatrice started out characteristically,
beginning with a suggestion to switch the energies of the young

men and women whose collaboration she was anxious to secure from the dying N.C.P.D. to the very practical project of setting up a Research Committee and Committees of Inquiry which were intended to do for the principal problems of modern society what she had already done for the Poor Law in the Minority Report.[1] The idea, in itself, was an excellent one, and looked like being a resounding success. The new Research Committee acquired a paid secretary, Julius West, the historian of Chartism; and the young men flocked in. Money was raised, and an impressive list of projects drafted. A very great deal of useful work was in fact done, without serious controversy, through the Committees of Inquiry, including a devastating analysis of insurance companies—the Webbs' revenge for their Poor Law defeat—and, at a later stage, one of the first drafts for a League of Nations, prepared by Leonard Woolf, as well as several other publications; and the tradition of research and inquiry thus begun is very much alive in the Fabian Society of to-day. But on one committee, that charged with inquiry into the Control of Industry, the fat was bound to be in the fire very soon. Beatrice had envisaged a report which would investigate the functions of professional associations in the modern world and would put the Syndicalists and their comrades in their proper place; but she found, to her pained surprise, that the young men of the Research Committee (who in 1915 founded the National Guilds League to give expression to their views), had quite other ideas. Their intention was to rewrite *Industrial Democracy* with a Guild Socialist slant, and they were prepared to fight for their opinions.

The details of the dispute would be out of place here. On the immediate issue, the Webbs were beaten. They succeeded in preventing, in the stormy 1915 Annual Meeting of the Fabian Society, the capture of that body by the insurgents; but the Research Committee, on which Beatrice had centred such high hopes, was effectively collared by them. It turned itself into an independent body (of whose Executive Committee Beatrice for some time remained a member); it subsequently changed its name to the Labour Research Department, a body with its own

[1] The Fabian Society also joined with the I.L.P. and the British Socialist Party in a "Socialist Unity" campaign which was intended to press important measures upon Parliament through the Labour Party. This campaign, however, produced little result, partly because the Fabians and the other Socialist groups were always uncomfortable bedfellows and partly because Arthur Henderson, soon to become the Secretary of the Labour Party, was gravely—and not always without reason—suspicious of both. In later years, of course, he became a firm friend of the Webbs.

extensive affiliations with Trade Unions and local Labour Associations, and abandoned even vestigial connection with the Fabian Society.[1] The major effect was that vigorous youth, just before and just after the outbreak of war, gave up working for the Fabian Society and the Webbs, and worked for the Fabian (or Labour) Research Department or the National Guilds League— the active membership of both bodies being almost coincident. The "Old Gang" triumphed for the last time in 1915, but at the price of condemning the Fabian Society to a stagnation from which it did not recover until 1939.

To the latter-day historian, this unhappy dispute, in which persons of equal ability, equal disinterestedness, and equal concern for the interests of the working classes, spent a great deal of time and energy quarrelling with one another, has something of the character of shadow-boxing. The differences were real, but they were differences of emphasis rather than of fundamental principle; and the combatants give the impression of rushing violently along parallel lines without ever quite coming to grips. There was, it is true, an antagonism between the philosophy of collectivism, with its insistence on the supremacy of the political machine, and the political pluralism of the Guild Socialists, of which the latter were very conscious. But to Beatrice, at that stage of her development, fundamental philosophy was not interesting or important. She had accepted Fabianism, and found it sufficient; accepting it, she found the practical tactics and proposals of her opponents unpractical and often shocking. But the dispute was not, as she tended to see it, a contest as to whether reason or emotion should prevail in human affairs. The advocates of self-government in industry were emotional, certainly, and reflected the passions of the agitators; but they had a faith in human rationality no less immense than Jeremy Bentham's, if they really believed that ordinary Trade Unionists or ordinary striking workmen could take over and administer the complicated business of the country on the morrow of a revolution without further ado. But neither did the Webbs themselves face up to the problem of providing an adequate personnel for a Socialist state; they ignored the hint given them by Wells in *A Modern Utopia*

[1] Later, the L.R.D. came under Communist control. But the tradition of accurate information and inquiry, which was its inheritance from its Fabian ancestry, persisted strongly enough to save it from the panic banning of everything savouring of Communism which was one of the contributions of Transport House to the politics of the 'thirties. The L.R.D. flourishes yet.

until, twenty years later, they went to the U.S.S.R. and there discovered its importance; in 1912 they had as much simple faith in the British civil servant, as trained in the Civil Service examinations, as their opponents had in shop stewards and Trade Union branch and lodge secretaries. Neither side really understood the other, though Beatrice, reining her natural impatience, from time to time made gallant efforts to discover what these trying young men were up to, and to find them jobs which they would like and which were suited to their capacities. The trouble was that the young men did not want to be found suitable jobs. They felt quite capable of choosing for themselves; and in the course of the dispute a great many hard words were used. The Syndicalist-Guild Socialists were not guilty of the foulmouthed abuse which some Communists, and nearly all Fascists, have employed on their enemies; but they did indulge in undergraduate insolence which Beatrice, who had never been to a university, appreciated as little as she did their idea of humour.[1] She could not understand why Cole and Mellor and their friends thought it necessary to be so rude, or why they enjoyed breaking all the regulations of the Fabian Summer School, for example, and generally making a nuisance of themselves. But, to a most creditable extent, she kept this to herself, and apart from a few explosions of irritation, treated the rebels with far greater courtesy than they showed to her. (In a small degree, this clash of behaviour was intensified after 1914 by disagreement over the war, which the Webbs, in common with the official Labour Party, supported, whereas the rebel ranks contained a number of pacifists and of others who for one reason or another were in opposition. But in 1914–18 disagreement over war policy among Socialists was less fundamental than this generation would imagine.)

These half-dozen years, from 1909 to 1915, were the period of the Webbs' greatest unpopularity. They suffered from having proved themselves, both in "permeation" and agitation, successful enough to be formidable without being successful enough quite to succeed; and they were attacked heartily from both left and right. Not for the first time, it was discovered that qualities

---

[1] The writer, when a very humble employee of the Fabian Research Department, well remembers the unexpected entrance of Beatrice, then its Chairman, into the office on a summer afternoon when she and another employee were playing tennis with two fly-whisks and a ginger biscuit. Nothing was said; but the atmospheric tension made it quite clear that this was not the sort of behaviour which the eminent lady expected from those who were privileged to work in the Socialist cause.

which are admirable in people who agree with you become vices
in people who do not; their singlemindedness and steadiness of
purpose were termed illiberal pigheadedness and obscurantism,
and their efficiency and grasp of detail became dirty Machiavellian tricks—though in fact the Webbs were among the more
candid of political propagandists, and never made the mistake
of thinking that to outwit or outmanœuvre an opponent is the
equivalent of convincing him. Certainly Beatrice made human
mistakes—the curious will find most of them set out in detail in
The New Machiavelli. She pushed people around with too much
vigour and too little finesse. "You must be 'rich'," wrote Ellen
Terry to Shaw as far back as 1896, "with Mrs. Webb to 'arrange'
you. Do you think she'd arrange *me* if I asked her?" No doubt
she would have done; and she had a way of deciding, in a rapid
and sometimes inaccurate summary, exactly what anyone she
was introduced to ought to be used for—or that he was no use at
all—which aroused resentment. "People," she said to Mrs.
Hamilton, "are really quite simple"; but they were not quite so
simple as that and did not relish being so regarded. The absolute
conviction of Sidney and herself that they were perfectly right and
were equal to saying the last word on any subject of importance,
though rather disarming in retrospect, was not at all disarming at
the time, particularly when joined with such personal habits as
interrupting anyone who appeared to be talking nonsense or
taking too long to make a point, and peremptorily taking charge
of a conversation or a gathering and butting, rather than leading,
it in the right direction. Especially—if irrationally—irritating
was the fact that there were *two* of them, almost invariably in
perfect accord and reinforcing each other. People felt it unfair
that as soon as Beatrice stopped talking Sidney would begin; it
was a war on two fronts in which the point of view which the pair
of them were missing, or had decided to ignore, often never
succeeded in getting expressed at all. There must have been
many besides Wells who left an evening of political converse at
Grosvenor Road feeling themselves a seething mass of unuttered
esprit d'escalier.

To say this, however, is to say no more than that Beatrice had
certain personal defects which at a time when her opinions were
unpopular bulked larger than they warranted, which overlaid
her deep natural human friendliness and earned for her dislike
which she did not deserve and which sometimes troubled her.

As soon as the external conflict was lessened the friendliness reasserted itself and for twenty years and more became one of her dominant traits.

The last enterprise, however, which the Webbs set on foot before the outbreak of war turned out one of the most solid and enduring experiments in journalism. The *Crusade* was to die, inevitably, after the death of the National Committee for the Prevention of Destitution; but its demise would leave Great Britain without a serious journal of Socialism and social reform, suitable for reading by enlightened members of the *bourgeoisie* and similar minds in other classes. The young *Daily Herald*, which lived a hectic existence from hand to mouth under a succession of editors, could hardly be called a serious journal; in any event, its policies were explosive and semi-syndicalist. *Justice*, which belonged to the Social Democratic Federation, and Hardie's *Labour Leader*, were sectarian organs, appealing principally to their own faithful; *Fabian News* was a parish magazine; the *New Age* was determinedly Guild Socialist; and Blatchford's *Clarion*, for all its extensive circulation, did not provide the sort of reading which would attract thoughtful civil servants. A new paper was required; and that paper turned out to be the *New Statesman*.

In founding the *New Statesman*, the Webbs showed remarkable judgment and acumen. What they wanted was a Fabian journal, a journal which would put across Fabian principles and the results of the newly founded Fabian Research Committee,[1] which would promote discussion on the social questions of the day from a Fabian angle and generally carry on the work of permeating opinion. But Beatrice saw quite clearly that if such a journal were run and published by the Fabian Society itself it would inevitably be labelled sectarian and start its life in hobbles. The problem was how to secure Fabian support and influence without forfeiting the appearance of independence; and this problem she or Sidney, or both together, solved in a highly characteristic manner.

The *New Statesman* was founded as an independent journal run by an independent company. But it was announced that the leading lights of the Fabian Society, such as Shaw and the Webbs, would write for it regularly; and it was further announced that any member of the Fabian Society who took out an annual

---

[1] In fact, several of the reports of the Fabian Research Committee first saw the light as Supplements to the *New Statesman*.

subscription to the paper before a certain date would get it at a reduction. There were some who doubted the efficacy of this bait, who thought that the paper would struggle into existence and then die quickly; but the Webbs were proved right. Over two thousand Fabians took out annual subscriptions, and in those days a guaranteed circulation of two thousand was a pretty sound send-off for a weekly journal. Thus, in one operation, the Webbs secured for the *New Statesman* both Fabian contributors and a nucleus public which was Fabian. They appointed a young Fabian, Clifford Sharp, as editor; they gave him, subject to the control of his directors, a perfectly free hand. Then they sat back, and watched their offspring grow.

Its growth was not perfectly smooth. Shaw, though a great box-office asset, proved an unexpectedly difficult contributor, and after some time gave up writing regularly; the paper was little more than a year old when the war, with all its material and political complications, broke upon it; it was a long time before it became a paying proposition. But it survived; it maintained and increased its circulation; it became, gradually, as solid and as traditional a foundation as the London School of Economics. Under the editorship of Kingsley Martin, who succeeded Sharp, it remorselessly ate up at least three of its competitors in the weekly market, and to-day is not merely a valuable property but (in war-time) almost as difficult for a new-comer to obtain as *The Times*.

CHAPTER XII

WAR

BEATRICE'S plans for a new Socialist Party, or united
Socialist influence, came to nothing, as we have seen,
mainly because of incompatibility between those personalities which would have had to bring it into being. It was not
merely a question of organized opposition to the Webbs, or even
of resentment at some of their tactics; the I.L.P. of Hardie, now
with only a few years to live, of Ramsay MacDonald and Philip
Snowden was no more Guild Socialist than it was Fabian in the
old sense, and if its members, or some of them, made temporary
alliances against collectivism, they were purely temporary. But
even had the plans met with more initial success they would have
been bound to come to grief with the catastrophe of 1914, for
though the organized Labour movement, after a brief hesitation,
on the whole supported the war, many of the potential leaders of
the Left were either opposed to it, or very lukewarm supporters.
Where they did not attack, they disapproved, both of the war and
of the industrial and political truce to which it led.

In 1914, as in 1939, the mass of the workers and their representatives in the Trade Unions and in Parliament supported the
war. But in spite of this resemblance many of the conditions were
very different. In 1939 it was the opinion of the workers, formed
after looking at the events of the months immediately previous,
which forced the most hesitant and timorous Government we
have ever known to take action; it was the Labour Party which
feared that there would be another retreat, another broken
pledge, another Munich; it was the leader of the Labour Party
whom excited Tories, changing their emotions at the last minute,
urged to "speak for England." In 1914 it was quite otherwise.
The general sentiment of the organized working class, in all
countries where it was organized, had for a generation taken the
line that war between nations was both a crime and a disaster
and furthermore was perfectly avoidable,[1] if not by sensible

[1] Nor was this view confined to illiterate underdogs or sentimental Socialists.
Sir Norman Angell's *The Great Illusion* had a very wide influence in those years;
and Dr. Gooch's *History of Our Own Times*, published in 1913, ends with the words:
"We can now look forward with something like confidence to the time when war
between civilized nations will be considered as antiquated as the duel, and when the
peacemakers shall be called the children of God."

statesmanship then by the rational refusal of the working classes
to allow themselves to be organized for killing their fellow
creatures. It was generally assumed, save by fire-eaters or
Germanophobes like Robert Blatchford, that the workers of all
countries would unite in some way or other to prevent war. The
fact that no machinery was created to bring about this desirable
result, that the anti-war resolutions of international gatherings of
Labour—as at Stuttgart in 1907, for example—were entirely
without precision on this point, proves that the sentiment was a
sentiment rather than a conviction making for action, but does
not prove that it was unreal. Right up to the eve of the declaration
of war, British Labour was demonstrating against it and it took
the invasion of Belgium, with its strong appeal to outraged feelings
for justice, to kindle national patriotism sufficiently to induce
British Labour leaders to take the same line as their Continental
brothers. Even then, the conversion, though complete for the
moment, was not very long-lasting. There was apparent before
long a strong undercurrent of opinion that the war ought never
to have happened, that somehow or other it ought to have been
prevented; and this was reinforced, as time went on, by the
muddles and disasters, by the patent way in which the owners of
property and the jumped-up munition contractors were waxing
fat, until, long before the Armistice, organized Labour was
demanding that there should be discussions of peace terms and
laying down, in such pamphlets as *Labour's War Aims*, what it
thought those terms should be. As the war continued, in spite of
the violent treatment meted out to a few conscientious objectors
by tribunals of old men, hysterical women with white feathers,
and the kind of crowd which can always be gathered in times of
collective emotion, differences of opinion about the war came to
matter less and less fundamentally within the Labour movement.
Soldier and civilian, munition worker and pacifist, they had all
alike been caught in a violent world-storm which was none of
their making; and their business was to mitigate its effects and
try to guard against its recurrence.

The Webbs followed fairly closely the development of the main
Labour movement—thereby, as we shall see later, eventually
attaining, though by an unexpected route, the object Beatrice had
dreamed of long before of being "clerks" to Labour. They had
not foreseen the war any more than anyone else outside a very
tiny inner circle. They had never been much interested in

European history or European problems; and though Beatrice
liked and respected some of the Continental Socialists she had
met—comparing them with the I.L.P., much to the latter's
disadvantage—it does not appear that she discussed problems of
war and peace with them. Nor had they any real understanding
of the way in which emotional storms could sweep whole peoples;
they might have had more if they had pondered more deeply the
book, *Human Nature in Politics*, in which their old comrade Graham
Wallas made his extraordinarily acute and penetrating analysis of
the motives and processes which move ordinary men to political
action. (It is one of the tragedies of political history that neither
Wallas himself, nor any of those of his compatriots who read and
admired his book, ever got beyond his analysis. If British politicians, particularly Radical politicians, could have carried the
lessons of the passage in *Human Nature in Politics* which begins,
"When a man dies for his country, what does he die for?" to
positive conclusions, the world might well have been less helpless
in the face of Nazi propaganda—of the one politician of our times
who fully applied the discoveries of Freud to the myth of the
Racial State.)

This being so, the Webbs almost literally followed the crowd,
at least the Labour crowd, on the war. They were not, at the
start, at all interested in its issues or in the invasion of Belgium.
Beatrice cynically recorded[1] that in one week they were twice
visited by the same group of politicians demanding on the first
occasion that the Webbs should take part in an agi ation for
preventing the war, and on the second that they should demon-
strate in the opposite direction. Their immediate reaction to the
war was that it was a nuisance, even though a potentially tragic
nuisance—an interruption to serious business. But nuisance or
not, it was a fact, which they accepted, and prepared to make the
best of it. In Sidney's case, making the best of it meant serving
on the War Emergency Workers' National Committee, a clumsy
name describing what was in fact the first real national combination of all the working-class and Socialist forces. The Conference
which founded it—it is interesting to note, as an indication of the
swift change in working-class opinion, that it had been originally
summoned as a Committee for Peace—was attended by representatives of the Labour Party, the Trades Union Congress, the
General Federation of Trade Unions, the Co-operative Move-

[1] In an article published much later in a symposium entitled *What I Believe.*

ment, the more important of the individual Trade Unions, the National Union of Teachers, and the Socialist Societies. As Hardie and MacDonald, owing to their anti-war attitude, were out of the picture, Arthur Henderson became chairman of the Committee, his assistant, J. S. Middleton, its secretary, and Sidney Webb, in effect, its draftsman. It is entirely in the Webb tradition that Sidney, within the first week of the Committee's existence, wrote a thirty-two page pamphlet which both urged working-class bodies to demand representation on all the Distress Committees which were then being set up all over the country to deal with the dislocation arising immediately out of the war, and suggested the lines of policy which such representatives should adopt—and refused to sign the pamphlet on the ground that "it will have far more influence without my name than with it."[1] The National Committee continued in being right through the war as the general representative of the working class on what might be called "consumer problems" such as rents, food prices, canteens, maternity homes and day nurseries, and the treatment of war casualties. Effectively, Henderson and Webb ran it together, and its work helped to build up Henderson—a member of the Coalition War Cabinet after 1915—into the real leader of the Labour movement, and Webb, who came on the Labour Party's Executive Committee in 1916, into its most capable and most trusted adviser, although the closest association between the two of them did not begin until after the middle of 1917, when Henderson had been summarily banished from the consultations of the War Cabinet over the abortive Stockholm Conference.[2]

This first pamphlet of the War Workers' Committee was only one of many documents—pamphlets, resolutions, manifestoes— the great majority of which Sidney supervised when he was not the actual draftsman. Concurrently, as might have been expected, he was occupied with many other jobs. In addition to the continuing work on local government of which the volumes on Statutory Authorities and English Prisons were being prepared during the war, he wrote, to take only three examples, (1) a little

[1] M. A. Hamilton, *Sidney and Beatrice Webb*, page 227.
[2] The Stockholm Conference was to have been a gathering of the Social Democratic Parties which had been members of the pre-war Labour International (including the Germans), with representatives of the Russian Soviets, in order to discuss a People's Peace. The British Labour Party at first supported the proposal by a large majority; but after a vigorous campaign by the fight-to-a finish elements this majority was reduced sufficiently to make the Government feel safe in refusing passports to Stockholm, and the attempt came to nothing.

I

book on the restoration of the Trade Union practices which had
been voluntarily abrogated by the Unions in order to facilitate
the introduction of women into industry and the quick production
of munitions of war—a book which caused an angry storm among
shop stewards and Socialists of the left; (2) a volume of expanded
lectures called *The Works Manager of To-day*, which anticipated,
in 1917, many of the problems of the management, as distinct
from the control, of industry which had not been solved by 1944;
and (3) aided by members of the Fabian Research Department, a
comprehensive study of *How to Pay for the War*, which included
detailed proposals for the nationalization of banking, of insurance,
and of the railways.

Furthermore, he took part in discussion in Government circles.
In 1916 he was appointed one of the first members of the enormous
after-war Reconstruction Committee, which spawned so many
sub-committees and led to the formation of the Ministry of
Reconstruction which gave birth to many more. He was not by
any means new to this type of work; as already related, in the
'nineties he had been a member of the Royal Commission on
Labour, and before the war had served on the Royal Commission
on Trade Union Law, on Departmental Committees dealing with
Technical Education, Agricultural Settlement and Education,
and the Territorial Army, and on the Committee which arranged
for the first Census of Production. The Reconstruction Committee, however, seemed at the time as though it might lead to
something more fundamental in the way of social change. That
it did not do so, that the best of the many reports it produced
were pigeonholed and forgotten, is part of the melancholy history
of the "back-to-normal-capitalism" scramble which followed the
first defeat of Germany; but the experience Webb gained in this
and in his other work bore good fruit as the war drew nearer to
its end and the Labour Party nearer to its break with Lloyd
George's Coalition.

For some time after the outbreak of war, there is little to
chronicle about Beatrice's own activities, though at the beginning
of 1916 she was made a member of the Government's Statutory
Pensions Committee along with G. N. Barnes and Harry Gosling,
leading Trade Unionists in the engineering and waterside trades
respectively. She was also putting a good deal of work into
research into the state and future of organization among "black-
coated producers" (teachers and the like), since the similar

investigation into the organization of manual workers had been frustrated by the disputes mentioned in the last chapter. In 1916 she had a serious illness, which more or less completely stopped her from working for a while.

But the real reason for her comparative inactivity seems to lie deeper, and to derive from the fact that she had no organization and no group with which she could effectively work in harmony. The Fabian Society, though she continued to serve on its Executive Committee and to lecture for it upon occasion, was half-dead; the young recruits who had swarmed into it during the exciting pre-war years had mostly gone away either into the armed forces or into the National Guilds League or both. The Fabian Research Department, of which she had hoped so much, was full of young and active Guild Socialists whose politics and practice she thought foolish and who responded with the kind of cheerfully violent hostility which is a characteristic of youth to the Webbs and Pease and all their works. The project of a strong independent Socialist Society, led by the Webbs, had vanished altogether, for neither the pacifist leaders of the I.L.P. nor the equally anti-war weekly *Herald*[1] of Lansbury and his supporters, appealed to her at all. Nor was she any happier when she turned her eyes to the official side of the working-class movement. She had little but a good-natured—and not always good-natured—contempt for the solid sleepy Trade Unionists who formed the bulk of the small Parliamentary Labour Party; and though she accepted the war, she had no enthusiasm for it or for the anti-Prussian eloquence which Lloyd George, for example, employed with such skill on the Trades Union Congress. Haldane, her friend, had been driven from office soon after the war broke out because of a ridiculous rumour that he was a "pro-German"; and she felt little sympathy with those of her former acquaintance who were busily engaged in war prosecution. (The only piece of war propaganda which she produced, a tiny pamphlet called *An Appeal to Women*, written for the War Savings Committee, is almost comically inadequate and childish.) Moreover, the wastage of young life in the most humanly extravagant war that this country has ever waged, which became apparent to all, even before Passchendaele, in the senseless slaughter of the 1916 battles on

---

[1] The *Daily Herald* became a weekly shortly after the outbreak of war, and did not resume publication as a daily until 1919. Its right-wing rival, the *Daily Citizen*, disappeared altogether.

the Somme, could not fail to depress her, particularly as some of
her own sisters' sons gradually came to be involved in it.

For all these reasons the first two and a half years of the war
were a gloomy and ineffective time for Beatrice. But soon after
the beginning of 1917 things began to look brighter.

Part of the reason lay in the slow change of atmosphere in the
country, which affected her though she was not conscious of it at
the time. By that time the phase of uncritical enthusiasm, the
indignation at the invasion of Belgium and the execution of
Nurse Cavell had passed, drowned in a sea of blood; the masses
of the working class were beginning to swing to the Webbs' view
that the war, even if inevitable, was a great and a tragic nuisance;
further, the workers in the huge war industries, now organized
as they had never been organized before, were beginning to feel
their strength and their feet and, as they watched the development of the war and war profiteering, to conclude more and more
that theirs was a battle on two fronts and that whichever side
was victorious in the military struggle, the working class was safe
to be a loser unless it took up the cudgels for itself. Beatrice might
not agree with the leaders or the programmes of the forward
movements among industrial workers which were coming increasingly into the public eye with every month of 1917; she
might regret that the officials of the Shop Stewards' Committees
—which under war conditions had largely taken over the job
of the official Trade Union machinery in the industrial plants—
were so often Syndicalists or Guild Socialists; she might think
that the Conference of Soldiers and Workers held in June, 1917,
on the model of the Soviet organizations being developed in
revolutionary Russia, was silly and hot-headed. But she could
not be, and was not, unaffected by the knowledge that the home
front, where her real interests and knowledge lay, was on the
move.

Nor was the change confined to home affairs alone. The
United States came into the war in the spring of 1917; it was
believed to have come in to save the principles of democracy and
to be free from any sordid taint of territorial or colonial ambitions.
Long before the Fourteen Points were formulated, supporters of
democracy throughout the world were learning to look to President Wilson and the coming armies of the Yankees as their
champions. More important for the immediate moment was the
March revolution in Russia, the collapse of the Tsarist régime

like the rotten apple it was, the appearance of orgnas of democracy in the form of Soviets all over the country—including the
armed forces—and the inevitable progress towards the greater
revolution of October. For a time, it seemed as though the
peoples of the world might really agree upon a democratic
"people's peace" and thrust their masters aside. The immediate
results of these developments were the Stockholm Conference
already referred to, and in Great Britain the pamphlet on Labour's
War Aims, drafted by Sidney during the late summer, and the
moves towards making the Labour Party a full political party,
with a new constitution and a Socialist programme, which are
described in the next chapter. The drafting of the War Aims
pamphlet, among other things, brought both Beatrice and Sidney
into much closer touch with other Socialists from Allied countries,
several of whom, such as Camille Huysmans and Louis de
Brouckère, remained their firm friends after the war.

It was a happy coincidence which in the spring of the same
year saw Beatrice appointed to the Reconstruction Committee,
where she was placed upon the panels for Local Government,
Labour, and the Control of Industry, for it meant she could
immediately start to work at the congenial task of trying once
more to force a group of supposedly influential people to accept
Socialist solutions for their problems. On the two latter panels
—one of which produced the famous Whitley Report on Joint
Industrial Councils for industry—she did not in fact play any
great part. But on the Local Government panel, presided over
by Sir Donald Maclean, she came to grips again with her old
enemy the Poor Law, and succeeded in inducing the Committee
to accept a report which practically repeated the suggestions of
the Minority Report of 1909. This time she was successful in
carrying her fellow members with her, but she had yet to carry
the Government and the "hard-faced men" of whom Lord
Keynes spoke in *The Economic Consequences of the Peace*. The
Maclean Report went down the drain with most of the other
reconstruction reports when the Armistice was signed; it took
another ten years, and a slump which destroyed the basis of local
authority finance, before another Conservative Government
finally made up its mind to grapple with the problem of local
government and the Poor Law.

A somewhat similar fate overtook the second important Committee of which Beatrice was a member during the war, the War

Cabinet Committee on Women in Industry, set up during the
summer of 1918 to decide whether the Government had or had
not observed its war-time pledge that where women were employed
on work which had previously been done by men, they should
be paid the men's rates. Here Beatrice, reaching the conclusion
that the pledge had been flagrantly broken, failed to convince
her colleagues. She found herself, actually, in a minority of one;
and accordingly put in a Minority Report[1] which not merely
dealt with the Government's record, but traversed the whole case
for equality of remuneration between the sexes—it remains a
minor classic. Whether Beatrice convinced the Committee or not,
however, did not in this case matter a jot; before the Reports
were completed the Armistice had come, and neither Majority
nor Minority were ever heard of again. The women who had
flocked to the industrial and Civil Service colours flocked—or
were pushed—back again almost as fast as they had come in;
and the problems of women's remuneration—except for a few
obstinate feminists who perversely continued to grumble—seemed
to be painlessly solved without any State action at all.

By this time, however, the war was over, and the new Labour
Party, now a year old, preparing to play its part in the post-war
world.

---

[1] Republished by the Fabian Society as *The Wages of Men and Women—Should they
be Equal?*

CHAPTER XIII

RISE OF THE LABOUR PARTY

THE modern Labour Party was born at its Nottingham Conference in January, 1918, and Sidney Webb, with Henderson, was the architect of its constitution and the framer of its first political programme. By many of the present generation, to whom the Labour Party seems nearly as ancient an institution as its Tory rival, the change made in 1918 is hardly realized. Before 1918 the Labour Party was little more than a group. Constitutionally it was a federation of Trade Unions—not all Trade Unions, by any means, but most of the more important ones—with the Socialist Societies and one or two Co-operative Societies.[1] The Trade Unions then, as now, provided the bulk of its scanty funds, raising them by a political levy collected from those of their members who had not signed a form saying that they did not wish to pay it;[2] the Socialist Societies naturally paid on the whole of their membership, which, however, had never amounted to more than a score or so of thousands all told. At any conference, therefore, the Trade Union element, with its vastly greater voting power, could always carry the day if it were united.

The Party had no defined form of local organization, though there were "Local Labour Parties" in a good many areas, and as already mentioned, it had no individual membership. Nor had it any defined policy; resolutions passed by its Annual Conference were not binding on the Parliamentary Party, and though some of the Labour M.P.s, such as Lansbury, were avowed and lifelong Socialists, many were not Socialists at all, and had never been asked to be. In the minds of the majority of the public, the Labour Party, apart from the handful of anti-war pacifists,

[1] Co-operative Societies, in general, took little or no interest in politics until in 1917 the Government proposed to bring their dividends under the Excess Profits Duty. When they did so, however, they formed their own Co-operative Party, which remained on terms of friendship with the Labour Party but without any formal connection.

[2] This formula was laid down by the Trade Union Act of 1913; it was reversed, and Trade Union members forced to declare in writing that they did wish to contribute, by the Act of 1927, passed as part of the Government reprisals for the 1926 General Strike.

meant, if it meant anything at all, a Liberalism slightly more advanced than the Liberalism of the old Asquith Government and a particular concern for the interests of Trade Unionism and Trade Unionists.

The Nottingham Conference and its outcome effected a considerable change. The new constitution—which is still, with minor modifications, the constitution in force—retained the federal character and the predominance of the Trade Union vote; but it introduced an entirely new element, that of the Divisional Labour Parties composed partly of individual members and partly of affiliated branches of Trade Unions. A certain number of the members of the National Executive Committee were thereafter chosen from the representatives of these Divisional Labour Parties.[1] This change meant, moreover, that individual persons could now become members of the Labour Party in their constituencies, and could thus have a chance of influencing Party policy otherwise than by joining one of the Socialist societies. It also involved in the end the doom of the I.L.P., which had hitherto been the main recruiting ground for individual Socialists in the provinces, though the full story of the decline of the I.L.P. first to a turbulent minority within the Party and thence to a small outside body of Socialists dependent on the prestige of two or three leaders falls outside the scope of this book. The constitution of 1918 implied that the Party was now set to become an adult political organization, ready to challenge either or both of the two older parties. (It must be remembered that it was a Liberal Government which embarked upon the war of 1914.)

But the Party could not appear as a major Party and issue its challenge, without a policy; it could not fight on a hotch-potch of resolutions passed at one Annual Conference or another, often at the end of a session as a result of pressure by one group or interest on a matter with which the majority of the delegates were not concerned one way or the other.[2] Accordingly, shortly after the January Conference the Party produced, in *Labour and the New Social Order*, its policy for the post-war world. This was a Socialist policy, and it was drafted by Sidney Webb, though in

---

[1] In 1937, the number of these representatives was raised to seven, and they were elected by the Divisional Parties themselves, instead of by the Conference as a whole—i.e., including the Trade Union vote.

[2] E.g., a resolution, moved annually by the Amalgamated Musicians' Union, which declared against the employment of military bands upon civil occasions. There were other "hardy perennials."

accordance with previous practice, it was published without a name, and it was not generally known for some time that Webb was in fact the author. On this policy the Labour Party was prepared to do propaganda through the country and to fight the next general election.

Nothing much happened as an immediate result, for only two months after the Nottingham Conference came the German break-through at St. Quentin which produced Haig's famous "back to the wall" order, and public discussion switched from post-war problems to the danger of defeat and to arguments about the new Military Service Bill. All through the summer the Labour Party was tied to the Coalition and the war, for, as has been frequently recalled during the last few years, the Allied generals and still more, of course, the Allied public had no idea that the German collapse was coming until it actually came. Immediately after the Armistice the Party summoned a national conference and, aided by a brilliant speech from Bernard Shaw, called its representatives out of their uncomfortable association; but Lloyd George hit back with the notorious Hang the Kaiser election, in which he bought three more years of power for himself at the price of fatally splitting his own party and ending his own political career as soon as his Tory coadjutors felt strong enough to do without him.[1] The "coupon" candidates, those who could produce a letter from the Prime Minister certifying their good behaviour during the war, stampeded the new large electorate created by the Representation of the People Act of 1918, and almost every Labour candidate of any outstanding ability, including Arthur Henderson, was defeated.

None the less, to anyone who could read the signs, this crazy election, however disastrous its effects—as, for example, in the reparations clauses of the Treaty of Versailles—did not at all represent the real situation. Only three months after its results had been declared, Labour won a large number of seats in the elections to local Councils, where no coupon writ ran; more than that, the industrial unrest, which despite the military situation, had been growing steadily during the summer and autumn of 1918, and was increased by the news of the October Revolution in Russia and the other revolutions which followed

---

[1] Cf. the fate of MacDonald after 1931, and of the German Social Democratic leaders who during the life of the Weimar Republic collaborated with the Right. History contains many warnings.

the Armistice in Germany and Austria, in the New Year broke out in a series of strikes and strike-threats of which by far the most important was the demand of the Miners' Federation for increased wages,[1] reduced working hours, and the nationalization of the mines.

The Government was frightened; Lloyd George played for time. He had already bought off the returning soldiers and the dismissed munition workers by means of a weekly "dole" (that much-misused word can be correctly employed in this instance) at the unprecedented level of 29s. a week; but it was not so simple to buy off the Miners' Federation. The device adopted was the time-honoured one of a Statutory Commission, which, it was hoped, would recommend some rapid and comparatively harmless improvements in wages and conditions—which could be withdrawn when the post-war boom was over and the situation improved from the employers' point of view[2]—and would register a firm negative to wild-cat schemes for public ownership. The miners postponed their strike notices for three weeks; the Government pledged itself to carry out the recommendations of the Commission, whatever they might be. But it was impossible, in the state of the coal industry, to appoint a Commission resembling in personnel the Royal Commission on the Poor Law and consisting mainly of officials and supposedly "disinterested" members of the middle classes. It was necessary to include representatives of both the miners and the coal-owners, and it was further decided that of the six experts who, with Mr. Justice Sankey as chairman, were to complete the Commission's personnel, three should be chosen by the owners and three by the miners. The chairman and leader of the Miners' Federation was Robert Smillie, and under his guidance the miners selected as their experts Sir Leo Chiozza Money, Professor R. H. Tawney, and Sidney Webb.

As soon as the Commission met it became plain that there was no hope of a whitewashing or delaying report. The gross mismanagement and inefficiency of the mining industry presented the miners with a strong initial case; but in addition the representatives on their side were of much higher calibre than those who sat opposite them or those whom they examined, and Smillie, Webb, and Tawney made hay with the coal-owners' witnesses.

---

[1] It is not always remembered that, with the removal of controls, the cost of living rushed up far more rapidly after than during the war.

[2] This was done in 1921 and again in 1926, in both cases after bitter and long-drawn strikes.

The public sessions in the House of Lords, where Smillie, with his shaggy hair and brooding face, cross-questioned and browbeat the titled owners of mining royalties, and Webb drove their statisticians from point to point, filled columns of the daily press and suggested to more than one newspaperman comparisons with the tribunals of the French Revolution. The interim reports, of which there were three, all recommended increases in wages and reductions of hours; the one signed by the chairman and the three experts nominated by the coal-owners[1] stated in addition that "the present system of ownership and of working stands condemned and some other, unified system must be substituted for it." Bonar Law, who was Acting Premier in the absence of Lloyd George in France, stated in the House of Commons (and repeated the statement in a letter to the Miners' Federation) that the Government "are prepared to carry out in the spirit and in the letter the recommendations of Mr. Justice Sankey's Report." The strike notices were withdrawn; the immediate danger was over.

By June the further discussions upon the future of the industry were finished and the final reports were presented. There was a majority in favour of nationalization—the three miners and their three experts, and Mr. Justice Sankey—subject to some reservation by the experts and by Sankey on the question of compensation. Sir Arthur Duckham recommended rationalization and cartellization of the industry; the three coal-owners and the two remaining experts favoured a policy which amounted in effect to no change at all. In this case, a minority report triumphed. It was the recommendation of the five which, after some months of argument, carried the day; and in the story of the Sankey Commission, its fate, and the events which followed it the student of history will find the explanation of much which may have puzzled him in the war-time experience of the British coal industry.

For the history of the Webbs, however, the important fact is that the Sankey Commission and the publicity which it received put Sidney in the limelight as a political personality as well as a trusted behind-the-scene adviser. In July 1919 the solid vote of the Miners' Federation helped him to head the poll for the Labour Party Executive; by the middle of the following year his advice to the Trade Union movement in general and to the miners

[1] Sir Arthur Duckham, Sir Thomas Royden, and Mr. Arthur Balfour (now Lord Riverdale).

in particular to take more trouble over the selection of able men (rather than Union officials with a long record of faithful service) for Parliamentary candidates had been followed by the Durham Miners, who put him up for Lord Londonderry's colliery division of Seaham Harbour. When, at the end of 1922, Lloyd George was elbowed out of office by a meeting of Tories at the Carlton Club and the subsequent election sent to the House of Commons a Labour Party nearly doubled in numbers, Webb came in with the astonishing majority of 11,200—a figure, it would appear, too much for the compositors of *The Times* to credit, for they printed the result as a row of noughts. He was set now, with his wife beside him, on the road to Cabinet rank and the House of Lords.

For neither Beatrice nor the partnership as a whole had been idle. Beatrice read the signs of the times. Having known an earlier "khaki" election—that fought in the middle of the Boer War—she was not deceived by the huge Coalition majority of 1918, observing rather the large total of votes cast for Labour candidates, and the fact that even under the adverse conditions the number of Labour members had increased, albeit by only a small amount, and that the Party was now His Majesty's Opposition. She saw—or thought she saw—the Labour Party on the way to becoming a majority of the whole country. Furthermore, the Labour Party, as a result of the 1918 reorganization, had been very much improved as a possible instrument of government, and had also committed itself to a Socialist policy. It looked as though the Labour Party might be in process of becoming the "strong independent Socialist Party" the need for which she had foreseen in 1912; what was now required was to push it along in that direction, to make it more conscious of the implications of its policy, and above all to imbue it with the courage and adroitness necessary to carry it out—to make it, in effect, rise superior to Churchill's election gibe that Labour was "not fit to govern."

Immediately, the prospect was not very promising. The sixty M.P.s who survived the 1918 election were not remarkable either for intellectual equipment, political ability, or grasp of Socialist thought; their new leader, William Adamson, was an honest and very slow-witted miners' official whose ideas of organizing a political party went little beyond the appointment of a messenger boy to run to and fro between the House of Commons and the Labour Party headquarters at Eccleston Square. Nor were the others particularly susceptible of being organized into an effective political caucus like the Haldane-Asquith caucus of Education Act days; they did not really appreciate being invited to lunch or dinner, to eat a rapid meal and be tutored by the Webbs in the principles and methods of politics. They preferred to sit in the smoking-room at the House of Commons and vote against the Government when called on by Whips or to make speeches upon the issues which they understood or upon which they had strong instinctive feelings.

Beatrice worked hard; after a year or two she decided—possibly with recollections of the part played in her earlier days by Mrs. Asquith and other brilliant political hostesses—that the women of the Labour Party needed educating for politics even more than the men; and accordingly at the end of 1920 she founded a women's society called, by reason of its limitation to one sex, the Half-Circle Club, which was intended to be a rendezvous where Labour women, and particularly the wives of prominent and potentially prominent Labour men might meet over coffee and cakes, discuss with and be addressed by interesting personalities, and generally be groomed and trained to take their part in public life. The aim was certainly admirable; it was a fact that the wives of Trade Unionists and Labour M.P.s, many of whom had had of necessity to stay at home in small houses, cooking and cleaning and bringing up children, while their husbands went about without them, speaking and organizing on their way to Parliamentary or official rank, were often singularly ill-equipped, as well as much too shy, to hold their own in an atmosphere of even moderately high politics.[1] But, as in the days of the Prevention of Destitution and *The New Machiavelli*, there was a touch of crudity in Beatrice's methods, and a not quite complete concealment of the view—to which she occasionally gave expression in private—that the Trade Unionists' wives were really "dreadfully unpresentable," which aroused feelings of resentment in some; and this may partly account for the fact that the Half-Circle Club, while it did some good work and promoted some gatherings which were greatly enjoyed, never gained a real hold and certainly never became anything like a force in politics. The Labour movement was prepared to accept the Webbs as

---

[1] The admirable political education given by Margaret Llewelyn Davies through the Women's Co-operative Guild to many women co-operators did not go far to meet the social difficulties of which Beatrice was thinking; in any event, as I have mentioned before, she never felt comfortable in a purely feminine atmosphere.

clerks, even, to a certain extent, as political advisers, but not as tutors in manners or methods.

As a matter of fact, Beatrice had set herself an impossible task, for her purpose was divided. On the one hand she was trying, as she wrote later in an anonymous article contributed to the *Political Quarterly*, to establish throughout the Labour movement a standard of social habits and practice which would be suitable to a democracy in which the main power rested with the common people;[1] on the other, she was seeking to groom her Labour friends for political association with persons of a quite different class, who had no such standard nor any intention of adopting it, even if MacDonald and more than one other of the members of the minority Labour Governments had not plainly showed that they infinitely preferred cultured and expensive society to intercourse with members of their own Party. The difficulties of a minority Government are just as real in the social as in the political field; the controversy about the wearing of Court dress which arose immediately upon the formation of the first Labour Government provides an excellent example of them. It is doubtful whether, at the time, anything less than a political Society organized as strictly as the Russian Communist Party, with equality of rights and responsibility between the sexes, could have achieved what Beatrice was aiming at; and though by the mid-'twenties she was beginning to talk about the need for a "dedicated Order of Socialists" like the Society of Jesus, her mind was still sternly averted from Lenin, and she carried the idea no further.

In "our constituency" of Seaham, however, she was very much more successful. Here she appeared, and was accepted, as an educational force, and she was dealing not with a mixture of classes but with a nearly homogeneous community whose members were of the type she had learned to love long ago in Bacup and in the Co-operative Movement, and whose natural good manners she had always greatly appreciated. The relations of Seaham Harbour with its candidate and its candidate's wife were uniformly happy and fruitful. They studied the ground in Seaham as thoroughly as they had studied it for the Minority Report campaign; they read up the history of mining and of County Durham

---

[1] "If you really desire," she wrote, "successive Labour Administrations, continuously devoted to the welfare of the common people, you will need to maintain, by precept and example, the modest personal expenditure and unpretentious ways of social intercourse implied by the ideal of equality between man and man—an ideal which is the very soul of the Labour Movement."

—Sidney in 1921 published a short *Story of the Durham Miners*—
and they mapped out through the whole division the many
existing institutions, from chapels to clubs, through which they
might influence the electors and their wives. From 1919 to
1928, when Sidney decided that he was too old to fight another
election, they visited their constituency as often as, if not more
often than, any other candidate or M.P.; more, they started and
kept up a regular series of educational activities which went far
beyond mere political instruction or canvassing. Beatrice gave
to these the name of "the University of Seaham," which vastly
pleased her new students; she provided them with a circulating
library of solid literature sent down from London, and, in
addition to all her lectures and meetings, while Sidney was in
Parliament she wrote every month a News Letter to the Women
of Seaham. "Our candidate's *wife*," said one of the electors
proudly, "can answer questions better than the other man can
himself"; and while under the circumstances that was not surprising, anyone who has ever lectured or held classes in mining
areas will remember the eager, stimulating, and friendly audiences,
so different from some of the jaded groups in the south. The
great majority of 1922 was attributable to Beatrice's work quite
as much as to Sidney's; so was the solid build-up which made
the constituency so faithful that even the "Red Letter" election
of 1924, when one-third of the Labour M.P.s fell by the way,
only reduced that majority by five hundred. It is interesting to
speculate what would have happened in the débâcle of 1931 if
Webb had remained there to fight the National Government,
instead of handing over the seat in 1928 to—of all people—the
very leader who later abandoned his Party.

All the while, the Webbs were continuing the more strictly
intellectual side of their work—the writing of books, during this
period with the main purpose of explaining the Labour movement
and its policy to itself. Though *English Prisons* appeared early in
1922, and *Statutory Authorities* later in the same year, the bulk of
the research for those two books had been done earlier, and the
characteristic products of the period were the revised *History of
Trade Unionism*, which in cheap form was gobbled up by Trade
Union branches, adult education classes, etc.,[1] the large study of

---

[1] The fact that the Webbs, like Shaw, were their own publishers enabled them to
make use of any and every means they pleased for rendering their books available
immediately upon publication to readers of small means, as they did also in the case
of the *Minority Report* and of *Soviet Communism*. They were in a position to do this, of
course, because they were not dependent on immediate returns from royalties.

The Consumers' Co-operative Movement, for which co-operators showed considerably less enthusiasm, *A Constitution for the Socialist Commonwealth of Great Britain*, which is their sole attempt at drawing the lines of a new Socialist society, and their only frontal attack upon its rival, *The Decay of Capitalist Civilization*.

Three of these publications need not detain us for long. Neither the revised *History* nor the *Consumers' Co-operative Movement* is in the front rank. In both cases they had lost the close touch with the actual life of their subjects which had given to the 1894 *History* and to Beatrice Potter's *Co-operative Movement* their peculiar freshness; they were working from available published documents and not on the spot, and the result is that the books tend to be dull. The *History* is further dated, and rather marred, by containing undigested lumps of the controversy with the Guild Socialists and Syndicalists which was still raging when it was written. Both books should be regarded rather as commendable contributions to the political education of the rising post-war generation than as major works.

The Decay of Capitalist Civilization is a long and vigorous tract "showing up" the capitalist system as both economically and morally bankrupt, with the strongest stress on the second adverb. It shows signs that one or both of the authors had read at least the historical chapters of *Das Kapital*, for Marx's view of history (though not his economics) is praised; it shows more trace of the influence of Thorstein Veblen and his biting comments on the moral and social effects of inequalities of wealth and of a leisured class, and of the information garnered by Sidney in the course of his service on the Government Committees on Trusts and Profiteering. Much stress is laid—one would guess by Beatrice in particular—on the bad social manners produced by capitalism between the rich and the poor.

"We do not, nowadays," says one paragraph, "think it compatible with the manners of a gentleman to give the governess a cheaper wine than is served to the other persons at table, nor even to put off the servants' hall with cheaper meat. But towards the great unknown mass of our fellow citizens, *who are really sitting down with us to eat at the world's table*, this principle of good manners is observed only by a tiny minority, even among those who think themselves well-bred"; and the same passage puts forward Matthew Arnold's forty-year-old maxim, "Choose equality and flee greed," as a motto for Socialists and for all who would have good social manners. In 1922 Beatrice, like Robert Owen and many other nineteenth-century thinkers, still believed that you could by moral exhortation persuade the well-off voluntarily to share their privileges. Save for a surplus of bloated footnotes, some taking up half a page and more, which should never have been allowed to intrude into a polemical tract, the *Decay* is excellently written and is as readable to-day as it was in 1923; this may be partly because Bernard Shaw, reviving an earlier practice, revised the whole text while its authors were engaged in their second election campaign. Such phrases as "if the people are not convinced that the police are morally right, they will finally burn down the police-station, and nobody will give evidence against them" smack of Shaw rather than of either of the Webbs.

A Constitution for the Socialist Commonwealth was written originally at the request of Camille Huysmans, then secretary of the International Socialist Bureau, which asked all its constituent bodies to send in reports upon "the socialization of industries and services, and upon the constitution that should be adopted by any nation desirous of organizing its life upon Socialist principles"; and it is important reading for anyone who wants to study the development of Beatrice's thought. Not because it is a good book; in many respects it is the least good, as it has undoubtedly been the least influential, of the Webbs' books, and this for two main reasons. First, it is not well written; the long, top-heavy sentences, the catalogues, and the excessive use of strings of words headed by capital letters, which are the vices of the combined Webbian style, are nowhere more conspicuous; and like the revised *History*, it is burdened with argument about Syndicalist theories which gets nowhere. Secondly, and more important, its main suggestions for the reform of the British political system are impossible. It proposes to deal with the problem of national government by cutting Parliament into halves and calling one half a political and the other a Social Parliament.

"We regard this splitting of the House of Commons as regards powers and functions," it states flatly, "into two co-ordinate national assemblies, one dealing with criminal law and political dominion and the other with economic and social administration, not merely as the only effective way of remedying the present congestion of Parliamentary business, *but as an essential condition of the progressive substitution, with any approach to completeness, of the community for the private capitalist.*" (My italics.)

K

The plan for the reform of local government has an equally drastic simplicity. It proposes to scrap, in principle, the whole of the system at present in existence, and to replace it by establishing all over the country "a common and approximately equal unit of representation which we call the Ward." These Wards, or strictly speaking the Councillors elected for them (who would all be paid), should then be combined in various ways, according to what turned out to be most convenient, for running the various local and regional services.

"In this way it would be possible to have one area for the administration of paving and cleansing, the management of the elementary schools and the provision of allotments, under its own directly elected Council; and quite another area, *equally under its own directly elected Council*, for the supply of gas, water, and electricity, and the management of tramways; and yet another, *equally under its own directly elected Council*, for the organization of medical services, the provision for the sick and infirm and the promotion of the public health."

Beatrice must take a large share of the responsibility for the second suggestion, for it was in substance the idea which had "flashed" across her mind long previously while listening to Wells's first paper.[1] But no one who looks at either of the suggestions can help noticing that they imply a revolutionary change in the whole of the British political system, to be put through from no motive except tidiness and a problematic efficiency. They ignore history and the historical growth of institutions altogether (in spite of the long researches into local government); they propose to wipe them out by an Act of Parliament and replace them with artificial creations for which nobody could conceivably feel a spark of real affection or loyalty. Napoleon's *Départements* of France after more than a century's trial have signally failed to come to life; but Napoleon never suggested such a fearful and rigid atomization—a critic called it "A Globe-Wernicke system"—as the Webbs proposed for local government. It is small wonder that their *Constitution* fell on very stony ground.

But if one leaves aside the main proposals of the book, the suggestions thrown out by the way are of great interest, and some curiously anticipatory of what was actually done in the Soviet Union years later. Their remarks about vocational organization and the need for Trade Unions to take on quite new functions

[1] See page 66.

in a Socialist State might almost have come from leaders of Soviet Trade Unions[1]—though they would have been expressed in rather different language—and their suggestion that in a Socialist society the unwanted mansions of the rich should become convalescent homes, colleges, and residential hostels, or "under various forms of voluntary association, the holiday homes and recreation grounds of the urban toilers by hand and brain" has been almost literally carried out in the U.S.S.R. So also has their hope of "socialist emulation" between towns and villages—they would have added factories, had they been writing of industry—to show the greatest progress in health and happiness, the best libraries, picture-galleries, and concerts, or the finest literary, artistic, or scientific, output. The passages dealing with these various subjects show how practically the Webbs saw the kind of motives which must operate in a Socialist society and the ways in which they could be encouraged—even when they were wrong and unpractical in their major proposals.

Neither "socialist emulation" nor social progress, they further saw, could be made a reality unless the facts—correct and established facts—were available for proper comparison. This led them to the famous slogan "Measurement and Publicity," which first occurs in this book—the demand that every enterprise in society should be made to account, and to account accurately and publicly to the community for what it had done; and, as a necessary corollary, to the demand for an enormous increase in research in the social sciences.

"What is no less needed," they write, "than this greater knowledge of things (the physical sciences) is greater knowledge of men: of the conditions of the successful working of social institutions. That on which the world to-day most needs light is how to render more effective every form of social organization: how to make more socially fertile the relationships between men."

To this end they had in their day done their bit, by the foundation of the London School of Economics and its Social Sciences Department; but their example was not followed to any extent by the controllers of university courses, and the need of which they spoke is little less crying to-day than it was in 1920.

---

[1] See, for example, *Our Soviet Ally* (Ed. Margaret Cole), chapter on "Trade Unionism."

CHAPTER XIV

LABOUR OPPOSITION AND
LABOUR GOVERNMENT

FOR nine and a half years, from February, 1922, to August, 1931, Sidney was continuously in Parliament, either in the Government or on the Front Bench of the Opposition. It was not, in retrospect, a very happy period either for him or his wife. Sidney was sixty-three when he was elected, too old to relish the great change in hours of work and rhythm of life which being an M.P. involves; and though he became recognized as an authority on subjects which he had made his own, and was bidden to office as a matter of course in both Labour Governments, Parliament was never his *milieu*. Beatrice, for her part, was also feeling her years; though she did all and more than was required of her as a political helpmate, she was not able to play the vigorous organizing part which she would have played twenty years earlier. She found inter-war London, with its crowds, its cars, and its noise, increasingly difficult to endure; and the result, particularly in the latter years, was a partial separation, both in physical space and in work, which was agreeable to neither partner. Beatrice, in effect, gave up a large part of Sidney to his country's service, and though she bore it as inevitable, she did not like it, and liked it less and less the more doubtful she became of the Labour Governments achieving anything.

In the November of 1922, however, most of this lay in the future. Sidney had just been elected with his thumping majority, and was joined in the House of Commons by over a hundred and fifty Labour colleagues. The present generation has forgotten the excitement of that election, when the Lloyd George coalition was broken after three dismal years of post-war muddling, and the Labour Party came back, not as a titular, but as a real tangible Opposition—no one then knew how short the time was to be before it was asked to become a Government—and an Opposition, moreover, which included a large number of the intellectual and left-wing personalities who had been kept out in the coupon beanfeast of three years back. The Clydesiders were

BEATRICE WEBB
in the lounge at Passfield Corner

the chief surprise. Thirty-four of the seventy-one Scottish seats were won by Labour, whose champions, including several out-and-out opponents of the late war, captured ten out of the fifteen divisions of Glasgow, six out of the seven divisions of the County of Lanark, and several more near by. It is a bitter irony that it was this Scottish triumph which actually helped to produce the Labour Party's major disaster. For it was generally felt that this new and vigorous party required a leader of more forceful and striking personality than Mr. Clynes, who had recently taken Adamson's place; and Henderson not being in Parliament[1] the obvious candidate was the hero of the war resisters, the leader and darling of the I.L.P., Ramsay MacDonald. The Webbs did not care for the choice: they could hardly have done so, for they had never really respected or completely trusted MacDonald, and he on his side had never liked them. But they were prepared loyally to try to make friends, and MacDonald, in great good humour and not yet taken up by high London society, at least appeared to be reciprocating. Beatrice admitted that he certainly looked very nice as a leader.

Immediately, she increased her own efforts. In addition to the Half-Circle Club, now just over a year old and going strong, and to her individual work in the Seaham division, she made it her business to become personally acquainted with all the Labour M.P.s, by asking them to lunch or dinner. This she continued throughout Sidney's Parliamentary career—no light undertaking when, after 1929, the number to be entertained had risen to nearly three hundred. But at least she found, within the 1922 Party, some individuals of more intellectual interests, such as the present Lords Ponsonby and Arnold, with whom she could discuss general questions of Socialism and politics.

She was trying very hard to make of the Labour Party a compact force fighting for Socialism; but she was not prepared, and could not afford, to give her full time to it. A sign of this was her gradual change of residence. In the summer of 1923, before the first Labour Government took office, she gave the first overt signs of the loosening of her ties with London. Early in August there appeared the newspaper advertisement which caused so much amusement, to the effect that "Mr. and Mrs. Sidney Webb would like to buy a site for a country cottage *with no dogs or cocks*

---

[1] Always unlucky in general elections, Henderson had lost his seat at Widnes and had to be brought in for the earliest available vacancy.

within hearing"; and by the end of the month they had acquired as a week-end and holiday residence Passfield Corner, which became their permanent home six years later. Forty-one Grosvenor Road turned into the residence of Susan Lawrence, though the Webbs for some years retained a part of it for their own use.

At the end of 1923 the Conservative Premier, Stanley Baldwin, announced that he had become converted to the necessity of Protection, and appealed to the country. The election of 1923 rejected his new policy, and resulted in a minority Labour Government, held in power for nine months by the support of the Liberals. Just previously, as President of the Labour Party Conference, Sidney, in full agreement with Beatrice, had clearly explained his views on future policy in the speech which contained the famous phrase "the inevitability of gradualness." So much misunderstanding has been attached to this phrase, which at one stage of Labour controversy was used simply as a symbol for reaction, that it may be well to set it in its context here.

Sidney had been arguing that one of the prime faults of the nineteenth century and of the first two decades of the twentieth, as exemplified in the Treaty of Versailles, was its *immorality* in the strict sense, its failure to take account of the fact that "morality, like economics, is actually part of the nature of things"—this, it will be remembered, was also the theme of *The Decay of Capitalist Civilization*, published in the same year. He lays down that any plan for the future of society is doomed to failure if it does not take account of three facts, that "free competition" as postulated by the *laissez-faire* school of Liberalism no longer exists, that the "overweening influence" of the rich in politics and society is an anachronism and a social danger, and that persistent unemployment on a large scale is equally a social danger and morally intolerable. He goes on to say: .

"Let me insist on what our opponents habitually ignore, and, indeed, what they seem intellectually incapable of understanding, namely *the inevitable gradualness* of our scheme of change. The very fact that Socialists have both principles and a programme appears to confuse nearly all their critics. If we state our principles, we are told 'That is not practicable.' When we recite our programme the objection is 'That is not Socialism.' But why, because we are idealists, should we be supposed to be idiots? For the Labour Party, it must be plain, Socialism is rooted in political Democracy; which necessarily compels us to recognize that every step towards our goal is dependent on gaining the assent and support of at least a numerical majority of the whole people. Thus, even if we aimed at revolutionizing everything at once, we should necessarily be compelled to make each particular change only at the time, and to the extent, and in the manner in which ten or fifteen million electors, in all sorts of conditions, of all sorts of temperaments, from Land's End to the Orkneys, could be brought to consent to it. How anyone can fear that the British electorate, whatever mistakes it can make or may condone, can ever go too fast or too far is incomprehensible to me. That, indeed, is the supremely valuable safeguard of any effective democracy.

"But the Labour Party, when in due course it comes to be entrusted with power, will naturally not want to do everything at once. Surely, it must be abundantly manifest to any instructed person that, whilst it would be easy to draft proclamations of universal change, or even enact laws in a single sitting purporting to give a new Heaven and a new Earth, the result, the next morning, would be no change at all, unless, indeed, the advent of widespread confusion. I remember Mr. Bernard Shaw saying, a whole generation ago, 'Don't forget that, whilst you may nationalize the railways in one afternoon, it will take a long time to transform all the third-class carriages and all the first-class carriages into second-class carriages.' Once we face the necessity of putting our principles first into bills, to be fought through Committee clause by clause; and then into appropriate administrative machinery for carrying them into execution from one end of the Kingdom to the other—and this is what the Labour Party has done with its Socialism —the *inevitability of gradualness* cannot fail to be appreciated." (Italics mine.)

The only comment needed on this passage is that it is phrased so as to apply to Britain alone, addressed to a Party committed to the promotion of Socialism by non-violent means and with the consent of the general mass of the people. Webb was not thinking of the politics of other European countries; and in any case it must be remembered that in 1923 the possibilities of violent political change had almost sunk below the horizon. Mussolini's grab at political power, which few even of the Left in this country regarded as a serious portent, had only recently happened, and he was still insecure in his seat; Hitler was the leader of a handful of maniacs of whom no one had heard; the U.S.S.R., since the inauguration in 1921 of the New Economic Policy, was generally supposed to be retreating rapidly from its revolutionary bridgeheads. The Labour Party, on the basis of its 1918 programme, had just made a huge leap forward towards power, and there was every indication that it would make another as soon as it was granted the opportunity. Given the political outlook of the time, from the standpoint of a home-keeping Briton, given the character of the instrument—the Labour Party—through which he proposed to work, and given the history of British politics and political institutions over many generations, Webb's argument, with its stress upon the difficulties and complexities inherent in making any Socialist measures effectively operative, is obvious common sense. Whether the ultimate objective could be attained by the means which the Labour Party proposed, whether the orderly progress envisaged would not in the event be prevented by revolutionary violence on the part of the present holders of wealth and power, is of course another question—at that time, a question of political prophecy. One would hardly expect to find it discussed publicly by the chairman of a Party which was just stepping out towards its first efforts at power.

At the beginning of 1924 the Labour Party entered upon its first term of "office without power," which ended somewhat ignominiously in October, when the Liberals turned it out as the result of a dispute over the prosecution of a Communist journalist, and in the subsequent election the "Red Letter" scare[1] brought a number of timid citizens out of their holes to vote against the Party which they believed was going to hand them over lock, stock, and barrel to the dictatorship in Russia. When the Government took office, Sidney was immediately offered the important but not spectacular office of the Board of Trade, which involved a good deal of rather dull detail. Beatrice was asked to serve on some of the Committees appointed by the new Government, but refused; she was too old and not strong enough to undertake the drudgery. For the first time in her married life she was parted physically from Sidney for stretches of time, as she lived more and more at Passfield. She found it distressing, but we should be grateful. For it was during that time of partial separation that *My Apprenticeship* was written.

Beatrice had intended for many years to compose an auto-

---

[1] The "Red Letter" was a document purporting to be signed by the Soviet Commissar Zinoviev—probably a forgery, though this has never been proved for certain —which the Foreign Office produced and the *Daily Mail* and other papers published on the eve of the election. It contained instructions to the British Communist Party on how to obtain control of the Labour Movement. When the document appeared, MacDonald's haverings and his refusal to make any definite statement left his supporting candidates without a word to say in reply until it was too late. The election tactics thus disclosed, and the effect which they produced, might have warned the leaders of the Party what was in store for them later.

biography from her diaries as soon as she should have time; but she was curiously nervous about the result, as may be gathered from the fact that she spent an unusually long time on revision; the book was not published until 1926. This may have been because it was so long since she had appeared in print with a work that was not signed by their joint names or at least drafted in common. It will be remembered that the Minority Report was actually written by Sidney, and it is to be presumed that he collaborated in the preparation of her other Government reports; but here collaboration was not possible and she had to stand or fall on her own literary feet. She had also to stand upon her own personality. Reticent and detached as the book is—it is recorded that Sidney, when the idea was first presented to him, uttered a horrified caution, "No personalities, please!"—it was bound to contain a certain amount of intimate disclosure of thoughts and emotions hitherto confided only to her diary. Whatever the reason, she was as anxious about it as though it had been a baby and was perturbed far more than normally by any unfavourable criticism from reviewers.

There was some; in fact, it may be said that *My Apprenticeship*, though it was of course recognized as an outstanding book, did not immediately meet with the appreciation it deserved and has since obtained. It is in itself an autobiography of a remarkable kind. It is astonishingly candid, within the limits of what it allows itself to disclose. Beatrice criticizes and appraises her own early self with as much detachment, and as much but no more interest than she shows in describing the other actors in the story of her life; she makes no excuses for faults, but neither on the other hand does she blame herself or others for actions which their own natures or the conditions of their time made inevitable. Her autobiography shows no trace of the desire, common to so many, to hit back at those who annoyed or frustrated her in her earlier days; she writes as a historian.

Furthermore, the book is far from being a book of simple reminiscence. It sets out to tell the story—largely a spiritual story—of one mind in its search for a profession and a faith to live by; and it does this by interweaving, in the most adroit and fascinating way, pieces of vivid contemporary picture quoted directly from the Diary into the long historical essays of which the book is built. One indirect result of this method of writing is that *My Apprenticeship*, beside being an extremely well written personal record, is a great contribution to the social history of the latter half of the nineteenth century, and should be prescribed reading for any serious student.

As its readers know, *My Apprenticeship* comes to an end in 1892, the date of Beatrice's marriage. It would be extremely interesting to see how far the technique then developed served her for the obviously more difficult task of continuing the story of her life after it had become closely knit with the life of another; but this will never be known in full. It was her intention to follow up *My Apprenticeship* with three further volumes, to be called *Our Partnership*. Of these the first, covering the period down to the Royal Commission on the Poor Law, was begun in the late 'twenties, and completed before her death; the others were never written at all.

After the fall of the Labour Government, though Sidney remained in Parliament and played his part as an Opposition leader of knowledge and commonsense, particularly during the passage of the De-rating Bill which became the 1929 Local Government Act, and whose subject was of course particularly his own, Parliamentary affairs occupied him less, and the partnership was able to spend more time together. They had decided that he was really too old for Parliamentary life, and that he had well worked out his time in a form of public service which, after the first novelty had worn off, he found exhausting and unpleasant; he would sit out the life of that Parliament (which could not be longer than five years) and then he would go. One sign of the slow withdrawal, which they supposed would be completed by 1929, was that in 1926 he went off the Executive Committee of the Labour Party, though he continued after that date to serve on the elected executive of the Parliamentary Party. Both he and Beatrice, they felt, and told the many visitors who came to spend week-ends with them at Passfield Corner, were moving quietly towards an old age of retirement.

For Beatrice the period was one of mixed experiences, some pleasant, some the reverse. Pleasant was the completion of the last of the great works on local government—*English Poor Law History*—of which the first volume, taking the story down to the Act of 1834, was published in 1927, and the two remaining ones in 1929, just in time for the authors to be able to add a triumphant appendix on Neville Chamberlain's abolition of the Boards of Guardians, twenty years after they had first advocated this in the

Minority Report. Local Government, it would seem from the references to it in *Methods of Social Study*, was until 1932 the research which Beatrice found most fascinating; and in 1927–8 they were close at it again, once more, as in the days of the *History of Trade Unionism* or *The Parish and the County*, visiting on the spot and talking to local officials and local recipients of relief—in South Wales, for example—in order to find out how the Poor Law was actually working in practice. The final product was the largest of all the Local Government series, 1,502 pages in all, handling its mass of detail in a thoroughly masterly way. It shows absolutely no signs of loss of grip or technique, or of the old age of which Beatrice was then particularly conscious—she told the writer, just before the last volume appeared, that she and Sidney "would never undertake another large book. At sixty-eight and sixty-nine, we are too old to begin again. We have finished our work."[1]

Pleasant, too, was the gradual recognition of good service done, coming from a variety of quarters. The "top-notches" of the intellectual world had shown a singularly grudging unwillingness to appreciate the intellectual work of the Webbs. Perhaps they had never forgiven them for the period of almost successful permeation and their subsequent abandonment of the respectable political parties; perhaps they resented the fact that neither of them had had a university education or showed any interest in the curricula and problems of Oxford and Cambridge; perhaps they realized subconsciously that the subject of the Webbs' research was dangerous, and however scholarly, was liable in its results to blow sky-high the islands of economic security on which they were living. As Sidney once said to the writer in the course of a discussion, "Capitalists will endow research into the causes of cancer, because they are afraid they may suffer from cancer; they won't endow research into the causes of poverty, for they don't suffer from poverty." It took Hitler, and a major war, to make it clear that the social results of the cancer of poverty are a major danger to the lives of many who are not poor; even now, it is doubtful whether that lesson has been fully learned.

Whatever the reason, the work of the Webbs had been grossly

---

[1] Throughout the period of "our partnership" Beatrice was always on the look-out for the approach of old age and its effects on the mind. Maybe this was due in part to her having married at an age which was advanced for a Victorian Society lady; it was of course an unwarranted apprehension, as the last chapters of this book will show.

neglected by those responsible for granting academic distinction, with the honourable exception of the University of Manchester.[1] But in 1927 Oxford asked her to deliver the Sidney Ball Memorial Lecture; and early in the following year the B.B.C., which she had begun to find a great solace while alone at Passfield, invited her to broadcast upon Herbert Spencer. The subject of course was congenial, and she was delighted to find that her voice went over well, that she was considered to be a radio success. She was asked to speak upon the way in which she and her husband had conducted their social research work, and in February and March of 1929 she gave a series of talks which formed the basis of the book, *Methods of Social Study*, published in 1932. Further broadcasts followed; and the British Academy made her its one and only woman Fellow. Finally, in 1928, the London School of Economics honoured its founders by asking Sir William Nicholson to paint their portraits for it. The result, the picture of the main living-room at Passfield Corner, with Sidney standing by the mantelpiece and Beatrice sitting in a low chair, with Sandy, her absurd and spoilt Dandie Dinmont, at her feet, was unveiled at a reception given to its subjects in January, 1929, and remained one of the sights of the School buildings until at the outbreak of war they were taken over by the Air Ministry and closed to the public.

These were pleasant incidents; but her thoughts in general during this period were less agreeable. Whenever Sidney was away she suffered from loneliness; and as she grew older she began to feel more the spiritual separation from her own blood-relatives which had sat much more lightly on her at the beginning of her career and her marriage. Beatrice was much fonder of her sisters and interested in her sisters' children and grandchildren than most people believed; she followed the careers of the younger generation with great interest. She did not appear to regret the decision made at the time of her marriage to have no children of her own; but my own impression is that after her retirement to Passfield she would have been glad to become more of an aunt and/or great-aunt in the conventional sense, to be liked and visited and confided in even by those of her relations who dis-

---

[1] And, later, of the Universities of Edinburgh and Munich. Much the same fate befell J. A. Hobson, an economic teacher and prophet who was also almost entirely neglected in his own day. Only after his death have his views about trade and unemployment become (without acknowledgment) part of the official policy of the British Government.

agreed with her politically.[1] Although many of the relations felt real affection and admiration for her, it was only with her niece Barbara Drake that she had a real and continuous friendship.

At the same time, she was becoming more and more pessimistic about the political outlook. She did not find the Labour Party inspiring; she thought the minority Government had shown itself on the whole weak and inept, and she saw little hope of tempering its leadership into a strong and disciplined society of convinced and determined Socialists. On the other hand, she was no better pleased with the left-wing opinions which had been wafted over to British Trade Unionism from the Soviet Union, and which showed themselves strongly in the Trades Union Congress of 1925 and the brief triumph, in the same year, of an organized strike threat against a drastic reduction in mining wages; she thought they savoured of emotional syndicalism. When, in April of 1926, the threat was renewed and had to be implemented in the face of much more extensive preparations by the Government for strike-breaking (and no preparations whatever by the Trade Unions) she thought the resulting General Strike a disastrous mistake, and deplored equally both it and the 1927 Trade Union Act which was designed to punish the strikers and to prevent the possibility of recurrence. Their attitude towards the General Strike must have created an awkward situation for the member for Seaham and his wife, and may have contributed to Sidney's defeat for the Labour Party Executive in the autumn of 1926.

Nor, when she looked outside Great Britain, did Beatrice see much more ground for hope. At this time she was still a strong opponent of the Soviet system and all its works; she saw little difference between it and the Fascism established by Mussolini four years before, and labelled them both "creed autocracies." One of her main themes of conversation with her visitors during the period between the two Labour Governments was that the world was moving towards a struggle between two "creed-autocracies," the Communists and the Fascists, with an uncertainty as to where Great Britain would be found or whether, indeed, it would survive at all. If Britain could not acquire for itself a creed, or at least a faith strong enough to take the place

---

[1] A case in point is her continuous interest in the doings of Malcolm Muggeridge, her journalist nephew-in-law who wrote some very "between the wars" novels, and subsequently, after a visit to Russia, became a bitter opponent of the Soviet Union at a time when his aunt's enthusiasm for it was almost at its zenith.

of the religious impulses which had given the driving force to its past history and which she herself had replaced by a faith in Socialism, and if it could not produce an Order, as she called it, of dedicated persons, something resembling the Jesuit Order or the Russian Communist Party,[1] trained and pledged to work for their political end, she doubted whether Britain would have any future. As regards the greatly increased role of ideology or creeds in modern world politics, she was obviously right, as subsequent events have proved; and both Russia and Germany have shown the tremendous effects of a trained and disciplined Party organization. But even in 1926 it is surprising that from the point of view of a British Socialist she found so little to distinguish between the contents of the rival creeds.

But before these speculations had got much further than table-talks, reflections on the future were stopped by the arrival of a new Labour Government. An election was due in 1929; it came in the early summer, and the working classes were able to show some of their resentment for the loss of the General Strike. They brushed aside Lloyd George's Liberals, with their carefully worked-out Yellow Book programme of moderate reform, and returned a Labour Party, still without a majority, but two hundred and eighty-seven strong. MacDonald was asked to form a second Government, and he asked Sidney Webb to take office as Secretary of State for the Colonies, and to go to the Lords. The Webbs were not prepared for any such event. In the previous autumn Sidney had said good-bye to Seaham with the simple words, "It (Parliament) is too much for me, and in two years time it will be very much too much for me"; and they were making arrangements to give up Grosvenor Road altogether and live entirely in the country. But when, after a spring holiday which included a visit to Trotsky, then an exile in Prinkipo, they returned to a demand for renewed political service, they accepted the burden. They would not give up Passfield, or return to Grosvenor Road; but they took a flat in Artillery Mansions in Victoria Street to enable Beatrice to do the entertaining necessary to a Cabinet Minister's wife.

She was prepared to endure—it amounted to that—a certain amount of inconvenient and distasteful social functioning in the service of the Labour Government. But not all that was demanded

[1] Mr. Wells must have smiled, if he heard it, at this revival, after a quarter of a century, of the Samurai of his *Modern Utopia*.

of her. The new episode opened with an amusing and characteristic brush with tradition. For a variety of reasons, Sidney had
agreed to take a peerage, to become "the fantastic personage who
goes by the name of Lord Passfield";[1] but Beatrice refused to
become a similarly fantastic personage; her name was Beatrice
Webb, and she would not be Lady Passfield. She had some slight
precedent for her refusal. Scottish Supreme Court Judges used not
to give their titles to their wives. But the precedent was slender,
and her attitude aroused a storm of opposition, the strength of
which shows incidentally how little progress the Labour Party
had made towards getting rid of social class distinctions. Mac-
Donald, already on the way to cultivate the "less disagreeable
society" of which Webb wrote in his article analysing the catastrophe of 1931,[2] bitterly resented the implicit criticism of it;
officials of the Civil Service pointed out how unthinkable it would
be to issue invitations to people "To Meet the Secretary of State
for the Colonies and Mrs. Webb"; Society ladies entreated her
not to let the side down; but in vain. Beatrice knew the social
hierarchy from inside, and had had more than enough of it.
She refused firmly, and she won her battle, although she lost on
another round, having to submit to being presented at Court
and to curtsy. (At a later stage she went to dine at Buckingham
Palace, and was also entertained by the Prince of Wales at York
House—on which occasion the Prince found her so interesting
that he kept her for half an hour talking about religion.)

These were amusing skirmishes. But when they were over, it
was not long before the Labour Government, which had taken
office with such high hopes, ran into stormy weather. Sidney
Webb suffered misfortune early, for before the year was out his
Ministerial duties had involved him in the insoluble tangle of
British policy in Palestine, which in the autumn broke out into
the open warfare of the Wailing Wall "incident." The winter
of 1929–30 was no pleasant time for the Colonial Secretary. But
much worse was to come. The trade boom of the late 'twenties
was about to break.

During its time in Opposition, and for many years before, much
of Labour's propaganda had been directed against the evils of
unemployment, and the persistence after the war of an army of
unemployed which never fell below the million mark had made
all its supporters conscious that this was the most outstanding

---

[1] M. A. Hamilton, *Sidney and Beatrice Webb*.   [2] *Political Quarterly*, January, 1932.

enemy which a Labour Government should tackle. But the Government had not been in existence many months before it became apparent that while it would make efforts to mitigate the lot of the unemployed, it had no idea whatever of how to tackle unemployment at its roots; the special commission, consisting of George Lansbury, J. H. Thomas, and Oswald Mosley, which was set up in 1930 to consider—and if possible to shelve—the problem got nowhere. Mosley produced a scheme of his own which was turned down by a narrow majority at the Labour Party Conference, whereupon he resigned from the Party in a fury and took to the road which led him in the end to overt Fascism and to Brixton Gaol; the I.L.P. and the other left-wing members of the Party grumbled impotently.

The while, the outlook for international trade was growing worse and worse, and the figures were declining to the great slump which brought down the Government with a crash as it brought down Brüning in Germany and overwhelmed the Republicans in America. Few foresaw the unprecedented size of the slump, more particularly as it began in the States, the golden land of prosperity, whose economists had been explaining, even in 1928, that there could never again be a slump in America, because her internal market was so vast that it could absorb increases in production to any extent. A slump in the States, in fact, was as wrong (and therefore as unthinkable) from the economists' point of view as a successful revolution in Russia was from that of the Social-Democratic followers of Marx. The Labour Government cannot be blamed for lacking the gift of prophecy. But as the clouds gathered and the unemployment percentages rose, the fact that it had no positive policy whatever became painfully obvious.

There is no need, in this book, to retell the melancholy story of 1931 and the ignominious death of the Labour Government at the hands of forces outside its own control—forces which on the other side of the Atlantic swept the more fortunate Roosevelt into power a year later. This much, however, must be said. The catastrophe was more than the mere fall of a Government; it was a sign of things to come. Because of the mildness of British party strife, as compared with Continental conditions, most people do not realize to this day that the British Labour movement was, after the Italians, the first of the Social-Democratic parties to sustain defeat in the counter-revolution whose developed pattern was soon made manifest, in greater or less degree, by events in

Austria, in Germany, and in France. Yet many of the factors correspond to the pattern. There was a Social-Democratic leadership, cautious and slow in action, with a programme of gradual reformist evolution which presupposed by implication the maintenance of the economic fabric and a steady increase in general productivity and had never faced in any practical sense the problems of economic collapse. When the collapse came there was a prompt move by the anti-Labour forces to throw all the blame upon the "impossibly high standard of living" enjoyed by the working classes, to demand instant reductions in wages, and through their command of the machinery of finance, which the Labour leaders had never touched and had barely understood, to strengthen those demands by conjuring up the spectre of inflation, which since the time of the French occupation of the Ruhr had loomed like a nightmare before the eyes of anyone who possessed the tiniest scrap of property and even of many who possessed none.

In Britain these ends were achieved by the report of the notorious May Committee—appointed by the Labour Government itself in an attempt to pacify its opponents—which announced an impending deficit of a hundred and sixty millions in the Budget and demanded drastic cuts in the pay of those whose living depended on the Government, including the miserable pittances allowed to the unemployed; and in the fantastic negotiations which were supposed to have taken place between the Bank of England and the bankers of America. The stage thus set, three of the most prominent of the Labour leaders, including the Prime Minister, were induced to save the sinking pound by deserting their colleagues (after they had failed to induce them to accept the cuts) and to become garlanded prisoners in what was designed to be in effect a single-Party government with a programme of restoring British confidence and prestige—i.e., the British capitalist system—by whatever means should turn out to be necessary. The subsequent election was conducted on the lines of naked appeal to fear, without unnecessary regard for truth. Labour was represented as incapable of dealing with the problems of finance (which was partly correct); MacDonald appeared on public platforms waving a million-mark note, symbol of what had happened in Germany and would infallibly happen in Britain if he and his colleagues were not returned to power with their "doctor's mandate"; and Snowden, Labour's Chancellor of the Exchequer, went so far as to put about over

L

the radio the story that the Labour Government had intended
to raid the workers' savings in the Post Office and pour them down
the drain of the Budget deficit.

The British Conservatives made no use of Mosley and his
small semi-fascist gangs; they were too firmly based to need him
as Hugenberg and Thyssen needed Hitler. But *mutatis mutandis*
the tactics were the same as Hitler's, and the results were sufficient.
Though the solid mass of Labour voters held firm, as did the
German Social-Democrats in the last Reichstag, the waverers
and the middle class, large and small, poured out in terror to the
polls, and the Parliamentary representation of Labour was
reduced to a handful of fifty. The Conservatives came back as a
National Government with an all-powerful majority; though
they needed no concentration camps they made it plain, by their
treatment of the unemployed in the winter of 1931–2, that they
were intending to stand no nonsense: and the Labour Party
received a blow from which it had not rallied by the outbreak of
war. Snowden partially recovered his senses after the policy of the
new Government with regard to trade and international relations
had become apparent, and left it, though retaining his embittered
hatred of his former colleagues. MacDonald, when he had served
his purpose, was thrown aside without ceremony.

MacDonald's own personality and the peculiarly contemptuous
and secretive way in which he effected his *coup d'état*—on the vital
24th of August, having received overnight permission to tender
his own and his colleagues' resignation, he reappeared before
them, without any word said, as Prime Minister of a National
Government including Baldwin and Neville Chamberlain—
obscured for most people at the time the underlying realities of
the situation. Even Webb, in his *Political Quarterly* article already
quoted, ascribes a rather larger share in the débâcle to MacDonald
than that woolly-minded *poseur* could ever have thought out on
his own.[1] Members of the Labour Cabinet and the Labour
movement regarded it as a simple, if scandalous, case of treachery
on the part of a handful and looked forward with some measure
of unjustified confidence to the coming election. They were
disappointed, not to say staggered. So, to some extent, were
the Webbs.

Beatrice had not mourned greatly the fall of the Labour
Government. She had grown to hope less and less from it. She

[1] For MacDonald, see L. MacNeill Weir's biography, *Ramsay MacDonald*.

drew, in fact, some satisfaction from the manner of its fall, which confirmed her thirty-year-old distrust of MacDonald; she thought the Labour movement well rid of him. With her habitual under-valuation of the emotional forces in politics—even after experiencing 1906, 1918 and 1924!—she had not anticipated the overwhelming verdict of the election; but she was not unduly perturbed by it. It made her doubt "the inevitability of gradualness"; and she thought it showed up the incompetence of the leaders of Labour in general, and would be a lesson to them. Sidney added, in the *Political Quarterly*, that "the whole episode is a manifestation, which the world will not fail to note . . . of the extraordinary strength of the position of British capitalism, and the British governing class"; and went on to add

"The Labour Party has now the opportunity, during the next few years of (1) applying itself continuously to the ubiquitous educational propaganda by which alone it can double the number of its adherents; (2) of quietly working out in greater detail its constructive programme, without prematurely committing itself as a Party to any but general principles; (3) of steadily accustoming the public to one item after another in that programme by the publication of an incessant stream, not only of popular pamphlets, but also of books, lectures and articles in the weeklies and monthlies by individual members; and last but not least, (4) of seeking to develop, within the Party itself, more of that friendly social intercourse among fellow-workers in a common cause which so effectively promotes its success."

This calm reception of the disaster may have been partly due to political prescience; but a more potent reason was undoubtedly the fact that their mental gaze, particularly Beatrice's, had turned away from the unsatisfying contemplation of the British political scene. In May, 1932, they left England for the U.S.S.R.

CHAPTER XV

SOVIET COMMUNISM

IF Beatrice had died in January, 1932, round about her seventy-fourth birthday, the historian of her life would have had to chronicle a rather grey twilight. He would have described a woman of remarkable capacity, infinite energy, and compelling ideas who met with the common fate of reformers, that of living to see that in the practical world they were not practical and could not be put into effect. As it was, however, the event was quite different. In her eighth decade she found a new hope and a new enthusiasm, saw many of the social reforms for which she had agitated since the 'nineties being put into effect in a new and vast country, entered upon a new piece of research comparable in size and complexity with anything which she had done before, and died, when she did die, secure in the knowledge that the new civilization with which she had fallen in love had successfully resisted the attacks of the most powerful and menacing enemy in all history.

Beatrice was not always a friend of the Soviet Union; far from it. Mrs. Hamilton's careful biography, in a laudable desire to defend its subjects against the charge of inconsistency, distinctly underrates her early hostility, which was as absolute as the most anti-Communist member of the Labour Party could possibly have desired. Neither the sheer romance of the *fact* of the Revolution, which in November, 1917, made most of the left-wing Socialists lift up their hearts and sing, nor the bold humanitarianism which even in the midst of war and civil war introduced complete equality between men and women, laid down the most enlightened labour laws in Europe, provided pay for the pregnant mother, and envisaged a universal system of education for a country ninety per cent illiterate, moved her at all. Revolutionary romance never appealed to the Webbs—it was part of their failure to understand the springs of emotion—and the humanitarian side she dismissed as silly Utopianism, something like the I.L.P.'s "Socialism in Our Time" programme, only more obviously unrealizable. For the rest, she regarded the Bolsheviks as a new and unpleasing variety of anarchists or syndicalists, who had unfortunately obtained a chance of putting their ridiculous theories of workers' control into practice,[1] and would thus add strength and vocalism to the anti-collectivists within the British Labour movement. She had Litvinov and Kamenev to lunch at the beginning of 1918 and received their statements with polite incredulity; later in the year, when the editor of *Pravda* invited her and Sidney to come to Russia and see for themselves, she retorted grimly that she knew what happened to hostages. Three years afterwards, a suggestion by Philips Price in his book *My Reminiscences of the Russian Revolution* that the Russian Communist Party in its post-revolutionary organization of the state had "something in common with the English Fabians" roused her to indignant protest. Reviewing the book in *Fabian News* she remarked contemptuously that Lenin may be all right for the Russians, who deserve no better. "But it seems hardly worth while for Western democracies to go through a similar experience of famine, disease, civil war, and the rapid decay of urban life, in order to come out at what Mr. Price, somewhat unkindly, believes to be the programme of the Fabian Society."

She was not, of course, interventionist—as was Churchill, who called Lenin and his colleagues by the singularly inapposite name of "crocodiles"; she had no use for the *cordon sanitaire* or the attempt to destroy the Soviet Government by external armed force. She looked forward to its either perishing of its own inefficiency or becoming gradually assimilated to capitalist states —in fact, she agreed with Marx's opinion of sixty or seventy years before that it was impossible that Socialism should be established first in Russia rather than in a more developed Western country. As time went on, she could not fail to observe that the new order in Russia was neither falling to pieces nor, in spite of the 1921 "step backwards" of the New Economic Policy, showing any marked tendency to change into a capitalist society; but her view of the U.S.S.R. in the 'twenties was taken almost entirely from the angle of the right wing of the British Labour Party. She judged it, largely, by the effect which the "splitting tactics" prescribed by the Comintern (which she always disliked heartily) to its constituent Communist Parties had on British working-class organizations, and she concluded that it was an

[1] Immediately after the Revolution, the Soviets in Russian factories did set up a form of unrestricted control by the workers working in them. This rather anarchical state of things quickly came to an end, however, when the Civil Wars made necessary the stern centralized control which was called War Communism.

ignorant and immoral force which made for disunion, ill-feeling and anarchy.[1] We have already noticed that in 1926 she practically equated Russian Communists with Italian Fascists; and a year later, in one of her letters to the women of Seaham, she called the Revolution "the greatest misfortune in the history of the Labour movement"; and added that "just as the French Revolution in 1789–93 kept back the advent of political democracy in England for a hundred years" (a somewhat surprising view of history!) "so the Russian Revolution of 1917 may, if we are not careful, prove to keep back the advent of economic democracy in England for half a century." As late as May of 1929, she and Sidney visited Trotsky on Prinkipo; but though they formed no high opinion of Trotsky and firmly denied that it was the duty of the Labour Government to offer him asylum in England,[2] it does not appear that it made them feel any more kindly to Trotsky's rival.

This is the more surprising as by 1929 the first Five-Year Plan, in which they might have been expected to show some interest, was already under way; but the Webbs were slow to believe in the existence of Socialist planning in the U.S.S.R., though the necessity for it had been clearly stated by Lenin at the outset of the Revolution. Some years before the meeting on Prinkipo, when Leonid Krassin came to the Fabian Summer School and spoke on the possibilities of planning in Russia, they could find nothing more helpful to say than that they thought he was proposing to establish a caste system. In point of fact, for as long as they were trying seriously to work for Socialism through the Labour Party, Beatrice's attitude towards the U.S.S.R. was one of mild curiosity tempered by hostility; it was not until the second Labour Government was beginning to get into difficulties and "gradualness" seemed to come very near to meaning complete immobility, that she really turned her eyes and her attention to what was happening to the east.

The change came somewhere about the middle of 1930. Sidney was in the Cabinet, and was therefore leaving Beatrice alone for long periods during which she read a great deal, and in the course of her reading she came across books, particularly

---

[1] Beatrice's criticisms were more apposite to the German branch of the Comintern than to the British. See Jan Valtin, *Out of the Night*, for a devastating account of its effects in Germany. But understanding of conditions in the Western Labour movements was not the Russians' strong point during the formative years of the U.S.S.R.
[2] See Trotsky, *My Life*.

by Maurice Hindus and W. H. Chamberlin (before the latter changed his views as a result of the mistakes made in the first Soviet drive to collectivize agriculture and the severity of the authorities). These books, reaching Beatrice at a time when her mind was particularly ready to receive their message, drew for her the picture of a society, covering a sixth of the world's land surface, run on assumptions entirely different from those of capitalist society, and continuing to exist and apparently to inspire its subjects after more than ten years of bitter struggle against the legacy of Tsarist inefficiency and corruption, the backwardness of its people, the hostility of nature in the 1921 famine, and the opposition of the whole of the "civilized" world. She was interested; she bade Sokolnikov, the Soviet Ambassador in London, and his wife to dinner and asked them about the Five-Year Plan; she turned from journalistic accounts to absorbing the solid facts of consular reports.

The Ambassador suggested that she should come and see for herself. This time the suggestion was not received with scorn; but it was obviously impossible to make the journey while the Labour Government was in office. A year later the opportunity came; the offer was renewed and accepted. Meantime Beatrice had been avidly reading more and more books, and had become more and more impressed with the moral fervour of the Soviet enthusiasts; and Bernard Shaw, who had visited Russia during the summer of 1931 in company with Lady Astor and others, came home bubbling with excitement and delivered a lyrical address to the members of the Fabian Summer School. The Webbs spent the winter making characteristically thorough preparations; they did not try to learn the language, which they felt would be impossible in the time available, but they read everything they could lay their hands on, and hired a Russian-speaking secretary to translate anything that was not available in English. They left in May, 1932, two months before a party from the New Fabian Research Bureau set out with a more modest inquiry in view.[1] Those who remembered only their early fulminations wondered what they would make of the Soviet system, whether they would return indignant or bewildered; but others[2] who had followed more closely the development of their

[1] See *Twelve Studies in Soviet Russia* (Ed. M. I. Cole).
[2] For example see G. D. H. Cole's essay on the Webbs written for *Current History*, while the Webbs were in Russia, and subsequently republished in *Persons and Periods*.

thought as well as the changes in the organization of the U.S.S.R. since the Revolution prophesied with some confidence that, whatever they had said about Lenin's Russia, Stalin's would be very much to their liking.

The U.S.S.R. in 1932 was exciting tremendous interest in the West. The first Five-Year Plan, now nearing its completion or near-completion in four years, in accordance with the slogans proclaimed by the Soviet planners, had succeeded in penetrating to English newspapers and the common talk of English people. Two facts were becoming apparent. First, that the first plan of the first Socialist state in the world was a plan for the future, not for the present. One of the stock arguments of anti-Socialists, that a Socialist community would be bound to be an economic failure, because it would inevitably divide up and instantly consume all its goods and would not save at all, fell to the ground with a bang, as the Soviet leaders told their people to tighten their belts and reduce their immediate consumption, putting their main effort into the production of capital goods—coal, steel, and heavy engineering—in order both to lay the base of future plenty and to make them independent for all time of foreign loans and the stranglehold of foreign capital.

Secondly, at the moment when the Great Slump was nearing its lowest depth, it was said that in Russia there was no one out of work, that, without employing huge masses of men on war or preparations for war, the Soviets had actually solved the problem that had baffled every other government in the world. Many of their political opponents declared that all their claims were lies, others that, in so far as they were true, they had only been achieved by turning the whole of Russia into a vast slave camp, where cowed and starving millions toiled under the whip of Stalin and his secret police, and no one dared utter a syllable of criticism; they further remarked (without seeming to notice the contradiction) that articles in Russian journals complaining about the inefficiency of the new factories etc., proved that State ownership and planning was a disastrous failure, and that the last state of the Russian people would be far worse than the first. In this heated controversy, in which many of the partisans of both sides argued entirely from *a priori* assumptions, the Webbs and the New Fabian Research Bureau were not by any means the only people to be moved with a desire to look at the facts for themselves. From 1931, and for the next few years, eager tourists flocked to *Intourist*, the Soviet travel bureau, in order to spend anything from a fortnight to three months in "Sovietland"; the Soviet Government, confident that it was over the worst of its troubles and on the road to success if only it were let alone, and also with the highly practical purpose of acquiring a certain amount of foreign currency, heartily encouraged these visitors.

The Webbs, however, were visitors of a very special kind. In the first place, they were people of very much higher calibre and standing than the majority of the flock of tourists; to convince them of the rightness of the Soviet system would be well worth while. But it is not necessary to attribute the eagerness of the Soviet Embassy to practical motives alone; the name of Webb had an almost mystical prestige in the Russian Communist Party, since it was their *History of Trade Unionism* which Lenin had read and translated during his exile and which he had recommended to all Party members. Their subsequent attacks on the Soviet Union were forgotten or ignored—as the Webbs themselves ignored them when they came to write *Soviet Communism*; they were to be received as the father and mother of the Revolution.

Of the Russia which they entered I can speak with some first-hand knowledge, since I went there myself during that same summer. It was not a well-fed or luxurious country; in fact it was only just beginning to recover from the mistakes of the first hasty efforts towards collectivization of agriculture,[1] and the standard of living was probably lower than it had ever been since the time of the civil wars. Such ordinary necessities as clothes, paper, household goods, etc. were in equally short supply and when obtainable of poor quality and dismal design. Nor was it an efficient country: the process of turning peasants into machine hands was proceeding rapidly but not without a great number of casualties both of humans and of the far less plentiful machines. The new houses and flats were often abominably built; roads were full of holes; trains ran irregularly and sometimes came in half *en route;* Low's friendly caricature of a Russian peasant girl trying to milk a tractor[2] was not at all far from the truth. Sabotage—which in Russia meant almost any avoidable accident—was rife. Visitors with experience of Western

---

[1] For this, and all subsequent Soviet history, see the late Sir John Maynard's invaluable book, *The Russian Peasant*.
[2] Low and Martin, *Low's Russian Diary*.

methods read the angry protests about inefficiency which filled the columns not merely of *Pravda* but of all the minor Russian press, wagged their heads and talked about the generations of practice needed to build up a machine-tool industry—the record of Russian war production during the last few years has made these vaticinations look rather silly.

It was not a very well-informed country. Though the Russians were moving towards universal education as fast as they could, they had still far to go before they rid their country of "analphabetism"; and the education, even of the best educated, stopped short at the boundaries of their own country; they tended to believe that in Great Britain women still worked underground in the mines and that such a thing as a children's day nursery had never been heard of. But it was a country of enormous enthusiasm, one which was building a new world as fast as it could make it, which felt that the new world was its own and was intensely proud of it. The Russians had already astonished themselves; soon they believed they would astonish the universe.

The Webbs arrived in Leningrad on the 25th of May, when that city, somewhat incongruously, was preparing a great reception for the King of the Hedjaz. But they had no fault to find with the quality of their own. They were met and welcomed by representatives of the Soviet Foreign Office, the consumers' co-operatives, and the Soviet of Leningrad. Sidney commented: "We seem to be a new type of royalty." From Leningrad they went straight on to Moscow, where they were similarly received, housed in the big Foreign Office Guest House—where Litvinov and Tchitcherin, among other commissars, were also living, and where they enjoyed a level of comfort, good food and good service which they afterwards discovered to be far from typical.

After staying for some time in Moscow, making their first general investigations, visiting places such as the Institute of Mothers and Children and a Russian theatre, and working up the enthusiasm which they had already begun to feel on the boat from London to Leningrad, they proceeded via Nijni Novgorod (where they saw the Autostroy motor works, one of the great admitted failures of the early Soviet industrialization) to the Volga steamer and so down to Stalingrad. In Stalingrad, which greatly impressed them, they attended conferences and inspected the Stalingrad tractor plant—"as great a success as Autostroy was a failure"—which bulked so large in the story of the 1942 defence. They then went on to Rostov, from which they under-took a hectic three days' tour of collective and State farms in the neighbourhood, including the famous "Gigant": their admiration of the rapid building up of these new agricultural settlements was perhaps a trifle premature and not too well informed, as a month or two later the New Fabian Research Bureau's agricultural investigator, the late John Morgan,[1] found the standard of cultivation in the same area to be regrettably low. (It was not until after the experiences of the winter of 1932–3 that the Soviet collective farming really got on its feet.)

As a result of this vigorous sight-seeing Beatrice fell ill in Rostov, and was thereby enabled to sample at first hand the medical services of the Soviet Union. Two doctors were provided to attend her, and when she had recovered sufficiently she was sent with a nurse and an interpreter to recuperate at Kislovodsk in the Caucasus, whilst Sidney continued the tour by himself to the Ukraine, to Kharkov and Dnieprostroy. At the end of June they came back to Moscow and stayed there until it was time to return to Leningrad and home.

The above brief itinerary shows the extent of the Webbs' travels in the U.S.S.R. They did not, of course, attempt to see the whole of the vast area, or even a fraction of it. They did not penetrate to the Far East, or to Central Asia, or even so far as Magnitogorsk in the Urals, where was being built up the immense new heavy industry which proved its value during the war; they confined themselves to European Russia west of the Volga. Even within that area they did not try the impossible task of sampling all the available institutions; except for the rapid three-day tour from Rostov, they did not personally investigate Soviet village life, or Soviet agriculture—which they were in any case ill qualified to understand. They looked in the cities to see what Communists said about Soviet agriculture; they talked to important people and to those who could tell them, as frankly as was possible under the circumstances, the aims which Soviet planners were setting before themselves and where they thought that they had succeeded or failed, though they endeavoured also, where they could, to talk with ordinary people as well and to use their eyes and ears for general observation, for staring and listening intently, in the streets of Moscow, for example, as well as for general and specific interviewing.

[1] See his chapter in *Twelve Studies in Soviet Russia.*

It should be emphasized that throughout they were treated as the honoured guests of the Soviet Union and were thus given a good deal more opportunity for free investigation than fell to some of the smaller fry who streamed in and out of Russia during those years. Within reasonable bounds, they were allowed to go where they liked and to see what and whom they liked; and though Beatrice regretted that she did not succeed in attending a meeting of the Central Executive of the Communist Party, she realized that the request would be tantamount to a demand that the sessions of the British Cabinet should be open to foreign visitors.

In August they came home, having accumulated, in Britain and in Russia, a mass of material which might have seemed an ordinary person's lifework to digest and to arrange. They set to work at once, however, and by the beginning of the following year the plan of the new book was already in being. The work proceeded rather slowly, partly because they were anxious to get their facts checked and their opinions fully criticized before finally publishing them, and partly because the U.S.S.R., unlike English local government institutions, did not stay put while they were writing a book about it; it changed rapidly and the opinion of some of its supporters and some of its critics changed too.[1] before the book was fin hed, the shadow of the Nazis had fallen over the Soviet régime, with many important results. The murder of Kirov in 1934 and the violent reprisals which followed it had disclosed the possibility of treason within the Soviet State—a prospect harshly underlined by the great "trials of the generals" in 1936 and 1937; on the other hand, by applying for admission to the League of Nations and by drawing up the new constitution of 1935, which *inter alia* ended the disfranchisement of individuals on political and social grounds, the Soviet leaders seemed to be drawing nearer to the Western democracies. The Webbs did what they could to keep their book in pace with the changing situation; in the autumn of 1934 Sidney—this time with Barbara Drake as his companion, since Beatrice was not considered fit to face the journey—went back to Russia to check their facts, and was able to note the beginnings of the long discussion on the new constitution, the appraisal of which appears as an appendix to

---

[1] Chamberlin, for example, whose book had been one of the forces leading Beatrice to Russia, changed sides after 1932 and wrote in *Russia's Iron Age* a violent attack which the Webbs were at pains to combat.

the second volume of *Soviet Communism*; but in main essence the book, which appeared in the autumn of 1935, is a study of the U.S.S.R. in 1932-3. The revised editions which came out later differ from the first chiefly in that the query disappeared from the title, which was originally *Soviet Communism: A New Civilization?* and that polemical prefaces were added defending the Soviet Union and attacking its critics. These changes reflect chiefly the uneasiness felt among Socialists about the treason trials and their doubts about Soviet foreign policy (as crystallized in the 1939 Russo-German Pact), together with the stout and growing confidence of the Webbs in the U.S.S.R.; but their significance is ephemeral.

Soviet Communism was not published until 1935; but all uncertainty about the Webbs' attitude towards the U.S.S.R. had vanished long before that time, at least among those who were well acquainted with them. Immediately upon their return they had proclaimed, he to the Fabian Summer School and elsewhere, she through the medium of the B.B.C., that here had risen the hope of the world; and through the years which followed all visitors to Passfield had that fact impressed upon them; they ate, drank, and talked Soviet Communism—and the Webbs were in no way ashamed of their preoccupation with it. "Old people," said Beatrice upon one occasion, "often fall in love in extraordinary and ridiculous ways—with their chauffeurs for example: we feel it more dignified to have fallen in love with Soviet Communism." It is a good defence; and as the years went on they only fell in love more deeply.

Soviet Communism (1,257 pages), though not quite the largest, is one of the largest of the Webbs' books; it is as fully documented as any of them, and though in the nature of the case it could not have the intimacy of their studies of the British Labour Movement, it is extraordinarily comprehensive and at one stroke rendered obsolete some dozens of books previously written by visitors to the Soviet Union. It does not, of course, say the last word upon its subject, or indeed upon any part of its subject. Quite apart from the very rapid rate of change in the U.S.S.R., even during the past few years, the Webbs were not at all soaked in the earlier history of that vast territory and its peoples. They learnt its history *ad hoc*, in order to understand its present; and their book needs filling out with such a profound historical study as Maynard's *Russian Peasant*, if the reader wants to give the picture depth. *Soviet Communism* is a large-scale photograph, far more detailed than any writer had yet given—or has given since —of the new civilization at a certain point in time.

Equally, of course, it is not impartial, in the sense that the studies in local government, with the possible exception of the Poor Law, were impartial. It could not be. The majority of the local government books were historical; they described institutions which had long since passed away and had ceased to excite passions, whereas the Soviet Union was alive and growing and the subject of fierce controversy. Besides, the Webbs fell in love with the Soviet Union as it is not possible to fall in love with the Parish and the County or with a Commission of Sewers; and you do not paint the features of those you love so as to bring out their worst points. *Soviet Communism* is, therefore, in some sense, an enormous propagandist pamphlet, defending and praising the Soviet Union; and the criticisms which the Webbs had to make of it are not emphasized. Nevertheless, the criticisms are there; it is surprising how many readers have attacked the book without, apparently, having read it through; the authors' dislike of Soviet foreign policy, as expressed through the Comintern, and the espionage system of the G.P.U. (secret police) is perfectly plainly stated.

What the Webbs found in the Soviet Union, as Cole had prophesied, was, with one important exception, almost exactly what they had demanded for Great Britain, at one time or another, during the whole of their working lives. They found a society based on the principle of production for use and not for profit, in which the motive of personal gain had ceased to count except in a quite minor degree, and in which neither considerations of private profit nor the ownership of large incomes played any part whatsoever in determining the course of production. The means of production were owned by the people, either through the State or through collective organizations,[1] and their use was planned nationally and locally, over periods, through the enormous State planning system. It was a Socialist Society.

It was a Socialist society, moreover, which aimed to use its resources for the benefit of the whole people. It was the "welfare State" which Marx had contrasted with the power State; its projected—and partially completed—universal services of educa-

---

[1] "Artels" of producers, or collective farms—though the Webbs' visit antedated the enormous growth of the collective farming system.

tion, health, etc., carried out the programme which dozens of Fabian Tracts had urged upon successive British administrations. Unemployment it had abolished; it was abolishing want and ignorance as fast as it could; and into its 1935 Constitution it had written the kind of rights for all citizens which the Webbs had long ago described rather more prosaically as "the National Minimum of Civilized Life." They found in it all the passionate enthusiasm for science which they had foreseen in the *Constitution for a Socialist Commonwealth*, the "Religion of Scientific Humanism," as they called it, which denied supernatural elements and yet provided the driving force which Beatrice had found lacking in post-war Britain; and by 1932, though the words "Religion is the Opium of the People" were still incised in the Red Square, the attacks upon priests and congregations as counter-revolutionary forces had been modified sufficiently not to offend against Beatrice's ideal of good manners.

And this society, after some experiment, had settled down to organize its social life through institutions of the type which had been the Webbs' chiefest study in Britain. They had studied Trade Unionism; in the U.S.S.R. Trade Unions were the keystone of industrial organization. Beatrice's first independent book had described Co-operative Societies; the U.S.S.R. had a co-operative movement of enormous size, supplying all the main demands of ordinary consumers,[1] and was even solving the problem, insoluble under capitalist conditions, of co-operative production by quasi-independent groups of producers. They had worked on local government, and had urged consistently that the "democracies of consumers" known as municipalities should take on more and more positive jobs of provision for their citizens; in the U.S.S.R. they found thousands of regional, district, town, and village soviets all free to initiate all manner of experiments for themselves, subject to their working efficiently and fitting in with the overriding Plan.

To see all this in one country would itself be a Fabian's paradise. But the new factor, the one they had not foreseen, was even more exciting than the rest. This was the Communist Party, the body which existed to provide what *Soviet Communism* calls "the Vocation of Leadership."

Beatrice had dreamed of a "strong and independent Socialist

---

[1] Subsequently, the urban co-operative societies became part of the State machine; rural co-operatives remain.

Society," which might have borne some resemblance, allowing for the very different conditions in British politics, to Lenin's Bolshevik Party before the Revolution. But the Socialist Society which she envisaged was essentially a society of politicians in Opposition, and its purpose was the gaining of power. What she had not imagined was the part which such a society might play when power was won, the part of seeing that the political revolution became a real, working, and continuous social revolution, that the first and third-class carriages were actually transformed into second-class carriages—if that were the object—and, most important of all, that the individuals of the classes freed by the revolution were enabled, trained, and compelled to take their share in the running of their own new country. "Every kitchen-maid," Lenin had once said, "must take a hand in running the State"; the Communist Party was the school through which the kitchen-maid learnt the art of self-government, or, to change the metaphor, it was the driving-belt by which the whole of the machinery of the U.S.S.R. was made to move. The most vigorous and enthusiastic chapters in the book are those which describe the organization of the Party and its working.

The Party was an Order, Beatrice was eager over and over again to explain, an Order or a College, not a political Party in the sense in which the Western world understands the term. It was not easy to enter, nor did it tout for membership. It exacted a high standard of training, discipline, and self-control in its members, and—a point which appealed particularly to Beatrice —it endeavoured to set a standard of social manners for the whole Union, to discourage slackness, extravagance, display, anti-social behaviour, and sexual promiscuity. It was with obvious satisfaction that Beatrice noticed the austerity of life under the Soviets —an austerity which may have been due less to principle and more to the economic stringency of conditions in 1932 than she had imagined,[1] but which was, nevertheless, an expression of the Communist view, which had always been Beatrice's view also, that when there was real work to be done in the building up of a new social order, minor luxuries and minor pleasures mattered nothing in comparison with the job.

Finally, the Webbs observed, as none could fail to observe, the widespread and enormous enthusiasm, and the hope, almost amounting to conviction, which was so strong a contrast to the

---

[1] Compare the recently published *I Married a Russian* (Hutchinson).

depressed misery of 1932 in every other major country. The people of the U.S.S.R. were making Socialist civilization, and they were admiring and *enjoying* it. The basis of their admiration was rational, as Beatrice saw; it was an attempt to solve the problem of living-together in the twentieth century by means of scientific knowledge coupled with practical political ability and commonsense; but the driving force which made the whole huge organization work was a passionate faith amounting to a religion. This Communist faith, which Beatrice had once coldly labelled "creed-autocracy" and equated with Fascism, she now found herself accepting to the full; and the chapter in *Soviet Communism* which is called "The Religion of Scientific Humanism" shows quite clearly that the Communist faith, as she found it in Russia, had filled for her the fifty-year-old gap which had troubled her in more or less degree ever since she had abandoned her belief in Christianity; she needed no other religion.

All these facts combined make it small wonder that the Webbs returned to England in love with the Soviet Union with a love which grew steadily stronger during the years before the Union had triumphantly proved itself, before the eyes of its harshest critics, in the defence of Stalingrad. They were convinced that it was a success and was going to be a permanent success, and that the features of it which they most disliked were temporary, products of the practical difficulties of the Revolution and the persistent hostility of the old governing classes and their supporters all over the world, and would in due time "wither away" —as the Comintern did in fact wither away until its final abolition in 1943. The rest, they believed, would become part of the world's solid possession, and in that belief Beatrice remained constant till her death. It has not been given to many reformers to see their early ideals take on solid political flesh within their own lifetime.

M

CHAPTER XVI

LAST YEARS

FROM the end of 1932 onwards, Beatrice Webb became gradually more and more retired from the world of political and social action; it is significant that in 1934 she acquiesced in Sidney's going to Russia without her, for she would certainly not have omitted that journey had she been strong enough to face it. Though not in the least "in failing health" she was beginning to feel her age; she had an operation in 1934 and a slight nervous breakdown in the following year, and she was definitely unable to contemplate such strain as would be involved in re-entering the London world of politics. She had given up Grosvenor Road, and her home was at Passfield. This did not mean, however, that she had become a stationary figure. Right up till the time when the blitz began she visited London regularly, appeared at lunches and At Homes—in Barbara Drake's house, for example—and occasionally at political gatherings.[1] She took holidays abroad, to Majorca and Portofino; in 1937 she went by air to Basle and greatly enjoyed the experience. (Some years previously she had been introduced to flying by Sir Horace Plunkett, who in his old age developed a great enthusiasm for the air.) But she made no more investigating journeys.

She did not cease to write. Preparing revised editions of *Soviet Communism*, with new and more polemical prefaces, occupied a considerable time; in addition, she added to the total of her output various articles, essays, and reviews, one of the latest, possibly *the* latest, being her farewell address to the Fabian Society which was printed in *Fabian News* of June 1941. By herself, and not for immediate publication, she continued to write the long entries in her diaries which packed in huge brown paper parcels await the excited attention of some social historian of the future; and she prepared, and almost completed, the companion volume to *My Apprenticeship—Our Partnership, 1892–1912*, which we may hope shortly to see in print. This reminiscent work was of great and continuing enjoyment to her; but though her interest in the outside world and in the problems of life and politics remained

---

[1] For her connection with the revived Fabian Society—her last appearance in English politics—see page 184.

BEATRICE & SIDNEY WEBB
in the garden at Passfield Corner, 1942

BEATRICE & SIDNEY WEBB
with the Ambassador of the U.S.S.R., M. Ivan Maisky

as keen as ever, her powers of sustained literary effort were slowly
waning, and as the years went on she found writing for external
consumption more and more laborious, until she finally gave it
up altogether.

Inevitably, her chief and abiding interest was in Soviet Russia.
Soviet Communism, in spite of being labelled by a sneering reviewer
"the Webbs' characteristically dull book about the Dictatorship
of the Proletariat," was immediately a resounding and continuous
success. By 1937, two years after publication, it had already sold
nearly 40,000 copies, many of them to working-class people,
Trade Unionists, and Co-operators—the audiences which she was
delighted to secure;[1] and it continued to sell, in revised editions,
until the remaining copies, together, alas, with all the sheets and
stock of the Webbs' other big books, were destroyed at their
publishers' offices during the City fire-blitz. Meantime she and
Sidney bought, borrowed, read avidly—and sometimes denounced!—everything of any importance published on the Soviet
Union; they were visited by, and corresponded with, those who
were going out to the Union to study and those who had come
back; and they developed a strong friendship, which lasted until
her death, with Ivan Maisky, who had succeeded Sokolnikov as
Ambassador, and with his wife.

As time went on, her utter absorption in the U.S.S.R., which
I have already mentioned and which was the source of some
amusement to her friends, became less marked. She could talk
on other subjects; it became possible to make a general remark
upon the weather without provoking a lecture on the North
Caucasus "famine" of 1932-3, and a hot assertion that it was due
to weather conditions solely and not to any political action by
the Union authorities—a point in which Beatrice had a fierce
dispute with W. H. Chamberlin, and one on which her passionate
partisanship, as is now clear, led her astray. But though she
moderated her transports she never moderated her love, and
never left anyone in the slightest doubt that she considered the
Revolution the most important event which had taken place in
her lifetime, and that for the future of the human race what was
happening or was about to happen in the U.S.S.R. was im-
measurably more significant than what was happening anywhere else. One received the impression that, compared with the
great reality of the U.S.S.R., every other country in the world

---

[1] She often told, with much pleasure, of her discovery that the taxi-driver who took
her and Sidney to a dinner at the Soviet Embassy had read and admired the book.

appeared to her as slightly shadowy and unreal—even Nazi
Germany. It is perhaps indicative that it was not until 1939,
when the shadow already lay black and heavy across the world,
that she read *Mein Kampf*; and though she was interested, for
example, in the Spanish Civil War, in the emergence of a dictatorship in Greece, in the transformation of Japan from the country
she had once admired into a world menace, and in the New Deal
in the States, it was with a remote and disinterested interest.
Roosevelt she tended to brush aside as "bound to fail in his
attempt to compromise with capitalism"—bound to fail, in fact,
because he was not Stalin.

Specific politics apart, however, she read a great deal on what
might be called the philosophy of history, and upon ethical and
moral problems. She was genuinely interested and anxious to
understand the kind of question with which the third generation
was faced, and—remembering perhaps the perplexities of her
own girlhood and youth—the kind of intellectual solutions, if
any, which it was reaching. And, being herself no longer a party
to the dispute, her efforts to understand were less impatient and
less wrathful than in the years of the battles within the Fabian
Society. Where she did not agree, her criticisms had no lack of
vigour; but they lacked bitterness. To give a few examples:
books which I remember her discussing with me include Arnold
Toynbee's vast *Study of History* (which she criticized violently),
Nehru's *Autobiography* and the Baroness Ishimoto's *Facing Both
Ways*, both of which she admired, Breasted's *Dawn of Conscience*,
which she found intensely interesting, Lawrence's *Seven Pillars of
Wisdom* and Aldous Huxley's *Point Counterpoint*—she thought both
disgusting—and the novels and plays of her nephew Malcolm
Muggeridge, to which, possibly because of their near relationship,
she devoted a great deal of thought and attention, and by which
she was as perplexed as she had been by the Guild Socialists. By the
touchstone of Soviet Communism, maybe, all this was of little
account; but she found it nevertheless of great secondary interest.

It was not only reading which occupied her increasing leisure
hours. Some years before, the B.B.C. had begun her musical
education; and more and more of her time was spent in listening
to concerts. Poetry she never grasped, even to the end; the
nearest approach I found was when on one occasion I caught her
swaying in time to the voice of James Joyce reading *Anna Livia
Plurabella*; and most persons would agree that it was the sound
and not the sense that was operative here. But her enjoyment

of music was real and growing; in the last year of her life she asked the 'cellist Juliette Alvin (Mrs. W. A. Robson) to play for her, and hinted that she would have liked herself to be a musician, had she had the gift.

Towards the Labour Party, and the Labour movement generally, she could not, for all her convictions about Communism and the U.S.S.R., maintain quite so detached an attitude as she felt, for example, to Roosevelt. The Trade Unionists and the Co-operators, after all, were her own people, among whom she had worked, and to whom she had for years hoped to give a lead. The immediate shock of the 1931 fiasco, combined with the tremendous impact of the Soviet Union, resulted in an angry despair; in the spring of 1932 she had already declared to a Fabian gathering that "the inevitability of gradualness" was dead. Later on in the 'thirties she was inclined to observe that Great Britain, as a political force, was finished—as indeed seemed to many others not an unreasonable conclusion in the days that led to Munich. But notwithstanding remarks of this kind, she maintained a keen and current interest in the Labour Party and in its leaders and still more its potential leaders. Her friendship with Arthur Henderson was strong and lasted until his death; for George Lansbury, who was leader of the Party in Parliament from 1931 to 1935, she had a great respect, though their mental processes were very different, and she did not agree with his tactics or with the uncompromising pacifism which finally drove him to resign the leadership; Sir Stafford Cripps, Deputy Leader during the same period, was her own nephew, and regarded therefore with peculiar attention. Many other present-day leaders such as Sir Walter Citrine, Clement Attlee, and Arthur Greenwood visited her at Passfield; and she was particularly pleased when in 1934 Herbert Morrison led the Labour Party to victory in the L.C.C. elections—"a Fabian triumph," she called it, remembering the Progressive majority of forty-five years back. But her most eager concern was with the possibility of new leaders emerging from the younger generation. "Who is coming forward among the young men?" was the question which visitors to Passfield were continually called upon to answer—she was never much interested in the young women; and almost any Socialist of twenty to thirty-five years who had shown ability was commanded to appear for a week-end to be given, as it were, the once-over. That she thus collected some geese as well as some swans, some whose after-careers disappointed her, did not surprise anyone who had known her for a long time and observed that her judgments tended to be made as a result of rather over-rapid summing up; in those later years the summing up may have been affected by the fact that polite young men, bidden as guests to the house of the *doyenne* of the Socialist movement, did not rudely obtrude their own opinions, but maintained a respectful silence which Mrs. Webb mistook for agreement with hers. Be that as it may, she immensely enjoyed these contacts, and gave excellent return in her own experiences and reminiscences of times past.

For to Beatrice, in her later years, a good gossip was as pleasant as it is supposed to be to all women, though the subjects of her gossip were semi-political rather than personal or domestic. No one who was a frequent guest at Passfield Corner during the 'thirties can fail to retain a vivid recollection of Beatrice sitting on a low stool in front of the fire, her skirt pulled back and her stockings as often as not in wrinkles about her ankles, seeking information about current politics and current relationships and proffering in return incisive recollections of Asquith, Haldane, Balfour, and other figures of her prime. The comments she made were not malicious, any more than *My Apprenticeship* was malicious; but they were often caustic and expressed in language which was certainly more Victorian-aristocratic than bureaucratic or benevolent.[1] The tone of voice in which Beatrice could refer to some well-known figure as "an *odious* woman," or "a very common sort of person," will probably never be heard again in our lifetime. But it was all very enjoyable gossip, and did nobody any harm. Nor did it, to anyone of the least intelligence, obscure for a moment her fundamental good will and friendliness, her willingness to try and understand, and to help as far as she could, anyone who was really anxious to serve in the cause in which she had spent her life.

Passfield Corner, in the days when it had become a place of pilgrimage, offered to its visitors a routine which was amusingly reminiscent of the Webbs' former routine at Grosvenor Road and elsewhere. The hosts rose early, owing to Beatrice's insomnia; but they imposed no early rising upon their guests, who descended about nine o'clock to eat their breakfasts to an accompaniment of political or similar inquiry from Beatrice, sitting on the dining-room window-seat. After breakfast there was a temporary separation until the time for morning exercise was announced, when the Webbs took their visitors—and their dog—for a rapid promenade

[1] See page 65.

through the neighbouring woods and heaths[1] until the lunch-hour. There was then just time to wash before a bell sounded, and anyone looking from the window could see the secretary running up from the garden-room at full speed in order not to be late. After lunch the Webbs rested, and the guests rested or not as they chose, until they were bidden to tea and conversation until the six o'clock news. Followed dinner, eaten rapidly, and further talk to an early bedtime which, again, was not enforced. The pair of Scottish maids whom, after some vicissitudes, Beatrice had finally secured, and who remained with her till she died, contributed in no small measure to the smooth working of this régime, to which all who visited Passfield Corner, small or great, conformed.

Small or great. There were great, as well as small, who came to visit the Webbs in their old age. It is true that the academic world, on the whole, held aloof. The suspiciousness of the really respectable, which I have mentioned in an earlier chapter, was maintained and strengthened by the Webbs' passionate support of the U.S.S.R. against all its opponents and critics of every kind, from the humanitarian Socialists who were shocked and frightened by the revelations of the treason trials to the blinkered economists who believed that the Soviet system was against nature and therefore could not exist, or was doomed to perish within a few weeks or months or years. "How right we were," one can feel them saying to one another, "not to bestow precipitate honours on persons whose political judgment has proved so unstable!" and with a few exceptions, such as Lord Keynes, the leaders of academic sociology in Britain, other than avowed Socialists or employees of the School of Economics, left the Webbs alone. But distinguished persons from other countries came to see them; to a certain extent they were, as they had been in Moscow, a kind of minor royalty, and Beatrice never seemed to suffer from a sense of being neglected. Meantime she gathered around her, in brief visits, old friends, sometimes with their families, promising young men, Potter descendants of the second and third generation —in June, 1937, over a hundred of these assembled and were photographed like a school treat at a tea-party on Passfield lawn —and visitors from the Webbs' political children, from the School of Economics, the *New Statesman*, and the Fabian Society.

---

[1] As they grew older, they sent the visitors out by themselves; but in the early 'thirties the morning walk was a great feature, though less strenuous and less oblivious of natural obstacles than in the first years of the century, when, as observers have testified, Beatrice strode as straight as a Roman road builder "thorough bush, thorough briar" and brought her juniors home in a state bordering upon collapse.

The Fabian Society, as it had been the first, was the last political body with which Beatrice maintained active connection. But in 1940–3 it was a Fabian Society considerably changed from the Fabian Society of the 'thirties, with its occasional tracts and pamphlets, its membership scarcely altered except by the hand of death and often not seriously harassed even by demands for subscriptions. That Society, from whose Executive Committee Beatrice had resigned in 1933 and Sidney in 1935, after fifty years' service, kept itself alive, though not without getting in debt, by running the annual Fabian Lectures, thronged by many who wanted to listen to Bernard Shaw, and by the Summer School whose patrons "grew old along with it." It did little or no other work, and but that its affiliation to the Labour Party provided a means of individual membership of that Party to some who for personal reasons could not openly join a local Labour Party and did not agree with the I.L.P., it might easily have faded away. It had just enough vitality left to repel some half-hearted attempts by Communists to rush prepared resolutions through its annual meeting, but hardly any more.

After the 1931 election, however, some of the leaders of the Labour Party, notably Clement Attlee and Stafford Cripps, were so strongly conscious of the Party's failure to think out a policy for dealing with the modern problems of government, that they cast round to find a nucleus grouping for a new intellectual leadership. After some discussion with G. D. H. Cole and others, including a group of young Socialists not long down from college —among them were John Parker, M.P., Colin Clark, the economist and statistician, E. A. Radice, E. F. M. Durbin, and H. T. N. Gaitskell—there was formed early in 1932 a small body called the New Fabian Research Bureau, whose purpose was to work out in practical detail the implications of Labour and Socialist policy. This body, inaugurated with the approbation of the principal Labour leaders, including Henderson, deliberately included the word Fabian in its title, with the consent of the Webbs, in order to emphasize to the outside world that its policy and practice were to resemble those which had for years been associated with the Fabian Society. Beatrice and Sidney attended the foundation dinner, held at the House of Commons; and Beatrice spoke of it as "a hopeful little venture," though during the time of her preoccupation with the U.S.S.R. she played no part in it.

The N.F.R.B. grew quietly and slowly; for some time it made

no real effort to attract members, and even after John Parker, who became its general secretary in 1933, had embarked upon a rather more forward policy, its numbers by 1938 had only risen to seven or eight hundred. But it was a picked, qualified, and active membership; it took its research and its responsibilities seriously, and its publications, from *Twelve Studies in Soviet Russia* to a score or so of research pamphlets and small books, represented almost the only concerted thinking that was being done in the Labour world and attracted a good deal of respectful attention.

Naturally, the membership of the N.F.R.B. overlapped to some extent with the less dormant portion of the old Fabian Society; the aims of both had a good deal in common, and the resemblance between their names sometimes created confusion. Accordingly, when in 1938 Galton, the Secretary of the Fabian Society, became due to retire, and its treasurer, Emil Davies, had by herculean efforts succeeded in wiping off its debt, an amalgamation of the two, under the older name, was proposed and carried through finally by the midsummer of 1939. The subsequent growth of the revived and amalgamated body to a membership (by 1944) of nearly seven thousand, with a working staff of over twenty, and a stream of publications limited only by the scarcity of paper, belongs to the history of the Fabian Society; what concerns us here is that Beatrice was asked to set her personal seal upon the union of the old and the new, and agreed. In 1939, when she had passed her eighty-first birthday, she became President of the Fabian Society;[1] she came up to London for the first Annual Conference of the new régime, and delivered a Presidential address which was published in *Fabian News*. A year later, when writing for the public had already become a great burden to her, she wrote a Presidential message which ended with the words "Long Live the Fabian Society!"; she asked leading Fabians, young and old, down to stay with her, and she was always glad to receive news and reports, and visits from residents at the Summer School when it was held at Frensham Heights in Surrey.

"Long live the Fabian Society!" As its honorary secretary, I am naturally a prejudiced witness; but I believe she meant what she said. More than once, she expressed to me and to others her belief that the Fabian Society was the most hopeful present-day development in the Labour movement. She knew, of course, that it was not the Socialist Order which she had imagined, on

---

[1] She resigned in 1941, after the London blitz; the office of President was then abolished.

and off, since 1912, and that it was very far from resembling Lenin's Bolshevik Party. But she recognized that among British Socialists, bred up in the British political tradition, and differing among themselves very widely on immediate questions—on their attitude to the Soviet Union, to take the most obvious example— there was no practical possibility of a disciplined and unanimous native party. (The British Communist Party she regarded as foreign-controlled and foreign-led; though her enthusiasm for the Soviet Union led her to friendly relations with some of its members, its tactics seemed to her fundamentally those of the Comintern, which she had always considered silly and dangerous.) She approved, therefore, of the Society's policy of allowing the largest possible latitude of opinion among its members and its publications, and of not putting forward any suggestions as "the policy of the Fabian Society." She made no secret of the fact that she thought the views of some of its leading members very reactionary; but she herself remained a keenly interested member, remarking with amusement that "the aged Webbs" were now well to the left of many of their juniors. She had promised to partake in some way in the jubilee celebrations of the Society on its sixtieth birthday, "if I live so long"; but she did not.

For a time, it seemed as though the long partnership was to be broken some years before her death. In March, 1938, a little while after Beatrice had celebrated her eightieth birthday to the accompaniment of admiring messages from all over the world, Sidney Webb had a stroke, which at first onset looked like being very serious indeed. Very fortunately—for, to most of her friends, it was inconceivable that Beatrice, without Sidney to support and strengthen her, should have gone on living—his vitality rallied from it. But the shock and strain, at her age, were very severe—the more so because, by the autumn, the world was marching close to war.

I do not remember that Beatrice showed any particular signs of foreseeing the war any more than anyone else. Her Russian friends did not tell her—as has since become apparent—that the purpose of the treason trials and the trials of the generals were to eliminate any possibility of betrayal within the gates in the inevitable struggle with Hitler. She defended them stoutly; but she defended them *ad hoc*, with a conviction that the Soviet leaders *must* be right, rather than in relation to wider issues. As I said earlier, she had not then read *Mein Kampf*. When the war did finally come, its issues were entangled, for her, with the issues of Soviet foreign policy, with Stalin's efforts to buy time and space by means of the Russo-German Pact and the Finnish war, which in the manner of their presentation no less than in the fact so deeply disturbed British supporters of the Soviets during the period of the "phoney war." Beatrice stuck staunchly by her faith; neither in public statement nor in private conversation did she admit for a moment that the Soviet policy was open to question. But she cannot have been really happy about it. The whole tone of the Soviet Foreign Office, particularly during the initial stages of the Finnish war, and the unblushing somersaults of Communist Parties outside Russia, savoured too much of the oft-condemned methods of the Comintern to live up to her standards of international good manners; and she cannot but have been relieved when the events of June 22nd, 1941, ranged the Soviets finally on the side of her own people. She listened, without despairing, to the news of the great German advances in 1941 and again in 1942, and lived long enough to see her faith justified in the surrender of von Paulus at Stalingrad.

For the rest, she maintained, right up to the early months of 1943, her close and lively contact, by letter and by visit, with friends and younger workers in the same cause. Perhaps the best way to express the impression given by Beatrice Webb before her death is to say that, apart from her looks—though these had changed little in twenty years—and apart from the fact that her physical energy was obviously reduced, one never thought of her or treated her as an old woman. One did not have to restrain one's tongue for fear of giving offence, or laboriously to select suitable topics of conversation; one talked to her as one would to an equal and interrupted or contradicted as freely—and could be assured of interest. For all her pleasure in reminiscence, she did not, in the slightest degree, "live in the past"; she was interested in the present and in what was to come, and she felt perfect confidence that there was a great future for the human race, though she would not live to see it.

She died, after a very short illness, on April 30th, 1943. After her death, the Churchill Government conferred the Order of Merit upon her husband. Lord Passfield was assured that this decoration was given in recognition of the social and political work of the partnership. A plain stone in Passfield Wood records the name of one of the greatest women of our generation.

CHAPTER XVII

CONCLUSION

IT is too soon, less than two years after her death, to attempt a definitive evaluation of the work and character of Beatrice Webb, even were that not a difficult assignment for one who for many years was her friend and her warm admirer. Something, however, can be said about certain outstanding characteristics which impressed themselves upon all who came in contact with her.

First among these is her extraordinary disinterestedness. Never, in all her life, did Beatrice—and this applies to Sidney also—have any personal axe to grind; her most Machiavellian efforts, in Poor Law days, for example, were directed to the promotion of public political ends and not to personal prestige or aggrandizement. She did not care in the least about public recognition or praise, although she was not so unhuman as to receive it without pleasure when it came. Public disinterestedness is, of course, not a rare quality, fortunately for the human race; the roll of those who have laboured in the cause of humanity without thought of personal gain contains many names. But disinterestedness which can endure not merely lack of ordinary reward but actual abuse and vilification from one's own side without becoming rancorous *is* rare; and Beatrice possessed it. She bore no malice; she accepted and forgave—and even forgot—insults and attacks which would have rankled for ever in lesser minds. She was almost entirely immune from those mental diseases of the enlightened which so often turn any community of the socially virtuous into an inferno of injured vanity and a succession of furious battles on points of prestige or principle. She was critical enough and to spare; but her criticism never had that venom which indicates unmistakably that it derives from a memory of personal injury. When her Diaries come eventually to be published, one can say with confidence that they will contain nothing more to give pain to anyone than did *My Apprenticeship*.

This calm spirit was acquired by her largely because her own personal life, after her marriage, was basically so completely happy. This might easily not have been the case. *My Apprentice-*

ship bears witness that as a child and a young woman she was often ill at ease with the world; she was sickly, lonely, and introspective almost to morbidity, and there was a distinct chance that in spite of her strong will and strong intellect she might have developed into a neurotic, and her gifts have run to waste. But in her early thirties she discovered, almost simultaneously, her life-work and her life-partner, and her satisfaction with both only increased as the years went by. Like the "happy countries," she had almost no personal history; the reader of this memoir must have realized how little of the story of Beatrice Webb consists of the personal details which bulk so large in the lives of most eminent women. Her life-history is the social history of two generations, and Sidney's exhortation, "No personalities, please," was obeyed almost to the letter. Incidentally to all her other work, she thus provided one of the most complete vindications of the institution of marriage that has ever been seen in British public life.

In the intellectual field, her most outstanding characteristics were her strong sense of the practical, her fundamental consistency, and her originality. For abstract discussion, whether of politics, economics or philosophy, she had really very little use; she was not without the strong religious strain of the mid-Victorians, which led her to seek for a faith to live by; but when she had found it she did not want to argue about it further, she wanted to accept and to act upon it. Discussions upon terminology, that beloved pastime of all naturally philosophic minds, bored and irritated her;[1] she wanted to express her own thoughts clearly and to leave it at that. If she had been able to meet Socrates or to sample the "Socratic method," she would undoubtedly have lost her temper. Her strength lay in her immense practicality, her ability to survey the human and institutional means by which any theory or any proposal might be translated into action, and to act promptly and without hesitation. Of course, she was not always right in her judgment of what was practical: sometimes, as in the case of the Poor Law campaign, she underestimated the forces against her—though in that instance the failure was well worth while for succeeding reformers—more often she went wrong upon the abilities or convictions of people

---

[1] She often recounted, with considerable amusement, the vain attempts of two eminent economists to arrive at a definition of economic terms which would be satisfactory to both of them.

whom she sought to appraise, attributing to them too readily her own single-mindedness, underestimating a fundamental disagreement which was unable to formulate itself in precise terms against her (or Sidney's) complete assuredness, or simply failing to "see the point," if it were a point in which she was not at the moment interested. Habitually, also, and partly because her own emotional life was so completely satisfied, she underrated the powers of irrational emotion and frustrated emotion in politics. "Measurement and Publicity" were the slogans on which she relied until she went to the U.S.S.R., and she thought that all sensible persons ought to be moved and convinced by Measurement and Publicity. Unfortunately they are not, and her failure to realize that, her continued acceptance of the rationalist premisses of nineteenth-century radical thought, would have prevented her from ever becoming a popular political leader. Certainly she never desired such a career, but her rationalism occasionally resulted in her presenting proposals—such as those contained in the *Constitution for a Socialist Commonwealth*—which whatever their merits were politically impossible.

Allowing for this limitation, however, her sense of what was practical was extraordinarily keen. She studied her material, both human and institutional, with the greatest care. To take only one example, she knew the nature of the individuals and organizations which made up the Labour Party as very few among the intellectual middle class knew it, and was therefore never tempted to quarrel with it, to abuse it publicly or to fling out into fractionalism, as others have done in their time,[1] because on closer acquaintance it turned out not to be composed of class-conscious Socialists and not to be endowed with much political daring; she knew it for what it was. At the same time, she was quite capable of realizing when a position was hopeless or an institution doomed to failure. She suffered from none of that sentimental clinging to organizations whose utility has long passed away which seems to be a peculiar defect of what Henry Nevinson once called "the Stage-Army of the Good," and which causes *Whitaker's Almanack* or any other directory to be peopled with ghost-like organizations from the past, which use up good space, good paper, and good energy on obsolete ends impossible of achievement. It may have been her early training as daughter of a business man which made her able to cut her political losses

---

[1] Mosley, of course, being the most notorious example.

—as she did in the case of the Poor Law campaign—coolly and
without unnecessary regret. Certainly she never *mourned* the loss
of a campaign.

But this power of cool judgment was not merely the result of
early training or disciplined common sense. It derived from a
deep fundamental consistency of purpose from which she never
deviated throughout her life. Once she had accepted the goal
of Socialism, i.e., the attainment of political and economic freedom by means of the abolition of private capitalism and the
communal planning of society, she held it steadily to the end,
and none of her secondary interests were anything more than
secondary to it. *Mutatis mutandis*, she acted up to the Fabian
practice as declared in Tract 70.[1]

This fundamental consistency covered a certain amount of
inconsistency in practice—covered it the more easily, perhaps,
because it was so fundamental. Beatrice pursued Socialism by
whatever means and through whatever instruments were available; if any particular means or instrument turned out to be
unsuitable, she used it no longer. Several times, during the
course of her life, she changed her mind and contradicted what
she had previously said. She made no bones about it; in fact,
she often did not trouble to mention that she *had* changed, she
was so conscious of still pursuing the same aim that it did not
seem to matter. True, she did publish a recantation on the
subject of women's suffrage, but that was in connection with a
particular political crisis in the Fabian Society; on the immense
question of Soviet Communism she was not in the least perturbed
by recollections of her earlier attacks; she simply ignored them.
It must be, she felt, if she felt at all, as obvious to everyone as it
was to herself that they were wrong. It takes a powerful and
impersonal mind to be so little concerned about possible charges
of inconsistency.[2]

Her originality needs little stressing. It was not, of course, the
type of originality which finds and proclaims a profound truth or
a new faith; it was the practical kind of originality which refuses

---

[1] See page 65.

[2] One apparent exception is, I believe, more apparent than real. She did, in 1932,
declare against "the inevitability of gradualness," upon which she had long insisted.
But I do not think that was a permanent recantation so much as an expression of her
opinion that in the second Labour Government, Labour's "gradual progress" had
become immobility or even retrogression, and that violent change could, by contrast,
get somewhere. She certainly never showed any signs of advocating violent revolution
in Britain, as she would have if her general views had fundamentally changed.

to be bound by traditional methods or traditional modes of thought, but chooses for itself whatever seems most fruitful. In her early years as a social worker she sensed that the traditional modes of those who were called political economists were wrong, that their work led nowhere because they ignored half the facts and institutions that were under their own eyes; she knew, before she became a Socialist, that for the practical betterment of society Co-operative Societies and Trade Unions were worth studying, and sweated East End sempstresses in comparison were not. She chose eclectically, from those who influenced her, what she found to be useful for her own work and its purpose, rejecting what was not, as she took from Herbert Spencer his passion for collecting illustrative facts without believing a word of his philosophy, from Booth his methods of investigation and sampling while disagreeing with his political views, and accepted Marx's history but not his economics. What was grist to her mill she gathered, and in collaboration with Sidney worked it into a *corpus* whose individual parts, in purpose and arrangement as in style, are so individual, so characteristic, that one can scarcely read a sentence or the table of contents of one of them without exclaiming "This is the work of the Webbs!"

Finally, it is quite in accordance with her own development that in her later years she was continuously and generally interested in the work of others, particularly if they seemed to be breaking new ground; she showed a lively curiosity in Mass-Observation for example, when it was founded. She did not ever imagine that the Webbs had said the last word, except temporarily, upon Trade Unionism, Local Government, or even upon the Soviet Union; and she was interested to read what others had to say, if she believed they were trying to get somewhere and were not spinning theories. She never became in any sense a Great Pundit whose word might not be questioned; and more than most she was kind and generous to younger workers in her field. That in itself produced the deep affection, as well as respect, with which she was regarded in her old age.

INDEX